FAIR
PLAY

FAIR
PLAY

HOW SPORTS SHAPE
THE GENDER DEBATES

KATIE BARNES

ST. MARTIN'S PRESS
NEW YORK

First published in the United States by St. Martin's Press, an imprint of
St. Martin's Publishing Group

FAIR PLAY. Copyright © 2023 by Katie Barnes. All rights reserved. Printed in the
United States of America. For information, address St. Martin's Publishing Group,
120 Broadway, New York, NY 10271.

www.stmartins.com

The Library of Congress Cataloging-in-Publication Data is available upon request.

ISBN 978-1-250-27662-9 (hardcover)
ISBN 978-1-250-27663-6 (ebook)

Our books may be purchased in bulk for promotional, educational, or business
use. Please contact your local bookseller or the Macmillan Corporate and
Premium Sales Department at 1-800-221-7945, extension 5442, or by email at
MacmillanSpecialMarkets@macmillan.com.

First Edition: 2023

10 9 8 7 6 5 4 3 2 1

For Andraya, Mack, Sarah, River, Lia,
Zoé, Kris, Becky, Luc, Fischer, Ember, and
the other transgender people playing sports,
young and old, known and unknown

CONTENTS

CONTENTS

FAIR
PLAY

INTRODUCTION

MY FIRST MEMORY is of playing basketball in my driveway. I was four years old. I have other memories from earlier in my life, but it's hard to know if I actually remember those moments or if I've just watched them on home movies. What I remember for sure is dribbling a pink rubber ball against the cement of my family's driveway in my rural Indiana hometown. I picked up my dribble and shot this small ball into the hoop only a few feet in front of me. This hoop was beat-up. Flakes of rust fell off the metal pole; the backboard used to be white but was now a dust-stained beige. The star-spangled net somehow remained fully intact. My little pink rubber ball was too small to make a sound as it fell through, but as I got older I came to love the thick swish of the net.

As with any good Hoosier, my basketball career was forged on that driveway, in one-on-one games against my dad, where he never took it easy on me. I would stomp away each time I lost, hearing him yell, "Why would I let you win? What would that teach you?"

He was not even a good basketball player; he was a wrestler. A really good one. And he was bigger, stronger, and faster than me, and for much of my childhood, that was enough to beat me. In my heyday, however, I was a better basketball player than him. I could hit more difficult shots; I could finish better at the rim. I knew how to attack his top foot to put him off-balance and how to use my body to shield the ball from him. Eventually, I could beat him. And if we played shooting games, it was a wrap. Those moments spent with my dad created a bond between us and also solidified "basketball player" as a core piece of my identity. Even as I've aged and my desires changed, I've continued to carry basketball through every phase of my life.

I played four years of varsity basketball at a medium-size high school, starting nearly every game in which I played. I coached basketball when I was in college. And I've made a career in writing about sports, mostly basketball. But as much as I enjoyed my time as an athlete, I often wonder if I would have had that same experience if I knew then I was nonbinary.

Gender has always been a place of difficulty for me. In a recent phone call with my mom, she said to me, "You've always been nonbinary." And she's right. I never neatly fit into the boxes provided for children. Sure, I was a tomboy, but it was more than that. Searching for answers, I once padded into the kitchen and stood next to my mother, who was cooking something—probably soup—and, stretching up on my chubby little toes, I asked her if I was supposed to be a boy. I was often mistaken for a boy, though I never particularly felt like one. But I wasn't a girl in the way my classmates or my sister were either. I played sports and hung out with boys, and I also wore clothes exclusively from the boys' section. My favorite church outfit was khaki pants and a green sweater with a yellow stripe across the chest. I wore my hair short, until I felt pressured by my peers to grow it out, but then I just popped it into a bun until I got the courage to cut it again at the age of twenty-seven. It was my mom who made me go to the salon. But in rural Indiana during the late 1990s, no one was talking about nonbinary or gender-expansive identities.

Basketball became my refuge. While adolescence brought pressures to be more feminine, basketball didn't require that of me. I could wear baggy shorts and cut-off tees to practice. I could gently sag the sweatpants I bought in the men's section, much to my parents' chagrin. Despite the pressure I felt from the girls in my classes to dress more like them during the school day and to shave my legs and grow out my hair, I was a ball player. That was enough to give me *some* cover. As an adult, far removed from my basketball career, I found the words to describe myself. I began using they/them pronouns. And still, sports have remained close to my heart, especially women's sports. Part of my love of women's sports comes from being a former athlete and a fan of the game I played. I grew up re-watching the 2003 UConn vs. Texas Final Four game on VHS, relishing the nine-point second half comeback by the Huskies each time as if it were the first time I'd seen it. Beyond just being a fan, however, when I reflect on the experiences I had playing sports, I see that basketball granted me a space to express my authentic self in a way I felt I couldn't in the halls of my middle school. When I watch a WNBA game and see the range of gender expressions and identities, it speaks to me as both an adolescent and the adult I am today.

I'm not alone in these feelings when it comes to sports. Almost every queer basketball player in girls' and women's basketball that I've interviewed—no matter at what level they played—has shared similar stories with me. The ability to carve out space for myself in basketball as someone who expresses myself in more masculine ways was not unique. But those experiences were also a double-edged sword: some athletes and coaches and leagues in women's basketball have been pushing back against the assumption that the sport is masculine for as long as women have been playing basketball. The WNBA, for example, put its stars in dresses and makeup in the league's early commercials.

Whether we realize it or not, our sports are coded, laden with allusions to gender and sexuality in ways that are fundamental to our collective understanding of both athletics and gender. It's the hypermasculine displays in football, the hyperfeminine expression in women's gymnastics. It's the implication that Supreme Court justice Elena Kagan must be a lesbian because she played recreational softball. It's the idea that men should bulk up and build muscle while women should "tone." It's the reason why Maria Sharapova made more endorsement money at one point during her career than Serena Williams despite not being the same caliber of tennis player at all.

Before your eyes glaze over and you try to tell me "it's not that deep," just think about it. Do you quietly assume that many male figure skaters are gay? Same with male gymnasts? What about WNBA players? What about women who play tackle football? Those questions and assumptions are driven by an endemic coding of each sport: gymnastics is feminine, basketball is masculine, figure skating is feminine, etc. And, well, we code sexuality too—being a gay man is considered to be feminine, and being a gay woman, or a lesbian, is considered to be masculine. So, if you're someone assigned male at birth and participating in a "feminine" sport like, say, figure skating, then the suspicion is that you must be gay.

I'm not saying that I believe these ideas to be true, rather that, culturally and collectively, we hold these assumptions. Lots of sports are unisex, but many of them are gendered. Boys play football and girls play field hockey. Boys play baseball and girls play softball. Boys wrestle and girls play volleyball. There are exceptions and examples of crossover, but not enough to break down those cultural structures. Built within these delineations and distinctions are cultural assumptions about *who* plays each sport. And many of those assumptions are gendered. Sports reinforce what we believe to be true about gender and vice versa.

There's this episode of *The Good Fight,* a television show about lawyers (stick with me here), where the protagonists wade into the topic of transgender inclusion in sports. The episode titled "The Gang Offends Everyone" introduces us to a swimmer named Melanie. Melanie qualified for the 2020 Olympic Team through a 2019 swim meet (I'm suspending my own disbelief here because the Olympic qualifying process happens weeks—not one year—before the Olympics, but I digress). But instead, the Olympic selection process was moved to a different meet in 2020, and Melanie (who is Black) was replaced by a white swimmer named Sadie. Turns out Sadie is transgender, prompting the judge in the case to tell the lawyers to change their discrimination argument. "From race to trans, let's go," he says.

Melanie's lawyers present arguments about testosterone and genitalia. They are accused of being transphobic by their own staffers. When they lose the case because the judge says "rules are rules," they refile to challenge another swimmer's participation on the basis of her having testosterone levels above the allowable limits. We come to find out that the woman in question, Piper Vega, is insensitive to androgen, meaning that her body doesn't process testosterone the way someone assigned male at birth would (more on this later). The judge sighs; he's confused. All the swimmers are confused. Everyone is conflicted. We're meant to walk away with the understanding that these topics are hard and barely understandable.

The merits of the case on the show are not of particular interest to me, but the fact that a television show attempted to treat the topic with nuance speaks to our current cultural moment. Difficult conversations about gender and sports, particularly those involving transgender and intersex athletes in girls' and women's sports, are happening in every community across the country. Sports have become a flash point for a broader conversation about transgender people on the heels of more visibility of that community, not dissimilar to the way "bathroom bills" served as a proxy attack on transgender people. Whereas those original bills mostly fizzled out, the question of transgender inclusion in sports has taken hold, and fueled a surge of anti-trans legislation, including a resurgence of bills regulating bathroom access. Transgender athletes participating in sports is not some new phenomenon. Renée Richards played professional tennis from 1977 to 1981. At the time, there was considerable fear that her participation was a harbinger of transgender women "taking over" women's sports. In the more than forty years since she retired, that has not come to pass, but transgender athlete participation is on the forefront of the so-called culture wars. It's being debated in statehouses and litigated in the press. It's on our television shows. A random guy on my flight out of O'Hare asked me my thoughts on the subject during a particularly long rain delay. Even my grandmother's Wisconsin dermatologist asked her about it while checking her moles. And while these conversations are complex, we are capable of having them without denying the humanity of many people who have a personal stake in the outcome.

I've spent the last five years reporting on transgender athletes competing in sports at all levels. I've covered Chris Mosier, who has represented Team USA in duathlon (running and biking); Jessica Platt, who played in the Canadian Women's Hockey League; Mack Beggs, who won two state wrestling championships in Texas; and Andraya Yearwood, who won multiple track championships in Connecticut; among others. This has been an issue I've followed up close in all its complexity. The question of gender in sports as it pertains to cisgender girls and women, transgender athletes, and intersex athletes has become the sports battleground of this generation.

Since Idaho's HB 500 was signed into law in 2020, barring transgender girls from high school sports—the day before Transgender Day of Visibility—scores of bills have been filed in more than three-quarters of the United States to codify the restriction of sports participation where it concerns transgender athletes, particularly transgender girls and women at the high school and collegiate levels. By the end of 2022, those bills have become law in Alabama, Arizona, Arkansas, Florida, Idaho, Indiana, Iowa, Kentucky, Louisiana, Mississippi, Montana, Oklahoma, South Dakota, South Carolina, Tennessee, Texas, Utah, and West Virginia—eighteen states and counting. For some, these bills and laws represent the necessary curtailing of physiological advantage, the continuing protection of the integrity of the female category of women's sports. Many others see the same pieces of legislation as dangerous, harmful for all participants in girls' and women's sports, and an invasion of athletes' privacy.

This book is about that complexity, revealing just how much sports and our enjoyment of them are wrapped up in identity and gender. It's on display everywhere, whether you're sitting in small-town Texas bleachers listening to kids boo wrestler Mack Beggs or you're observing the story of Connecticut athlete Andraya Yearwood move from simmering regional rage to boiling over across the nation. I've talked to lawmakers, scientists, and policy wonks on all sides of these issues. I've gotten to know transgender athletes who've trusted me with their stories. I'll also share my own experiences. If I've learned anything over the past half decade, it's that every single one of us brings our own experience with sports to this conversation, whether we are Olympic swimmers, last off the bench for our third grade soccer team, an enthusiastic spectator, a Division I quarterback, or, in my case, a perfectly serviceable varsity point guard who still smarts over getting beaten by my former summer camp teammates in the sectional championship during my senior year of high school.

I've also learned the importance of language. For the purposes of this book, I will be using the following definitions:

- **Sex assigned at birth**: used to describe how a person was identified by a medical professional shortly after birth, typically male or female
- **Gender identity**: the identity a person uses to describe their gender, such as man, woman, genderqueer, nonbinary, etc.
- **Cisgender**: a person whose sex assigned at birth and gender identity are in alignment

- **Transgender**: a person whose sex assigned at birth and gender identity are not in alignment; used both as a specific identity description (transgender man or transgender woman) and as an umbrella term to describe binary and nonbinary transgender identities
- **Gender expansive**: an umbrella term used to describe a variety of gender identities outside of the traditional gender binary, such as genderqueer, nonbinary, etc.

There will be other terms introduced as we go along, but I wanted to start here because making assumptions about what I might mean does no one any good, especially when confronting difficult topics.

This story isn't about one kid running track, or another trying to wrestle; it's about so much more. This book is about the changing culture confronting an immovable object in sex-segregated sports. It's about where we've been, where we are now, and where we're going. For me, the only way to have this discussion is to confront the complexity of the subjects. We're going to talk about the history of sex separation in our sports (briefly, I promise) and the passage of Title IX. We'll explore the science of the issues, and why it's so hard to get a definitive answer on anything when it comes to testosterone and policy, as well as the function of stereotypes in women's sports. And we'll take on the difficult questions, particularly as they pertain to transgender athletes competing in all levels of sports and the legislation that targets transgender youth.

I was asked by a lawmaker once, "If anyone can just declare themselves a woman, what becomes of women's sports?"

It's not so unreasonable a question. If gender is a construct, and it is fluid, and sex is a spectrum, then what, indeed, becomes of women's sports? Of any of our sports? Through the stories of athletes at the center of these debates, this book seeks to consider that question in a meaningful way. There are many athletes who have found themselves ensnared in conflict when all they wanted was to take the field. Some of them you may already know; others you may not.

But before we look ahead, we need to understand how we got here. And to do that, we've got to go back. Way back.

1.

THE TWO GENDERS

ON A DREARY day in April 1967, Kathrine Switzer did what was once thought unthinkable. She pinned a Boston Marathon race number to her sweatshirt and lined up at the start of the course to run 26.2 miles. She was joined by her training partner and her boyfriend. The latter had instructed her to take off the lipstick she'd put on so as to not draw attention to them, but Switzer refused.[1] No woman had ever successfully registered for and run the Boston Marathon before, but though men had been the only competitors up to that point, there was no official rule that kept women from participating, only cultural norms. So Switzer had registered to run, signing her name as K. Switzer. The lack of a clearly identified gender was what allowed her to obtain an official race bid.[2]

Switzer wrote in her memoir that she was welcomed to the starting line by many of the men she was running with and against. She and her two companions ran together, and for the first few miles everything was fine. They were a handful of miles into the race when things went sideways. Race director Jock

Semple swiped at Switzer's bib and attacked her, trying to remove her from the race. "I'd never been manhandled, never even spanked as a child, and the physical power and swiftness of the attack stunned me," Switzer wrote. Switzer's boyfriend trucked Semple and the three runners took off, pursued by journalists. A humiliated Switzer wrote that she briefly thought about leaving the course.

"I knew if I quit, nobody would ever believe that women had the capability to run twenty-six-plus miles," Switzer wrote. "If I quit, everybody would say it was a publicity stunt. If I quit, it would set women's sports back, way back, instead of forward."

Switzer carried on. According to Switzer, her boyfriend ended up leaving their group in dramatic fashion. He paused running and ripped up his numbers, blaming Switzer for ruining his chance at the Olympics because he'd hit Semple. For the record, Switzer said she never asked him to come; he'd insisted. But he made it her fault anyway, in the middle of a marathon in the snow where the literal race manager had just tried to remove her from the race because she was a woman. In the end, Switzer finished. Her boyfriend did too. They went on to get married, though they later divorced.

After the conclusion of that snowy race, the headlines and photos of Semple's attack on Switzer were what the world paid attention to, even though another woman ran the Boston Marathon that day: Bobbi Gibb. She'd had her registration rejected by the Boston Athletic Association (BAA) in 1966. She said that race director Will Cloney wrote her a letter that said "women were not physiologically capable of running twenty-six miles,"[3] but she joined the race unofficially for the second consecutive year and finished an hour ahead of Switzer. After Switzer's successful official run of the Boston Marathon, women were formally banned from running the race until a women's race was created in 1972.

Curtailing women's participation in sports has been a core part of sports culture for much of modern history. It is only relatively recently that women have had access to sports with even moderate encouragement for participation. "In fairness," Gibb wrote of her experience in the 1966 Boston Marathon, "it should be noted that prior to 1966, people did not know that a woman was capable of running twenty-six miles, even women didn't know it, and many women officials were opposed to it out of fear that it would cause injury or death."

The assumption that women were incapable of sports participation drove early policies to keep them out of competition. But as Switzer's experience showed, there was also fear that maybe women weren't so incapable after all.

The first modern Olympics took place in Athens in 1896, featuring athletes from fourteen countries. All of those athletes were men. The event was the brainchild of French aristocrat Pierre de Coubertin, who served as the first president of the International Olympic Committee (IOC), a position he held from 1896 to 1925. The stated IOC mission was "to help build a peaceful and better world by educating young people through sport."[4] Though women did not compete in the first modern Olympic Games, twenty-two women competed in five sports— sailing, tennis, croquet, equestrianism, and golf—at the 1900 Games in Paris. Women made up just more than 2 percent of the total number of competing athletes. It wouldn't be until 2012, with the addition of women's boxing, that women competed in every sport present at the Olympics. But in the early twentieth century, women were fighting to compete in sports outside of the emerging Olympic Games.

Sixty-five years before Kathrine Switzer ran the Boston Marathon, Madge Syers entered the 1902 World Figure Skating Championships because there was no explicit rule keeping her from doing so. Until her entrance into the competition, all of the events sanctioned by the International Skating Union (ISU) had been male only. She placed second among the four competitors. In response to both her entrance and her relative success, the ISU amended the rules at its 1903 conference to formally bar women from competing in the existing championship. Two years later, the ISU created a separate women's championship. When figure skating first became part of the Olympic program in 1908, it did so with separate sex competitions and was one of the first sports to ostensibly place women on an equal footing with men and have multiple opportunities for women to compete on the highest stage (a pairs competition also debuted in 1908).[5] Syers won gold.

Depending on your perspective, Madge Syers' saga, and that of figure skating, could be an example of the empowerment of women through opportunities that were guaranteed and protected. However, it could just as easily be an example of how sex segregation in sports may not have needed to happen in the way it has. What if, instead of banning women from competition and creating a separate category, the ISU simply created and sanctioned integrated competitions? Often when questions like that are posed, we try to answer them in today's context. There is no question that the iteration of today's figure skating would disadvantage women because of a scoring system that favors jumping skills. Only one woman has successfully landed a quad jump in Olympic competition: Russia's Kamila Valieva at the 2022 Beijing Winter Olympics (she was later at the center of a doping scandal). In men's figure skating, however, it is now impossible to be in medal contention without quad jumps. In Syers' era, however, such athletic feats were not the center of the debate. Degree of difficulty and how routines are scored are about values, and those are human decisions. Why is it considered to be more difficult, and therefore more impressive, to twist four times in the air than, say, to perform a series of complex spinning combinations? Perhaps if figure skating as a sport had developed differently, the scoring system might have also developed differently; the values of the sport might have developed differently; the power brokers of the sport might have been different.

Women were simply assumed to be inferior athletes and therefore were not considered as viable participants in the sport.

Even though the figure skating controversy ignited by Syers was more than a century ago, and Switzer's run more than fifty years ago, the arguments about what women can accomplish have not dissipated. In fact, they surface in some of the most surprising places. Including on our television screens.

MICHELLE WARNKY-BUURMA TOOK a deep breath and pointed to the sky as she collected herself after completing the Salmon Ladder obstacle on the eleventh season of *American Ninja Warrior* (ANW) in 2019. She gripped the handles of the ball on Slam Dunk, the course's eighth obstacle. She'd never made it past the eighth obstacle on a ten-obstacle city finals course. This one, however, was in her home state of Ohio. She was competing in Cincinnati, a couple of hours south from where she owned a gym in Columbus. She just had to jump this ball to another platform and then do that two more times with two different (and heavier) balls to meet her personal best. No big deal.

ANW is based on the Japanese television show, *Sasuke*. The show features high-flying laches—airborne swing-jumps between two hanging bars, ledges, dangling objects, etc.—and competitors, often referred to as ninjas, race through balance- and strength-defying obstacles in a bid to claim total victory and be crowned an American Ninja Warrior.

The show divides the courses into qualifying rounds, semifinals, and the national finals in Las Vegas. The qualifying courses are all six obstacles, though not always the same obstacles; the semifinals courses are ten obstacles; and the national finals course is divided into four stages: a timed course for Stages 1 and 2, a grueling upper-body-driven Stage 3, and a seventy-five-foot rope climb up the structure known as Mt. Midoriyama for Stage 4. The climb must be finished in thirty seconds or less for the participant to be eligible for the $1,000,000 prize money. In the first thirteen seasons of the show, only five people had ever made it to Stage 4. In season fourteen, however, five competitors made it to the fourth stage. But out of those ten athletes, only three completed the climb in under thirty seconds. None of them were women. A woman has never even made it to Stage 3, and only three have ever run Stage 2 in regular season competition. As a television program and a sport, ANW offers a unique window into the essence of sex separation in sports. Unlike in figure skating and what Syers experienced, women have always been welcome to compete alongside men. In theory, ANW is an athletic competition where gender doesn't matter. But women are still running a course designed to test the physical boundaries of men, which means the ultimate successes on the show and in the sport often evade all but the most elite of female competitors.

Only one woman had ever finished the type of course Warnky-Buurma was in the middle of running. That was Kacy Catanzaro in season six. Five years before Warnky-Buurma, Catanzaro made history atop the Spider Climb, successfully wedging her five-foot frame between the walls to climb the height of the obstacle to the buzzer. Hitting a buzzer, or collecting buzzers, means completion in ANW parlance. Every time a ninja brings their hand down on the cylinder to send the smoke into the air, it means they've conquered something nearly impossible. On the city finals (or semifinals, as they're referred to now) courses, though ninja superstars Jessie Graff and Jesse Labreck had come close multiple times, only Catanzaro had ever known the honor of standing atop the tenth obstacle to smash a buzzer.

When Warnky-Buurma cleared the eighth obstacle, she threw her hands up in the air in celebration. She'd been introduced to the show by friends begging her to watch it. Warnky-Buurma grew up playing sports, participating in a mixture of track, hockey, baseball, football, and rock climbing. She'd been climbing for years, and any ninja will tell you athletic fluidity and climbing are the fundamentals of a successful run on the show. After much encouragement, she finally watched it. "I was like, 'This is awesome,'" Warnky-Buurma said.

She looked up an event in New Jersey that had similar obstacles to the show and that invited folks to try them, but she couldn't get there in time for the event. She ended up going out to the course anyway and trying the Salmon Ladder. The obstacle is an ANW staple and requires a competitor to hang from a bar resting on a rung on either side and jump the bar up multiple rungs using a kip motion like in gymnastics. Warnky-Buurma got the ladder on the first try, and the guy spotting her was impressed. "He was like, 'I've never seen a girl get the Salmon Ladder before,'" Warnky-Buurma said. "I was like, 'Really?' It wasn't that hard." He also told Warnky-Buurma that he'd never seen a "girl" get the Warped Wall before, a curved fourteen-foot wall that served as the punctuation to every first-round ANW course. She worked on that the next day and was able to do it.

After that, she started building obstacles on her own. A producer saw her post in a Facebook group about getting building help and encouraged her to apply to the show. Suddenly, she was cast on season five and among the first group of women to hit a qualifying buzzer and find success on the course. Six years after her debut, she was staring down the ninth of ten obstacles on a city finals course, a place few women before her had ever been. All she had to do was lache perfectly across a series of hanging cylinders, then climb thirty-five feet and open three sets of doors along the way that weighed nearly as much as she did.

After successfully bypassing the last part of the ninth obstacle, throwing her body to the platform in a long dismount that was both a calculated decision and a prayer, Warnky-Buurma wedged her feet against the walls of the last obstacle and began the thirty-five-foot ascent. She struggled past the first set of doors, pushed past the second set, and, with excited glee, powered past the last set to become just the second woman to ever finish a ten-obstacle course. She touched the buzzer and fell to her knees against the railing, exhausted and grateful.

Warnky-Buurma's success was an incredible moment of athletic achievement, and her hitting the buzzer in semifinals was also the exception that has proven to be the rule. Later that night, Labreck also hit the buzzer in Cincinnati, in a historic moment that brought the total number of women who had hit buzzers on ten-obstacle courses to three. There have been three more seasons of the show, but the number of women who have hit semifinals buzzers remains at three. Labreck, however, has done it three times. Labreck also became the third woman to finish Stage 1 in the finals, in 2021, but the pattern of irregular breakthroughs and little sustained success for women on the television show has led some of the highest-performing women to ask hard questions about the future of ANW, both on television and off.

ANW is certainly athletic. I hesitate to call the show a sport because it's cast and produced like the television show it is, complete with tear-jerking stories pulling at your heart-strings. But the amazing thing about ANW is that, unlike most "sports," the entire concept was developed around the idea that each ninja competes against the course, and the course remains the same. That means, unlike almost everything else in our sporting culture, all athletes are measured the same, regardless of traits like height, size, and, yes, gender.

When the show started, it was aired on the now-defunct network G4, which was kind of a "nerd-bro" network. When Warnky-Buurma was watching the show with her mom to see if she wanted to apply, they paused the show to count the number of women they saw competing and in the stands. "We scanned the crowd, because I was like, 'I really want to do this, but are women even allowed to do this?'" Warnky-Buurma said.

Women were allowed to compete, and ANW wanted more women to participate. Seasons five, six, and seven were huge breakthroughs for female competitors. The aforementioned

Warnky-Buurma and Catanzaro started competing. So did Graff, who competed during her first season wearing a chicken costume before growing into one of the most successful women to ever compete. Meagan Martin, the lone woman of color in this pioneering group, became a buzzer-hitting mainstay. Labreck started competing during season seven and now holds the record—ten—for the most buzzers hit by a woman on the show.

Fellow competitor and elite ninja Allyssa Beird watched Warnky-Buurma finish the Cincinnati course in tears. She'd been competing on ANW since the seventh season, when she was among an elite foursome of women—which included Warnky-Buurma and Labreck—to hit qualifying buzzers in the same city, something that had never happened before and has not happened since. Beird teaches fourth grade in Massachusetts, but before she became a teacher, she was a gymnast for fifteen years. She first got involved in ninja training after looking for a gym where she could try out obstacles. One thing led to another and she was on the show hitting a buzzer.

ANW's relationship with gender has shifted over time. In the early seasons, the show employed the same advancement system for everyone. The top thirty qualifiers in each region moved on to the semifinals, and the top fifteen competitors in the semifinals qualified for the national finals. The field would be rounded out with wild cards to create the national finals field of roughly 100 athletes, many of which went to popular women competitors who either missed the cut in their regions, or fell early on a temperamental obstacle. That changed in season nine, when women were given their own advancement system. The top five qualifying women were automatically guaranteed a spot in the semifinals, and the top two from each region's semifinals qualified for Vegas. The number is now three women from each semifinal. No more wild cards. "I remember talking to a couple other female ninjas about it. We're like, 'Okay, this is actually better than crossing our fingers and hoping we're in the top fifteen, top thirty, or hoping for that wild card call,'" Beird said. "There's just so much on hope, rather than proving that you're, you know, a top female competitor. But it really hasn't made that much of a difference in my own like, pride on the course, you know, I've qualified both ways now."

"I wasn't a huge fan of it, because I felt like it meant something to make it into the top thirty," fellow top competitor Meagan Martin said. "I still would say I kind of like that better. I do like that now you can for sure have five or more women in the semifinals. But prior to that rule change, there were women already getting into the semi. There were more and more women getting into that top thirty. So, I don't know if the change was a hundred percent necessary."

The reality of ANW was that for as many women who have seen success, those successes have been more one-offs than sustained breakthroughs for high-level women competitors. That is not to say that Warnky-Buurma, Martin, Beird, Graff, and others aren't phenomenal athletes who can (and do) hit buzzers. But their successes are outliers. At least for now. And that uncomfortable truth has led to a lot of reflection among the ninja community about how best to move forward while holding true to the spirit of the emerging sport. "This is a hot-button issue," Warnky-Buurma said.

In addition to the show, a sporting community sprung up around ninja gyms and competitions. World Ninja League (WNL) holds competitions for kids, teens, and elite ninjas across the country. Just as with the show, all ninjas run the same course. Kids of all genders are competitive in the kid category, but fewer and fewer girls cleared courses during the teen competition, something that only became more pronounced among the elite competitors. For this reason, the athletes began to ask if they should change the course for women. "For so long, I was so adamant," Beird said. "This is exactly what we need. As women competitors, we can keep up with the men. And sometimes that's true. And sometimes it's not."

The question became how to get more girls and women to complete, or clear, more courses in competition. Lots of options were thrown out for consideration. The field could be divided by height. The field could be divided by sex. Adaptations could be made so the course was more equitable. "But there were some really interesting ideas that went further than just separating by men and women on the specific course," Beird said. "It's really coming down to thinking about which type of athlete the obstacle would benefit and how we can more evenly or equitably make the course accessible for all different types of skill levels."

Each idea opened more boxes (and caused more of what I'll call "spirited discussion"), but extending the time to complete an obstacle has been the one implemented so far. "And I think that's been a great change," Beird said. "You're now getting to see more female clears. As a competitor, you always approach a course wanting to clear. As an audience member, it's exciting to see people clear a course. So I think it's beneficial to like all parts of the sport involved."

Height has historically been an advantage on the ANW course. The height of an average American man is five foot nine. The height of an average American woman is five foot four. Smaller competitors of all genders have struggled on the course. Former Olympic gymnast Jonathan Horton has struggled on the more advanced courses not because he doesn't have the upper-body strength to complete it, but because it is just more difficult to traverse a course that is more or less designed for someone significantly taller. Longer arms and the ability to generate more torque help to lache bigger gaps; longer legs help to jump and traverse bigger steps. It's easier to get up the Warped Wall at five foot nine than at five feet. Kacy Catanzaro, who is five feet tall, was not just the first woman to complete a ten-obstacle course, but at the time she was also the shortest competitor to ever accomplish the feat.

In addition to height, there's also the simple fact that what makes ANW so compelling to watch is the strength obstacles. It's amazing to watch "regular people" do the most irregular things, like cling to a two-inch ledge with their fingers. In semifinals courses, the back half of the course is usually stacked with upper-body obstacles. It's a gauntlet designed to test grip and upper-body strength. Lots of athletes fail to finish because of exhaustion—getting "pumped out"—rather than from lack of ability.

When Jessie Graff finished Stage 1 in season eight, she did so on a night when only seventeen ninjas were able to complete the course, far below the average. Unlike the earlier courses, Stages 1 and 2 are timed. Graff was able to finish Stage 1 in time, but she was also among the top five fastest. Graff, Beird, and Labreck were the only women in the history of the show to advance past Stage 1 at the national finals. The rigidity of that barrier has proved to be formidable, exposing the inequities that exist within the show. Much of that barrier is due to course design. Women have failed to move forward in the national finals despite having guaranteed opportunities to run the course mostly due to three things: the time to run the course, an obstacle known as the Jumping Spider, which requires athletes to jump from a trampoline and land between two walls that are five feet apart, and a modified version of the Warped Wall, which uses a shortened runway.

For much of the show's history, the only prize money awarded was to the person who successfully claimed the mantel of "American Ninja Warrior" atop Mt. Midoriyama. That meant it took seven seasons for ANW to pay out anything to the competitors. That has since changed, with more money available at different stages of competition. Much of that moneymaking opportunity was skewed to favor male competitors. In the qualifying courses, top finishers received small cash prizes. There was also the Mega Wall, an eighteen-foot version of the Warped Wall. Any athlete who got to the top of that wall to hit a buzzer in qualifying was awarded $10,000. Now, every season, a prize of $100,000 is awarded to the "last ninja standing," meaning the athlete who went furthest on the course. None of these prizes are gendered, but no woman had ever seriously competed for them. Meanwhile, elite female ninjas were some of the most famous and visible personalities on the show. In 2021, ANW held the first annual Women's Championship as a special episode of the show. The winner is awarded $50,000.

"I liked the Women's Championship, mainly because it finally gave the women an opportunity to make a good amount of money," Martin said. "We're never racing, we're just trying to finish the course. So the real moneymaking opportunities aren't as prevalent."

"I love having the opportunity to compete among the men to show women are strong and capable, but I do think there should be awards for the top placing women," Graff said. "Which is not currently the case. I have won money in different rounds of competition by placing in the top three men, but I do believe because there is such a physiological difference between men and women, there should be a separate prize structure for the top women."

I was surprised when Graff said that. Not because I think she's wrong, but because of the perspective she brought. She has achieved at the highest levels on the show and is one of the best ninjas, regardless of gender. Of course she stands to benefit from a different prize structure, but why shouldn't she? One of the things that interested me about ANW was the tension between bias and physiological limits. There is absolutely no question that course design favors male ninjas, and yet women do find success. Statistically, though, they don't find the success one would expect. This is a sport being designed off of a television show, so it's not the same as basketball or tennis. However, as a sport and competition, ANW and WNL have strayed closer to separating by sex over time than dismantling the idea of it.

The prevailing system of sports being segregated by sex, as demonstrated by Syers and Switzer, has its roots in a lack of inclusion and sexism. But that same system also has roots in trying to ensure fairness for women competing in systems that historically have not been built for their participation. How to separate physiological reality from assumption while creating a place for women to access sports fairly has been a battle for as long as there have been women's sports. In the United States, that battle truly began with the passing of a law that was thirty-seven words long.

2.

THIRTY-SEVEN WORDS

"No person in the United States shall, on the basis of sex, be excluded from participation in, be denied the benefits of, or be subjected to discrimination under any educational program or activity receiving Federal financial assistance."—Title IX of the Education Amendments of 1972

A CENTRAL PILLAR of achievement by feminist movements in the 1970s was the passage of Title IX on June 23, 1972. The law banned sex-based discrimination in education and all of its ensuing activities, including athletics. What made the law stick was the perceived threat of losing federal funding should a school not be in compliance, something that, fifty years later, has never happened.

While the language of the law was broadly based, in effect, the law fundamentally changed the reality for women who wanted to play sports. Suddenly schools that had boys' basketball teams needed to have girls' teams as well; ditto for swimming, golf, and soccer. According to a 1971 survey by the National Federation of State High School Associations

(NFHS), the number of girls participating in sports that year totaled 250,776, which was less than the number of boys participating just in wrestling that year (265,039).[1] By the 1975–76 school year, girls' participation in basketball alone had jumped to almost 405,000 students.[2]

The reality of women's sports is that without some kind of legal requirement for funding, they would be a shell of what we know them to be now. That was made perfectly clear by the pre-1972 years. What else is clear is that without Title IX, the United States likely would never have enjoyed some of our favorite sports memories. It's hard to imagine a dominant U.S. Women's National Team (USWNT) winning the most Women's World Cups of any country without Title IX. The entire women's basketball universe likely wouldn't exist either. And the same is true for sports that have seen tremendous participation growth, like volleyball and softball.

Title IX created robust experiences for women at the high school level but more significantly at the college level. In the United States, only soccer and basketball have viable professional opportunities domestically. Even for two of the most popular college sports, volleyball and softball, there are no current leagues that are on the level of the WNBA and NWSL when it comes to sustainability. Athletes Unlimited (AU) is trying a new model that uses an individual scoring system for players, sort of like fantasy sports, instead of the franchise or team models most commonly used in American sports. AU sponsors both a volleyball and a softball league and has games on national television, but it's still a start-up. With so few professional opportunities for these sports, the collegiate experience is the premier one.

There is a narrative that women's sports are unpopular, but

the data say otherwise. As of this writing, the most watched soccer game in U.S. history was the USWNT 5–2 victory over Japan to win the World Cup in 2015, with 26.7 million viewers across Fox and Telemundo. ESPN reported that 22.6 million people tuned in to the 2022 College Football Playoff National Championship across all ESPN networks. In the ratings world, football is king, so it's not quite an apples-to-apples comparison, but both the World Cup and the College Football Playoff are special events and, frankly, 26.7 million is a huge number. It was also likely an undercount. That number doesn't exactly account for the watch parties around the country. But even outside of the absolutely monster number of the 2015 World Cup, the everyday data around women's sports viewership are promising.

In general, the value of women's sports is depressed by comparisons to football ratings, but the value of men's sports is inflated by football as well. In 2021, NFL regular season games averaged 17.1 million viewers, with the top ten games all garnering at least 25 million viewers.[3] College football posts big numbers, but not as big as the NFL. Outside of the bowl games, the top-rated college football game in 2021 was the SEC Championship Game between Alabama and Georgia, with 15.28 million viewers. The rest of top-tier men's sports do not come anywhere close to that viewership on a consistent basis. In 2021, the NHL playoffs went head-to-head with the Women's College World Series. The opening round of the NHL playoffs averaged 642,000 viewers and the first weekend of the WCWS averaged 755,000 viewers.[4] Women's March Madness doesn't post the same viewership as Men's March Madness, but the 2022 championship game between South Carolina and UConn drew 4.85 million viewers. That's not a small number! The 2021–22 NBA regular season averaged 1.6 million viewers per game.[5] I'm not saying that the WNBA and NBA rate the same, or that a championship match is the same comparison as a regular season average, but the reality is when it comes to eyeballs tuning in to sports, football is an outlier. When you get into the data, there is plenty to show that there is popular interest in major women's sports.

Corporate interest is another matter. WNBA Commissioner Cathy Engelbert has said that less than one percent of sponsorship dollars are allocated to women's sports, with much of that going to endorsements for individual athletes like Serena Williams and Naomi Osaka instead of team sports.[6] And it's not like cities and towns have been lining up to pay for stadiums and arenas for women's sports teams. All of this is because of Title IX! If Title IX hadn't passed, it's easy to see how all of the excuses made on Twitter about why no one cares about women's sports would have been projected onto college and high school sports as a means to resist calls for investment.

What's interesting about Title IX as a law, however, is that the text of it says nothing about a requirement to fund women's sports. Instead, it bars sex-based discrimination in education. In 1972, it was pretty clear what that meant, but the way we understand sex as a society has changed and evolved over time. In June 2020, the Supreme Court ruled that sex-based discrimination in employment *includes* sexual orientation and gender identity. It's not hard to see that same logic extrapolated to Title IX and how it governs education access in all forms, including athletics, which would enshrine protections for queer and transgender youth to access school sports.

But there was no guarantee that Title IX would create a slew of women's sports teams. When the law passed, it was part of a larger omnibus education bill. Three years later, hearings were held to decide how the law would be implemented. There was surprising disagreement that included a key question: Should there even be women's sports at all?

THE ATHLETICS SYSTEM we know today, of schools with both boys' and girls' sports teams, was not guaranteed upon passage of Title IX. Following the law's quiet enactment, huge questions of implementation were raised as the agency equivalent to today's Department of Education began to draft enforcement recommendations. Thirty-seven words, after all, was not a lot of words. One of the primary questions had to do with athletics. Did nondiscrimination and equal opportunity mean integrating women into the current athletic system with increased opportunities, or did it mean creating a separate system that would be equal to the existing one?

"There was debate in the seventies over the question of whether sex-segregated athletics was the best way to end exclusion and discrimination," Libby Sharrow said to me. Sharrow is a political scientist who studies how public policy shapes cultural understanding of sex and gender. "And that debate was fairly robust. In fact, many interest groups were concerned that a sex-segregated system will ultimately put a real ceiling effect on possibilities for women and girls as athletes."

Prior to the passage of Title IX, girls and women had very few athletic opportunities. That meant on a practical level, they'd been left out of the practice of skill building across sports. A person doesn't simply pick up a basketball and become a great basketball player. There's training and skill, in addition to athletic talent. A fully integrated system in the 1970s would have meant that high school–aged girls would be trying out for the same soccer and basketball and football teams as their male peers without nearly as much of the training. There was very little, and, in some cases no fundamental foundation for girls at that time because so many hadn't been given the opportunity to play sports as children. The idea of throwing women into a fully integrated system when, as a group, they were starting decades behind didn't feel like the best path forward to everyone, even those who were more interested in an integrated sports model.

The National Organization for Women (NOW) supported sex separation more as a means to an end, with the eventual goal being integration. In a 1974 memo, the organization wrote, "NOW is opposed to any regulation which precludes eventual integration. Regulations that 'protect' girls and/or women are against NOW goals and are contradictory to our stand on the [Equal Rights Amendment]."[7]

The core of the issue with sex integration—meaning no separate gender categories within or between teams—in sports was (and is) the question of how to do it. Because sports had been a male domain, it was built for men. Speed. Power. Strength. Those are traits that reflect masculinity, but that doesn't necessarily mean that they had to be the foundation for sports competition. However, by September 1975, when the Office for Civil Rights (OCR) in the Department of Health, Education, and Welfare (DHEW)—the predecessor of today's Department of Education—issued a memo on implementing Title IX as it pertained to ending sex discrimination in athletics, separate teams by sex were explicitly allowed, and in some cases recommended. For example, a school could not abolish women's teams and open up the men's teams but then cut women from participating. That didn't amount to equal opportunity to DHEW, and it spoke to the tension that NOW and other women's liberation groups felt at the time. Forgoing a separate category, at least in the short term, would have likely meant that fewer women played sports, which was not the intent behind Title IX.

The consequence of OCR writing sex segregation into the recommendations was that much of the debate happening among and between feminist groups about how to organize women's sports faded away over time. To those of us who grew up in the post–Title IX era, separating sports by sex feels like the only way to organize athletics, because that's how it has always been. It wasn't until I read some of Sharrow's writings that I realized there was more to that story.

"We seem to have lost and forgotten that history," Sharrow said. "And instead have sort of naturalized another understanding that segregation is the only way that we could possibly imagine this world of athletics best benefitting girls and women. We actually can question the structure. We've done it before; we just have not seriously done it in recent years."

With sex separation codified by the enforcement of Title IX, women's sports as we know them today became available for girls and women around the country. That does not mean, however, that equality was achieved.

"THIS IS OUR weight room."

University of Oregon women's basketball center Sedona Prince uttered those words on a video shared to TikTok and Twitter. The camera panned around to show a sad, lonely dumbbell tree with one set of weights and a couple of yoga mats that supposedly comprised the "weight room" for all the women's teams competing at the bubble site of the NCAA women's basketball tournament in 2021. The internet subsequently exploded. That dumbbell tree stood in stark contrast to the rows of squat racks and cardio machines that were available to the NCAA men's teams at their site in Indianapolis. The women's site in San Antonio wasn't just in a different location, it was of a different quality. That difference violated the spirit of Title IX, if not the letter, because the NCAA, which organizes all of the collegiate championships (except major college football), is not an education institution, and therefore is not subject to Title IX (this interpretation of the law had been upheld in 1999 by the Supreme Court of the United States in *NCAA v. Smith*).

Prince's video received millions of views and thousands of shares across social media. Television shows highlighted the disparity. Corporations tweeted that they'd be willing to help. The NCAA scrambled, with then-NCAA president Mark Emmert saying that the spaces "weren't intended to be weight rooms." Within days, a new weight room appeared in San Antonio, costing the NCAA $370,139. That did not end the conversation, however. Prince opened the floodgates with her video.

There were all kinds of disparities between the men's and women's tournaments that expanded well beyond the weight room issue. Questions about media rights, branding, and tournament format cropped up. The NCAA commissioned law firm Kaplan Hecker & Fink to study the issue of gender equity as it pertained to the organization's basketball championships. In a 118-page report released in August 2021, the law firm noted a number of differences between the championships: The women's tournament was not permitted to make an announcement of (or get approval for) its single bubble site until a month after the men, putting the women's tournament significantly behind the men's in terms of planning. The COVID-19 testing method was different at the two sites—men got daily PCR tests (the gold standard), and women used antigen tests supplemented by one PCR test per week. The food options were also different. Men got prepackaged meals during quarantine and then buffets for the rest of the tournament. Women received prepackaged meals for the entire tournament. The men's tournament used "March Madness" for tournament branding, and the women's tournament didn't. The men's tournament was sixty-eight teams, and the women's was sixty-four. The list just kept going.

What started as a video about a singular discrepancy ballooned into a much bigger conversation about the prevalence of gender inequity throughout the NCAA basketball championships, and other sports as well. Volleyball coaches spoke out about the conditions faced in their 2021 bubble tournament (delayed from fall 2020), including questions about locker room space and broadcasting arrangements, even though the field shrank from sixty-four to forty-eight teams due to the pandemic.[8] Softball coaches spoke out about the compressed nature of their tournament format and the impact that had on player safety. The Women's College World Series historically has been played over seven days in Oklahoma City. Every year there are weather issues that cause games to be significantly delayed, and in 2021, games were bumped an entire day. But even with the extra day, the WCWS still played a maximum of seventeen games in eight days, with teams in the losers' bracket staring down the barrel of the possibility of doubleheaders with zero days of rest. The Men's College World Series uses a twelve-day schedule for the same maximum number of games. The collective voices of athletes, coaches, and administrators speaking out in 2021 led to significant changes in

2022. Of course, some things were "bubble" dependent, but other things were not.

March Madness is now branding that is used for both the men's and the women's basketball tournaments. The women's tournament debuted a new format in 2022 with sixty-eight teams. The softball championship expanded its time frame to avoid the possibility of doubleheaders on consecutive days.

Before everyone claps for the NCAA "doing the right thing," however, it's important to note that the disparity rife within NCAA championships was always within the organization's control to address. Additionally, the existence of such stark treatment between men's and women's championships, though specific to this particular moment, was not *unique* to this moment. The NCAA wasn't even in charge of women's championships in the immediate aftermath of Title IX. In fact, the NCAA didn't exactly embrace Title IX when it was passed.

Before the 1975 and 1979 memos regarding Title IX implementation were published by DHEW, the men's college sports apparatus tried to extricate itself from having to comply with Title IX at all. John Tower, a U.S. senator from Texas, proposed an amendment to Title IX in 1974 that would have exempted collegiate athletics from the law. When it failed to pass, he introduced another piece of legislation a year later that would have exempted "revenue-generating" sports from the law. That also failed to pass. The NCAA supported such legislation. Then–NCAA president John A. Fuzak appeared before Congress to argue that the legislation would, in fact, create *more* opportunities for women by protecting the "surplus" generated from revenue sports.[9] The NCAA, however, had already acknowledged that at that time, its 750 member institutions operated at a $50

million deficit. Following the failure of these legislative projects, the NCAA filed a lawsuit against DHEW in 1976 in hopes
of circumventing Title IX enforcement, but it was dismissed
two years later.

Though the NCAA today hosts championships and governs the overwhelming majority of collegiate athletics in both
men's and women's sports, in the subsequent years following
Title IX's passage, the NCAA didn't hold women's championships. Instead, the Association for Intercollegiate Athletics for
Women (AIAW) did. The AIAW was founded in 1971 for the
explicit purpose of holding collegiate women's championships.
Originally, the organization barred member schools from offering scholarships and recruiting, instead focusing on a model
that was similar to what we expect (albeit somewhat naïvely)
from high school sports: colleges create teams, put them up for
competition against one another, and the best team wins. No
further incentive allowed.

In 1973, however, athletes and coaches in Florida sued for
the right to issue scholarships, which the school argued would
greatly enhance the ability of schools to attract talented athletes. The existence of the lawsuit pressured AIAW to allow
scholarships. Dale Plyley traced the battle between the NCAA
and AIAW.[10] Until 1982, the AIAW was the primary home of
women's collegiate sports championships. Aided by Title IX
and the growing investment in women's sports, the AIAW
had approximately 960 member schools in all fifty states and
D.C. by 1980. The following year, the National Association of
Intercollegiate Athletics (NAIA) entered women's sports by host-
ing nine championships. Then, in the 1981–82 academic year,
the NCAA finally entered women's sports as well. The NCAA
hosted a total of twenty-nine women's championships in twelve

sports across its three divisions. According to Plyley, the NCAA allowed all of its existing member institutions to participate in the women's championships without increasing membership dues, undercutting the AIAW. In addition to the NCAA entering women's sports, NBC also declined to show the AIAW championships on air in the fall of 1981, though it had done so in previous years.[11] The AIAW would cease operations following the 1981–82 school year, but not before suing the NCAA.

In the fall of 1981, while grappling with the loss of revenue and broadcasting from NBC and the entrance of the NCAA into women's sports, the AIAW filed a lawsuit against the NCAA accusing the organization of violating antitrust law.[12] The AIAW argued that the NCAA's bundling of media rights to men's and women's championships was illegal, and that the use of excess money to underwrite women's championships was also illegal because those actions created a monopoly. The AIAW lost the case in 1983 and lost its subsequent appeal a year later. But those losses were somewhat moot because the AIAW had already shuttered, leaving the NCAA as the last organization standing and shifting most of the women's championships to its purview. Of course, the NAIA technically still existed, but as an organization it was (and is) a much smaller outfit.

Interestingly, the practice of rights bundling, which the AIAW argued violated antitrust law, also came up in the 2022 Kaplan report following Prince's weight room video. The NCAA has long-term media contracts with three entities: CBS, Turner Sports, and ESPN. CBS and Turner combine to broadcast the men's basketball tournament *and* to sell the NCAA's corporate sponsorship program that blankets all ninety championships. They reportedly pay a fee of $1.1 billion per year for that privilege. ESPN broadcasts twenty-nine NCAA championships across men's and women's sports, including marquee women's championships like basketball, softball, volleyball, and gymnastics. ESPN reportedly pays $34 million per year total for *all* of those championships combined. The Kaplan report argues that the women's basketball championship alone should be valued considerably higher, perhaps three to four times more. The current arrangement with CBS all but assures that women's championships (and less-watched men's championships) will be unable to be evaluated at market value. It's impossible to know what the value of a property is when it's packaged with something else and sold at a discount. This hurts the amount of revenue generated by women's sports and payouts to conferences for making the postseason. Currently, conferences receive no money for participating or advancing in women's March Madness, whereas for the 2022 men's tournament, each conference received one unit (valued at $338,210.96) per team playing in the tournament.[13] Conferences earned an additional unit for every game won by each team. Those units are paid out each year for six years after the tournament year in which they are earned. Conferences then distribute that money to schools.

Though the sports themselves have remained sex separated, the NCAA has control over both men's and women's sports and, as such, provides a window into the barriers presented by a more integrated model foreseen by many women's organizations. Even if women were given the opportunity to try out for existing athletic teams, would they have been allowed to compete? Looking at how women's sports have and haven't evolved in the past fifty years, it's not hard to surmise the answer to that question. Even as a separate category and idea, women's sports have been systemically devalued; the NCAA women's basketball tournament is just one example of that. The media rights bundling practiced by the NCAA was also practiced in soccer, putting the rights of MLS and U.S. Soccer (including the popular U.S. Women's National Team) together. It's hard to determine how valuable a property is if it's not allowed to stand on its own. Sports, however, were not the only thing Title IX affected. As discussed earlier, sports weren't mentioned anywhere in the law. At its core, Title IX was civil rights legislation protecting all students from discrimination in education settings. While for a generation of athletes in women's sports, Title IX was defined by all of the opportunity it created for women accessing athletics, for another generation, Title IX came to mean something else entirely.

IN THE 2010s, Title IX once again became the center of a contested debate. This time, however, the debate had nothing to do with sports at all. Young women in college began filing complaints with the Department of Education, arguing that universities' lackluster responses to sexual assaults on campus were a type of sex-based discrimination and therefore violated Title IX. This was something the department itself had argued as well. In 2011, OCR released a Dear Colleague Letter—a type of formal guidance from the department—that stipulated "Sexual harassment is unwelcome conduct of a sexual nature. It includes unwelcome sexual advances, requests for sexual favors, and other verbal, nonverbal, or physical conduct of a sexual nature. Sexual violence is a form of sexual harassment prohibited by Title IX."[14]

Sexual assaults occurring on college campuses was nothing new. Entire collegiate subcultures existed as a means of encouraging partying and "getting women drunk" (looking at you, Greek life). Enthusiastic consent wasn't exactly a staple conversation in the public consciousness or in pop culture. If pop culture could be considered a mirror, then the movies about high school– and college-aged kids released in the '80s, '90s, and 2000s reflected a culture generally ambivalent about alcohol, sex, and consent, from *Animal House* to *American Pie* to *Bring It On*.

The activists in the early 2010s, however, successfully reframed the entire conversation, leveraging the guidance from OCR itself. Alexandra Brodsky and Dana Bolger cofounded the organization Know Your IX in 2013. Brodsky brought fifteen survivors together to file a complaint against Yale. Andrea Pino and Annie Clark filed a Title IX complaint against the University of North Carolina at Chapel Hill in 2013 and launched the organization End Rape on Campus. The actions taken by these students (at the time) were led by survivors. By sharing their experiences, they forced the culture to pay attention—and also learn about a lesser-known provision of education legislation: the Clery Act.

In 1986, Jeanne Clery was raped and murdered in her residence hall room. Following her death, Clery's parents lobbied for the passage of what became the Clery Act, which required colleges and universities to publicly report the crimes that happen on campus, support the victims of those crimes, and publicly state what policies and procedures exist to ensure a safe campus. The scope of the Clery Act expanded beyond sexual assault and harassment, but such offenses were absolutely included in reporting requirements. The Clery Act and Title IX were separate pieces of legislation, but their considerable overlap was successfully leveraged by students trying to hold their universities accountable for adequate support of survivors of sexual assault and harassment on their respective campuses.

In addition to confronting an important discussion that needed to be—and continues to need to be—front and center when it came to issues in higher education, the discussion about sexual assault wasn't harmonious. As more guidance was issued and policy implemented, disagreements emerged over how the issue should be handled. More conservative voices pushed back against regulations that made it easier for those accused of sexual assault to be punished by colleges. Following Donald Trump's inauguration in 2017, sexual assault and harassment in schools was one of the first pieces of guidance rescinded by the new Secretary of Education, Betsy DeVos. The other, of course, was the guidance regarding transgender students (we'll come back to that in a later chapter).

This period of time, however, began a resurgence of intense politicization of Title IX and regulations coming from the Department of Education. Title IX had always been political; that wasn't new. But the level of public awareness around mechanisms such as Dear Colleague Letters changed during this period. These political squabbles also began to happen in the wake of increasing gridlock in Congress and hyper-partisanship in our political system. Much of these battles have happened over *interpretation* of existing law. This ultimately served as a battleground for partisan warfare over Title IX regulations, especially over who the law was designed to protect. What did "on the basis of sex" mean decades after Title IX was passed? The work done by activists on the issue of sexual assault, though not directly related to sports, refocused Title IX in popular consciousness as an education equality law that affected sports rather than applying only to sports themselves. Furthermore, as the Department of Education received more inquiries about transgender youth in the subsequent years, the use of the department's ability to issue guidance on key questions would ignite the battle over transgender youth playing sports, something we will come back to later.

How the Department of Education handled Title IX enforcement in the past decade has depended on who was in office. But no matter which side of the political aisle you're on, it was impossible to ignore Title IX's impact on girls' and women's sports. More girls and women have had the opportunity to play on sports teams because Title IX was passed. Survey data from the NFHS counted 3,238,024 participants in girls' sports for 2021–22. To reiterate, the same organization put the number of participants in girls' sports in 1971 at 250,776. That's less than the number of girls playing basketball today. For many people, this remains the primary legacy of the law. All those questions around implementation and sex segregation, however, never left. But Title IX isn't just about creating more opportunity for sports participation; it's also about the way sexism operates in educational environments, down to the color of a visiting team's locker room.

THE VISITING LOCKER room at the University of Iowa's football stadium is pink. I don't mean that just the walls are pink. Everything is pink. Pink floor, pink ceiling, pink urinals, pink lockers, it's all pink. It was painted that way in 1982 by Iowa football coach Hayden Fry, and as an homage to the coach, Iowa renovated the locker room to add the additional pink accoutrements in the summer of 2005.

Erin Buzuvis was a visiting professor at the University of Iowa College of Law from January 2005 to May 2006. During the time she was in Iowa City, the university was conducting a yearlong self-study to examine compliance with NCAA standards in multiple areas, including gender equity. Buzuvis studies gender discrimination in sports and is an expert in Title IX law, especially as that law is applied to LGBTQ+ topics in sports. Part of Iowa's self-study was holding a public forum about gender equity in athletics. Buzuvis attended with the intention of sharing her perspective on the pink locker room. "It was as a way of exposing the visiting football team to the ignominy of having to change in a pink room," she said to me. "This was their master mental strategy."

It was very clear what the pink locker room represented to Buzuvis. Changing in a pink locker room was meant to be demeaning and cut to the heart of the visiting team's masculinity. What could be worse than a manly football player being forced to pee in a pink urinal or put on his cleats in front of a pink locker? The pink locker room was meant to be an insult. Bo Schembechler, legendary football coach at the University of Michigan, would have his staff cover the walls, a tradition carried on by current Michigan coach Jim Harbaugh. Fry studied psychology and has said that the color pink is calming, but he also wrote in his book *Hayden Fry: A High Porch Picnic* that the color was the color of "sissies" and conjured images of little girls' bedrooms. When Buzuvis got the perfunctory email to attend the public forum, she knew she had to go. How could she not?

On September 27, 2005, Buzuvis spoke at this public forum, saying what she thought was pretty obvious: that the pink locker room was misogynistic and homophobic. "What you're really saying is you're weak like a girl," Buzuvis said, according to *The New York Times*. "That belittles every female athlete out there." The rebuke for Buzuvis came swiftly. She was inundated with negative emails and comments from the Iowa community. They were not happy that she had just criticized their brand-new pink locker room, a locker room that, more than fifteen years later, still sports the pink urinals.

What I found interesting about the pink locker room, beyond my shock that such a thing exists in the world, was how it shows just how much sexism and homophobia lurks below the surface of sports culture. I would argue that painting a room pink to remind young men of "little girls' bedrooms" ahead of a football game is pretty overt, but it's the sort of thing that can exist just out of view for many people. Title IX did create more opportunity for women to participate in sports, but it did not remedy the assumptions and stereotypes faced by women like Kathrine Switzer. The question of sex separation in school sports was mostly answered, and the sports landscape was forever changed. But things like the pink locker room still exist.

3.

NO BOW LESBO

WHEN BARACK OBAMA nominated Elena Kagan to the Supreme Court in the spring of 2010, a particular rumor began to swirl about her. It seemed to derive from the fact that she wasn't married and had short hair. The whispers percolated in Washington, D.C., in politically connected corners and also, bizarrely, the gay blogosphere, combining to become dull noise that suggested that Kagan might be a lesbian.

"A White House spokesperson called me," journalist Ben Smith said. At the time, Smith worked at Politico, blogging about politics. (Most recently, he was the media critic at *The New York Times*.) "[The spokesperson] said, 'I'm going to give you the weirdest story. It's incredibly awkward, but we want you to report that she's not a lesbian, but it's fine if she was.'"

What spurred the White House to decide that something needed to be said about the sexuality of a future associate justice on the United States Supreme Court? It was a grainy photo on the cover of *The Wall Street Journal* of the aforementioned future associate justice playing slow-pitch softball, after weeks of the rumor mill churning out whispers of Kagan's sexuality.

Smith did report that Kagan, in fact, was not a lesbian, in the story "Elena Kagan's Friends: She's Not Gay."[1] In the piece, Kagan's friends say exactly what the headline says they said. It was straightforward. People thought she was a lesbian because of assumptions. She was not. Case closed.

Except that in the following days and weeks, *everyone* wrote about the softball photo and the media response to it: *The Guardian,*[2] the *New York Post,*[3] *The Daily Beast,*[4] even *The Washington Post.*[5] Days of blogs dissected one grainy photo and what it told us about the possible next Supreme Court justice. The International Softball Federation—now part of the World Baseball Softball Confederation—eventually sent out a press release titled "Softball References in Media Coverage of Supreme Court Justice Nominee" to address the issue.[6]

What I found to be interesting about this particular political moment was the clear association between lesbians and softball. "[The photo] clearly is an allusion to her being gay. It's just too easy a punch line," Cathy Renna, a noted communications guru within the LGBTQ+ community, said to Smith for his story on the photo. The implication here is that softball is culturally assumed to be a lesbian sport; therefore, the fact that Kagan played softball of any kind is a type of proof of her lesbian identity. Making those connections requires a lot of inferences, and it only works if, culturally, we are all making the same inferences at the same time.

"There was a ton of reaction to that comment because I think people were surprised that I called it out so strongly," Renna said to me. "I think for a lot of people, they didn't get it, in terms of the code, but for a lot of us, we were like, 'This is code.' The thing is that I always say, let's be honest about this stuff. The truth is that a lot of lesbians play softball."

That's the thing about stereotypes: there can be a kernel of truth to them. And in this case, the truth is that plenty of queer—meaning both lesbian and bisexual—women play softball. Plenty of queer women participate in all different types of sports. According to LGBTQ+ sports blog *Outsports,* at least 186 LGBTQ+ athletes competed at the Tokyo Olympics in 2021, with athletes in women's sports outnumbering athletes in men's sports by a nine-to-one ratio.[7]

But the prevalence of out queer athletes in women's sports today doesn't mean that it was always that way. In fact, the stereotypes of athletes in women's sports being part of the LGBTQ+ community historically drove behavior pushing back against those cultural assumptions. In its early years, the WNBA specifically marketed its players as being more conventionally feminine. It's not uncommon to see athletes in women's sports compete with a full face of makeup, long hair, and even fake eyelashes. Not every athlete with a feminine presentation is straight, or even consciously trying to present themselves in a specific way, but there is pressure to be feminine in women's sports.

But softball historically had a more recognized tell to communicate femininity to the outside world: hair ribbons. It was the sports equivalent of "no homo." No bow lesbo.

WHEN KAYLA LOMBARDO was in middle school in the 1990s, she'd walk the hallways of the building and sometimes the resident mean girls would call her "Gayla." The reason? Softball.

"They knew I loved softball and I was fairly good at it, and they would try to insult me [by calling me gay]," Lombardo said. "Isn't that ridiculous?"

Lombardo grew up in suburban New Jersey and began playing softball when she was six years old. Raised by a single father who was a Yankees fan, she fell in love with baseball at first. She and her dad used to listen to Yankee games on the radio and watch them on TV. Sometimes, they'd even trek up to the Bronx to go see games. But when it came time for Lombardo to start playing baseball, she ended up being funneled into softball. "There wasn't another option for girls at that time," she said.

Thankfully, softball was big in her hometown of Pequannock, New Jersey. The existing Little League infrastructure built around baseball had transferred to softball, so the town had a booming Little League softball program as well. And Lombardo was into it. She started playing travel ball in late elementary school and kept at it all the way through college. She's coached on the collegiate level and now, as an adult, still does private instruction and is the lead editor of softballamerica.com.

But for all the hullabaloo and being called "Gayla," Lombardo wasn't gay at all. She wasn't quite sure why her middle school classmates were choosing to insult her in that particular way. And she didn't grasp what it had to do with softball. It wasn't until she got to Fordham, where she played at the collegiate level, that some of what she experienced while growing up started to click. "Most of my teammates were queer, and are queer," Lombardo said. "That was really my first exposure to out athletes in softball."

In college, she commonly wore a hair bow. The ribbons were often a stretch of thin fabric loosely tied around a ponytail. Whole cultures were built around these ribbons. At Fordham, each player picked out a hair ribbon that symbolized them. Each player wore one as a way of honoring a teammate, sort of like a "player of the week."

"I was very much a ribbon wearer, but we all were ribbon wearers, even the queer people," Lombardo said. "It was more of what our team did and less of what you did if you were straight."

But that wasn't the case everywhere.

FORMER COLLEGIATE SOFTBALL pitcher Miranda Elish grew up during the 2000s in Crown Point, Indiana, a growing exurban town just a stone's throw away from Chicago's urban sprawl in the northwest corner of the state, sometimes referred to as "The Region." She started playing softball at four or five years old, and it came as a surprise to no one in her family. "My mom played softball, and my aunts played softball," Elish said to me. "I remember my mom coaching a high school–age rec ball team. I thought it was the coolest thing ever and idolized those girls."

When she started pitching in her local rec league, her parents would pull her out—they were the coaches—because, frankly, she sucked. "I would do terrible," Elish said. But she begged her dad to keep working with her. He ordered pitching books and softballs with numbered indents imprinted on the surface so Elish could work on grips for different pitches. She was ten.

"I'll say it 'til I'm blue in the face," Elish said. "If it wasn't for them pushing me as hard as they did, I one hundred percent would not be where I am now."

Elish began to realize that she was pretty good at this whole softball thing when she went out to UCLA for a camp. California was to softball what Texas was to high school football. One of her dad's coworkers heard she was going to the UCLA camp and quipped, "Oh come on, she's never going to be good enough to play in the Pac-12." The Pac-12 is one of the NCAA's major conferences and a historic softball powerhouse. When Elish heard that, she and her dad went to work. They trained nonstop to prepare for the opportunity to compete against some of the best young players in the country. The offers started rolling in, including from programs out West.

As Elish became more enmeshed in softball, she began playing on an elite travel team. It was clear to her middle school peers, especially the boys, that Elish played a lot of softball. She started getting questions from boys about whether she was a lesbian because she played softball. They often called softball "manly," and Elish was already a little self-conscious because she was taller than most of the boys in middle school. Plus, she had muscles. "I feel like I was always trying to over-feminize myself when I was younger because I played softball and the boys would make those comments to me," Elish said.

And then came the hair ribbons. "My first two years of elite competitive travel ball, you wouldn't have caught me without a bow in my hair," Elish said. She'd seen what happened if someone took the field without a bow in their hair. Suddenly there were questions about why the player wasn't wearing one. "And let her be the least bit masculine, they're like, 'She's a lesbian.'"

Wear a hair bow, and you're considered straight. No bow? Lesbo. The message was anything but subtle. Elish knew exactly what was expected of her from her teammates' behavior and her mom's quiet questioning whether Elish would be wearing a bow before games. Teams had bows in their colors, and ribbon kits in the locker rooms. If you didn't participate in this particular ritual, well, everyone knew what that meant. Elish put on the bow because she wasn't quite ready for the alternative, admitting to herself that she wasn't straight. If she couldn't admit it to herself, she certainly wasn't ready to tell the whole softball world in Indiana. "I kind of brushed it under the rug," she said.

She'd heard her parents' opinions and the hair ribbon judgement of her teammates. Rainbow flags weren't waving in Crown Point in the 2000s. They still aren't. Elish knew that being LGBTQ+ wasn't viewed as a good thing. "It just wasn't something that necessarily was going to be accepted," she said.

When Elish began her college career at Oregon, things shifted. She played with openly queer teammates. Sometimes she wore a bow, and sometimes she didn't. Sometimes she wore makeup on the field, and sometimes she didn't. She still dated men, but she was more open to herself and sure of the woman she was becoming. In her softball career, that showed. After playing two seasons at Oregon, she followed her coach, Mike White, to Texas and put up monster numbers for the Longhorns. In an impressive feat of stamina, Elish threw 429 pitches during the Longhorns' opening round of the 2019 postseason. She was named the 2020 Softball America Player of the Year during the pandemic shortened season. She transferred to Oklahoma State for her final season of eligibility.

She also fell in love.

Elish caught wind that O'Neil Roberson had a crush on her. They'd been friends for a while, but that's all they were. But Elish found herself open to the possibility of dating Roberson. And she developed feelings too. "I was like, 'This is what I thought I felt for boys, but this is different,'" Elish said.

Elish figured telling her parents wouldn't be that big of a deal. Elish figured her parents would be surprised, but fine.

Instead, her parents took it poorly. "That kind of slapped me in the face," Elish said. "Here we are, two years later, and I don't really talk to my parents. Hopefully they'll come around. I'm going to stand up for what I think is right. And I'm not one to budge."

Even though telling her parents didn't go over the way she'd hoped, Elish still found it important to share her love and her identity publicly. Her Instagram was full of photos of her and Roberson. "Maybe if some thirteen-year-old girl who is scared to tell her parents that she's gay or scared to let the world know that she likes women, maybe she'll see me and be like, 'Okay, like if Miranda can do it, then, you know, I can too,'" Elish said. "I would do anything just to make sure that they're happy and living their best lives."

I could hear her voice break over the phone, and just the faintest hint of a sniffle. In that moment, my heart clenched a bit. I originally spoke to Elish in the fall of 2021, just a few months before the softball season began in earnest. At some point over the next few months, Elish and Roberson broke up. As is typical of modern breakups, the relationship was scrubbed from Elish's Instagram. But Roberson wasn't the only thing that was gone—so was every reference to Elish being queer. There were no more Pride posts or a coming out announcement. It was all gone. I'm not sure when it disappeared, but by the time Elish played in her final Women's College World Series with Oklahoma State in June 2022, her world had seemingly changed. She played against her sister, who pitched at Arizona, and her parents were present. She looked happy, and I have no reason to suspect otherwise.

I reached out to Elish multiple times for an update, but she never responded. I don't know why she no longer has public references on her social media to the queer identity she shared with me. But I wonder about this moment in our interview often: a young woman struggling with being separated from her family and trying to embrace all of her authentic self. Though things may have changed for her, what she had to say at that moment in her life resonated with me deeply. We might be more than half a decade apart in age, but Elish and I were two sides of the same coin.

MY HOMETOWN WAS only fifty-nine miles from Crown Point. A lakeside resort town, Culver boasted a population of 1,400 to 1,500 people for most of my childhood. I grew up bouncing a basketball instead of hitting softballs, wearing baggy AND1 shorts instead of fitted pants made for sliding on infield dirt. Because of the lake and the boarding school in town, Culver was frequented by folks who didn't grow up in the area. When I go home now, the cashiers ringing me up at the local gas station usually assume that I'm one of those people from out of town.

Most of the kids I went to school with didn't grow up in town. Few locals could afford housing within town limits, a problem that has only been compounded over time. Almost all of my friends growing up lived out in the country somewhere. And almost all of those friends were boys.

I always seemed to relate better to boys in my childhood. We liked the same stuff and wore the same clothes. During recess, I was always one of the first picked for football and basketball. We have a word for that: tomboy. That was a word I heard everywhere as a child. In today's parlance, "tomboy" is often used to describe a young girl who does things traditionally associated with boys, like playing football at recess, rolling around in the mud, refusing to wear dresses, etc. But the word "tomboy" in the nineteenth century was used as a tool of white supremacy by the white middle class. In an effort to stave off the white population becoming a minority due to the combined forces of immigration and abolition, tomboyism was a movement that encouraged additional physicality among young white women and girls, particularly as a means to prepare them for the rigors of motherhood, and to ensure and protect white offspring.[8] I certainly wasn't preparing for white motherhood in the 1990s, but there is a fluidity to being a tomboy that is important to talk about.

Being a tomboy, culturally, is meant to be temporary. "Little girls" are allowed to participate in activities coded for boys—like playing with trucks, running around outside, playing football, etc.—without threatening the greater gender structure because, well, a tomboy is an identity and a word used to describe children. That was made increasingly clear by my peers as I entered fifth grade. I could be a tomboy at five or six or seven, but once I hit eleven and neared twelve, the tolerance for such behavior in my world was limited. That didn't extend to my parents, but it didn't need to. My peers were telling me to wear tighter clothes, and I was getting invited to sleepovers where trying out makeup was a common activity.

The one place where that pressure didn't exist for me was on the basketball court. I could wear what I wanted. I could flex after a basket. I could be aggressive; in fact, it was encouraged. But even that lasted only for so long. As I entered high school, I noticed that many of my teammates and opponents were wearing makeup while they played. And I began to hear homophobic taunts from the student section of the stands during some games, and sometimes from opponents. Even within my own teams, especially travel teams, the homophobia was palpable. I'd grown up hearing racial epithets hurled at me on and off the court, but the homophobia was new, and I wasn't ready.

One of my favorite movies growing up was *Love & Basketball*. I was nine years old when it first came out in 2000, but I don't think I saw it until years later. There's this scene where the main character, Monica, has a conversation with her mom in the kitchen. Monica's mom desperately wants Monica to be more feminine, and she says that she'd always hoped Monica would grow out of her tomboy phase. Without missing a beat, Monica says, "I won't. I'm a lesbian."

"That's not funny," her mom says.

It actually was pretty funny. And Monica, the character, was not a lesbian. But I was definitely gay. I probably knew it then, deep down, somewhere. That scene, however, seemed to present two options: grow out of your tomboy phase, or be a lesbian. At that age, I knew which door I was walking through.

The confession from Monica's mom about her hope for Monica to leave her tomboy days behind, and Monica's response, also says something important about how we see the relationship between gender expression and sexual orientation and the limits of an identity that bends those expectations, like being a tomboy. Monica's mom explicitly identified being a tomboy—someone assigned female at birth subverting gender expectations—as a "phase" and something to grow out of. It was tolerable at one point in time but became less culturally acceptable as Monica aged. And Monica's response was to say that she wouldn't grow out of it *because* she was a lesbian. Even in jest, this signaled that the masculinity Monica expressed as a "tomboy" could also be read as indicative of her sexual orientation, because lesbians are masculine, duh.

That core assumption, that masculinity among women equals an attraction to women, drives hyperfeminine gender expression in women's sports. That's what's behind the full faces of makeup, the long hair, the nails, the eyelashes, and even the hair ribbons in softball. The overt expression of femininity reflects female athletes' desire to be seen as continuing to belong within the gender power structures as they operate in society, and to avoid the stigma of being called gay—even if they are gay. The stereotype of being an athlete in women's sports is that you're queer, regardless of whether it's true. Kayla Lombardo was called "Gayla" in her middle school hallways for this reason. Within women's sports, there has historically been a desire to push back against these stereotypes, including among those who are queer. I'm not saying that every softball player who has ever worn a hair bow is homophobic, or that every basketball player who has ever worn makeup on the court holds prejudice against the LGBTQ+ community. It's complex: every LGBTQ+ person has their own journey of self-discovery that is informed by their personal experience and circumstances. Presently, being queer is much more accepted in a mainstream way than in previous generations. I'm in my early thirties, and the landscape has changed rapidly since I was an adolescent. For many people who came of age before the 2010s, LGBTQ+ identity was seen as unequivocally negative. The relationship between queer identity and women's sports, however, was reflective of conversations happening within feminist movements beginning in the 1970s.

Around the same time that women were fighting for access to sports with Title IX, sociologist Jan Felshin coined the term "feminine apologetic"[9] to describe a phenomenon of athletes in women's sports emphasizing femininity to "apologize" for sub-

verting gender norms and participating in masculinity by playing sports. Apologetic behavior can take many forms: makeup;
downplaying athleticism; participating in sports seen as more
feminine, like gymnastics or figure skating; adhering to Euro-
centric standards of beauty and emphasizing thin and smaller
physiques; and, of course, hair bows.

The feminine apologetic as it pertains to women's sports
has been studied by many sociologists. What the idea boils
down to, as Laurel R. Davis-Delano, April Pollock, and Jennifer Ellsworth Vose assert in their 2009 study, is that apologetic
behavior is "a form of cultural and economic capital utilized
by some women in sport."[10] Davis-Delano et al. surveyed forty
athletes in women's sports and found that three negative stereotypes were commonly shared: female athletes are masculine,
female athletes are lesbians, and female athletes are inferior to
male athletes.[11] Those negative stereotypes were likely things
these athletes had been hearing for as long as they'd been playing sports, hearkening back to the tie that is often made between gender, gender expression, and sexual orientation. If, as
an athlete, these are the stereotypes you hear all the time, they
become easy to internalize. Additionally, there's the sexualiza-
tion of athletes in women's sports: that the patriarchal system
in which they are operating sees them as sexual objects, and
there's also the longing among women's sports as an industry to
be desirable. That's where the apologetic comes from: the tension held in these ideas.

Growing up playing girls' basketball, I heard all three of
those stereotypes regularly. Two of them happen to be true for
me—I am both a masculine person and queer—but it took me
a long time to not consider either of those things to be negative.
It's notable to me that being thought of as masculine and/or a

lesbian is considered to be a negative stereotype among these surveyed athletes—and I would argue probably among most women playing sports. It's not just that for many people both of those stereotypes are false descriptors of who they are, it's that for everyone in women's sports, regardless of sexual orientation or gender expression, the message is that you don't *want* to be seen as masculine or queer. That's why no one would catch Miranda Elish without a ribbon in her hair while she was playing travel softball, and it's why I spent years growing my hair out after chopping it off when I was six years old. The fraught history of the WNBA's own gender politics demonstrates this complexity.

In trying to gain traction among the traditional (read: male) sports fan base, early WNBA marketing efforts spearheaded by the NBA focused on portraying WNBA athletes as feminine. "The first video shoot I ever did with the WNBA, they put my hair down, lipstick, I had a fucking halter top on," Diana Taurasi said in an episode of *Basketball: A Love Story,* a docuseries chronicling the history of basketball. "I've never felt so bad in my life." It's well documented that the WNBA offered its draft classes makeup tutorials. In 2002, lesbian fans staged a "time-out kiss" at a game in New York between the Liberty and the Miami Sol to protest a lack of explicit inclusion of lesbian fans and promotion of lesbian players. It's not that there weren't feminine, straight (or queer, for that matter) women in the WNBA; it was the perception of the league's preference to foreground feminine expression as a means to appeal to a straight male fan base that chafed against so many queer women.

I want to underscore that times have changed, however. The WNBA is the most queer-friendly professional sports league in the United States, possibly the world. It was the first major American professional league to establish a league-wide Pride initiative, in 2014. Lots of players share more about their lives and identities with the public, especially on social media. Players are encouraged to present themselves authentically, so when teams post the outfits of the players arriving for games, it's a beautiful range of expressions and fashion. But where we are now, with one or two professional women's sports leagues, is not representative of where we have been or the total experience of athletes participating in women's sports. The pressures of stereotypes and rigidity of gender, however, aren't present just in softball and basketball—they're in all of our sports. And sometimes written into the rules.

BLAKE BONKOWSKI KNEW it was time for him to leave gymnastics when he was thirteen. He'd been participating in women's artistic gymnastics—or WAG, as he prefers to call it—since he was a child, but his progress had stagnated. He also just didn't feel welcome anymore. "At the time, I thought that it had everything to do with body type," Bonkowski said. "And it certainly did have to do with body type. I am currently five foot ten. When I quit, I was like five eight. I now identify as a fat person; at the time I wasn't, but I was considered fat compared to everybody else around me."

As an adult reflecting on his childhood experiences, Bonkowski can identify the body discomfort he felt as gender dysphoria—the distress a transgender person can feel when their body does not align with their gender identity. That dysphoria was exacerbated by the very sport Bonkowski grew up loving. All of his teammates would get together and do their makeup, put on their sparkles, and get their hair perfectly done. "The expectation of being feminine just didn't resonate with me and made it difficult to connect with my peers," Bonkowski said.

When Bonkowski left gymnastics, he had been training for ten years. For the next decade, he completely ignored the sport. He wanted nothing to do with it. It wasn't until he came back to the sport as a fan in his mid-twenties that he decided to re-enter gymnastics in a significant way. He started training again, became a coach, and now cohosts the gymnastics podcast *Half In, Half Out*—devoted to discussing gymnastics through an LGBTQ+ lens. The only complication with getting back in the gym, however, was the fact that Bonkowski—who now identifies as FTM, short for female-to-male—was running into the expectation that he would have experience with gymnastics equipment that he definitely did not. "I wasn't even in a facility that had the men's equipment most of my life," Bonkowski said.

WAG and men's artistic gymnastics (MAG) are basically different sports; some equipment is shared, but there's very little overlap. WAG athletes compete in four disciplines: uneven bars, floor exercise, balance beam, and vault. MAG athletes compete in six disciplines: still rings, parallel bars, horizontal bar, pommel horse, vault, and floor exercise. In WAG, "feminine grace" is literally written into the code of points that determines how a gymnast is scored. MAG emphasizes strength and power and does not include dance skills like turns and leaps commonly seen on floor exercise and beam in WAG. For all intents and purposes, they are completely different sports. Athletes are separated into WAG and MAG when they start gymnastics, sometimes as young as three years old, the outcome of which is that there is no overlap in skill development. It's not like soccer or basketball.

In the United States, we *love* WAG during Olympic years. During the years between, there's less sustained interest. "We call you all the four-year fans," Bonkowski said. But *gymnastics*—culturally speaking—often refers to WAG. We win in WAG, and so the beloved athletes of the sport are often from WAG. The closest MAG superstar is probably Jonathan Horton, and, let's be honest, he's like a D-list gymnastics personality. There are twenty-five WAG gymnasts who could be listed before him (except for the *American Ninja Warrior* fans, who might list him first, but I digress).

The consequences of both the gendered differences of the sport enforced by the code of points and the significant popularity of WAG over MAG at all levels has created an expectation of hyperfeminine and hypermasculine expression that has traditionally left very little room for nuance. This is especially true for anyone who identifies as queer and/or transgender within the sport, but it's true for cisgender and heterosexual athletes as well. "There's the stereotype that dudes who do men's gymnastics are gay," Bonkowski said. "And so, if you're 'acting gay,' you're the reason why we have the stereotype. And so, you're the problem."

Meanwhile, over in WAG, the assumption is that no one is gay. Or at least the image that is put forward is one of structured ultra-femininity written into both the rules of the sport and its culture. But I do want to be clear here: a person's gender expression doesn't indicate sexual orientation. There are plenty of feminine queer women. And there are masculine queer men. But the way gender expression is regulated can repress queer identity. WAG is a good example of that. For example, in NCAA competition, teams must dress exactly alike, down to the sparkles and ribbons. But the pressure to fit into a specific box starts much earlier in the sport. "There's just so much pressure to be a little girl," said former NCAA gymnast and Team Canada member Ella Douglas, "not just a girl or a woman."

Douglas realized she was queer at twenty-two. She'd been doing gymnastics since she was seven, "which is a little bit later than most," she said. Douglas fell into the sport while attending a birthday party for one of her friends that happened to be at a gymnastics gym. Her balance and strength caught the eye of the coaches working the party, and suddenly she had an open invitation to try her hand at gymnastics. After just a couple of years at this first gym, Douglas moved to one of the most competitive gyms in Canada (she grew up in Etobicoke, a neighborhood in Toronto). The biracial daughter of a Black father who immigrated to Canada from Grenada and a white mother, Douglas already noticed that she was a bit different. Race and racism function differently in Canada than in the United States (that's a whole different book), but it was still noticeable to Douglas that she was one of the only non-white people at her very white gym and in her very white sport.

As she matured, both in terms of competition and in terms of age, Douglas experienced the social pressures that are common for teen girls. Everyone was texting boys and going on dates. And she . . . wasn't as much. Or at least she wasn't as into it as her friends and teammates were. "And I had always internalized that, as I'm just a little bit of a late bloomer and this will happen to me eventually, I'll start really, really falling in love with boys later in my life," Douglas said.

But then, when she was twenty-two, something unexpected happened. Douglas met Nia Hollie in a class during her sophomore year while they were both students at Michigan State. Hollie was a basketball player, and by the end of that year, they ended up in the same large circle of friends. Unbeknownst to Douglas, Hollie had been harboring a crush on her from afar, but had settled on the idea that "this girl is a gymnast. There's no way she's gay and there's no way she's going to date me," Douglas said.

"I attributed a lot of me not knowing to my environment," Douglas continued. "From the age of seven until twenty-two, I was put in this box and you don't even think you have any other options. When you grow up in this ultrafeminine environment where everybody is straight, there's no anything. And even the coaches when you're younger, always talking to us about 'When you get older and you have a boyfriend.' And that being the main message driven, you just don't really know any different."

Douglas had only dated men, but she felt similar feelings stir for Hollie. Even though she felt gymnastics culture wasn't open to queerness, that wasn't the case in her family. The message she'd received from her parents and those in her family was one of openness. Some of her family members had even come out and been accepted, which she took note of. But as she felt her feelings for Hollie grow, Douglas still felt shame, like it wasn't something she was supposed to feel. "I sort of said, 'Oh, okay, I recognize this feeling. I've had it before, but this is another woman and I'm not going to go there,'" Douglas said.

Her resolve barely lasted a week. Once she allowed herself to accept the feelings she had for Hollie, Douglas learned they were mutual. They started dating and, slowly, Douglas began sharing. First with the friend group she shared with Hollie, then with Hollie's team and community. But then she stopped telling people. "I was terrified," Douglas said. She was afraid of how her gymnastics community would react. How the gymnastics public would react. No one had done what Douglas was thinking about doing, what Hollie was asking her to do.

"Why are you so terrified?" Hollie asked her.

"I don't think you understand," Douglas said. "I think I'm the only one."

Hollie was confused. "What do you mean?"

"I think I'm the only one ever," Douglas said.

At that moment, in the spring of 2020, no collegiate gymnast in women's gymnastics had publicly come out. Ever. As of this writing, that is still true of elite women's gymnastics. Douglas truly believed she was a party of one. That's what was running through her mind when she sat down with Bonkowski to record an episode for his podcast titled "I'm the Only One."

The next episode, which ran two weeks later, was titled "You're Not the Only One." Florida gymnast Savannah Schoenherr was also queer, and she decided to share her story publicly after Douglas had. The moment sparked a revolution in collegiate women's gymnastics. UCLA had held its first Pride Meet event earlier in 2020, but by the 2021 season, Pride Meets were popping up all over the place. "The last two years have been an absolute revolution in WAG, in terms of people coming out," Bonkowski said. "By the end of the 2021 season, we had eleven openly queer college athletes on the WAG side."

For her part, Douglas has also seen the shift. "It's been really special to see this massive shift in gymnastics in the last couple of years," she said.

Douglas, Elish, and Bonkowski all challenged the rigid cultures around them in different ways. Their stories demonstrate the complexities of how individual cultures within sports shape our understanding of gender and vice versa. It's tempting to look at those stories and see just the positive gains, and there have been plenty! But it's worth noting that the growing acceptance of queer folks in athletics has, in many ways, been asymmetric. It is *because* of the stereotype of women's sports as being full of lesbians that there has been substantial work done in those sports to make them more inclusive, but the opposite is true for men's sports. There has been a significant shift in how athletes in women's sports come out, meaning they don't anymore. They just post photos of their lives on social media. Nearly half of the draft class invited to the 2022 WNBA Draft showed up in suits. As Bonkowski said, double digit numbers of collegiate gymnasts came out publicly. That's fantastic! But there are currently no active NBA players who are out. There is one active NFL player. The gains in women's sports have not led to a stampede of sharing in men's sports. There have been examples of men coming out in professional sports, but they are still few and far between. The sea change has been in women's sports so far. I think the primary reason why is that for all the angst felt in women's sports about appearing too masculine or being queer, the assumption in men's sports (with a few exceptions) is that masculinity and straightness are the default. It's exactly the opposite of women's sports. If we think of queerness in women as masculine, then I would argue we think of queerness in men as feminine. And in American male sports, femininity is not tolerated.

Why else would the visiting locker room at Iowa's football stadium be pink? The goal is not just to shame in the personal sense, but to demonize femininity more broadly. It's not so different from using the phrase "like a girl" to insult a boy or man's athletic ability. That doesn't create the most inclusive environment in men's sports, and it affects athletes in women's sports as well. Athletes in women's sports are constantly pushing back against the idea that they are inferior athletically, while also juggling the ways in which those sports butt up against cultural expectations of gender. We've seen movement toward a more accepting culture in women's sports, but not everyone who deviates from the norms of sporting cultures is embraced. Sometimes they're criticized and targeted. And in the most extreme cases, like that of Caster Semenya, they're completely excised from the sport itself.

4.

THE RUNNER IN SOUTH AFRICA

ON A CLEAR night in Berlin, Germany, in 2009, South African runner Caster Semenya made history. The eighteen-year-old middle-distance track athlete rounded the final turn in the 800m final and separated herself from the chasing pack. She sprinted down the stretch of the last 100 meters, crossing the finish line at 1:55.46, the fastest time of the year. She curled her arms into a flex as she peacocked around the track.

Her celebration was short-lived.

Semenya had shaved seven seconds off of her best time from a year prior. She was muscular, which members of the press (as well as her competitors) couldn't help but point out. And she was Black. Suddenly, there were questions about whether she should be running at all in the women's category.

"These kind of people should not run with us," said Italian runner Elisa Cusma, according to *The New York Times.* Cusma, who finished sixth, reportedly shared these comments in a postrace interview with Italian journalists. "For me, she's not a woman. She's a man."[1]

The *Times* also reported that Mariya Savinova, a Russian who finished fifth, told Russian journalists that she did not believe Semenya would be able to pass a test. "Just look at her," Savinova said.[2]

Instead of being present at the postrace press conference, Semenya was whisked away to undergo invasive testing that would determine whether she was a woman in the eyes of the International Amateur Athletic Federation (IAAF), now World Athletics—the international governing body for elite track and field.

This moment would launch Semenya into a decade-long fight with World Athletics that would lead from Berlin to South Africa to London and to Switzerland and the Court of Arbitration for Sport.

Following Semenya's win in 2009 and the subsequent evaluation, she was forced to undergo testosterone suppression drugs due to her high levels of natural, or endogenous, testosterone. Though she has never commented publicly on her medical status and her medical records are private, the press has speculated rampantly, and some World Athletics officials have commented inappropriately. "She is a woman, but maybe not one hundred percent," World Athletics secretary Pierre Weiss said in 2009.

WHAT DOES IT mean to be 100 percent a woman?

That question is what World Athletics and Caster Semenya have been arguing about for more than a decade. That question has also been continually asked of athletes in women's sports. For as long as there has been a women's sports category, there have been efforts to regulate it, especially on the elite level.

In general, the policing of elite athletes is an accepted practice, though there are some who think the scrutiny is too invasive. Most elite athletes, especially in Olympic and international-level sports, are consistently tested for doping. Doping is the use of performance-enhancing drugs (PEDs), such as human growth hormone (HGH), synthetic testosterone, erythropoietin (EPO), and a long list of medications—some of which can be bought over the counter—that confer a physiological and/or metabolic advantage outside of an immutable characteristic like height. An athlete can't exactly stretch their body and make it taller, but they can blood dope with EPO and stimulate red blood cell production. The desire to regulate cheating in elite international sports, particularly individual sports, is not unique to women's athletics. Many doping scandals (hello, MLB and Lance Armstrong) have happened in men's sports, but men do not have to prove they are men to be eligible. It would not be considered cheating, per se, for a woman to disguise herself as a man and compete. When Bobbi Gibb did it in 1966, that was a bit of a different story, but there is still a view that, because of the (assumed and real) physiological differences between men and women, women aren't an athletic threat to men.

The elevated scrutiny of elite female athletes, then, serves a dual purpose: one, to screen for and catch doping, and two, to "verify" eligibility. For decades, athletes in women's sports underwent verification tests to ensure that there were no men trying to infiltrate the sport to gain an advantage. Prior to 1968, athletes in women's sports had their bodies visually inspected by IOC officials in what were colloquially referred to as "nude parades." That practice was abandoned in favor of other, less invasive chromosome testing. Upon verification, each athlete was given a document that functioned as a gender passport of sorts. If they were asked to produce that card and not able to do so, all kinds of unwanted issues could arise. One of the most famous cases of that happening was with Spanish runner Maria José Martínez-Patiño, who was retested at the 1985 World University Games. Patiño learned that she did not have the XX karyotype of a typical woman, but instead had XY chromosomes.

On the surface, having XY chromosomes might seem disqualifying for women, but there are situations where that's not the case, such as an athlete being diagnosed with partial or complete androgen insensitivity syndrome (CAIS). This particular difference of sex development (DSD) means that the person doesn't process testosterone in the way most people with XY chromosomes typically would. Their serum level of testosterone may be similar to a person assigned male at birth, but their bodies are not affected by the hormone in the same way. For example, people with CAIS can develop vaginas but lack a uterus and ovaries. After petitioning her disqualification, Patiño was reinstated by World Athletics two years later. By 1999, the IOC did away with formal sex verification testing because of the inconsistency of results and the continued use of urine testing for athletes under the World Anti-Doping Agency (WADA). But of course, that didn't mean athletes couldn't still be forced to verify their sex. That's how Semenya ended up being whisked away after her victory in Berlin in 2009; she was accused of not being woman enough to compete in the women's category.

Semenya's case was the first to happen in the burgeoning era of social media and that of the constant news cycle. Whereas other athletes before her had experienced similar levels of scrutiny, they hadn't received the same level of publicity. This environment elevated awareness of Semenya and her case through

THE RUNNER IN SOUTH AFRICA · 71

international media that also brought heightened awareness of some of the scientific questions and language underpinning the case. It was with Semenya that language around testosterone levels and nanomoles per liter (nmol/L) entered the popular sports journalist and public lexicon. "It really just brought up the whole conversation about who counts as a woman," said Anne Lieberman, director of policy and programs at Athlete Ally. "And, how are we defining womanhood, either legally, or for sporting purposes, et cetera."

Following Berlin and the subsequent examinations, World Athletics required Semenya to suppress her testosterone through medication. In an interview with Andrea Kremer, Semenya described the medication as something that made her sick. "Made me gain weight," Semenya said. "Panic attacks. It's like stabbing yourself with a knife every day. But I had no choice. I'm eighteen and I want to run."

Semenya was cleared to resume her career in July 2010. At the next World Championships in Daegu, South Korea, Semenya again competed for the world championship in the women's 800m race. When she kicked away from the pack, Russian runner Mariya Savinova followed her and bested Semenya at the finish line. Semenya finished in 1:56.35, her best mark since Berlin. At the 2012 London Olympics, Semenya crossed the line second, again, behind Mariya Savinova. Savinova was later disqualified and stripped of her gold medal due to a doping violation. Semenya was consequently elevated to both the Olympic and World Championship gold medals.

Semenya, however, had been quiet following Berlin. She didn't fight the policy. But in 2015, another athlete did. A sprinter from India named Dutee Chand.

• • •

IN 2014, CHAND was summoned to Delhi by the Indian track and field governing body. She had been preparing for the upcoming Commonwealth Games after making a splash at the Asian Junior Athletics Championship, where she won an individual gold medal in the 200m and another gold medal as part of the 4x400m relay. Chand told *The New York Times*[3] she assumed the meeting was for a doping test, but instead she was given an ultrasound. Like Semenya before her, Chand had been singled out by competitors for her physique and surprising showing. Even though she was only five foot, she was told that her muscles were "too pronounced" and her stride "too impressive." The results of the ultrasound were relayed to the federation, which then requested a gender verification exam.

At that time, the World Athletics gender verification procedures had different levels of testing and measurement. The organization looked for cases of hyperandrogenism, or elevated naturally occurring testosterone. If an athlete competing in the women's category triggered that system, an in-person exam would be given to attempt to determine how the presence of testosterone had affected the athlete. What Chand reportedly experienced was a Level 3 assessment. Chand told *The New York Times* that she underwent a chromosome analysis, an MRI, and a gynecological exam. World Athletics protocols involved measuring the size of an athlete's clitoris, examining the labia and vagina, and evaluating breast size and pubic hair patterns based on a five-grade scale.[4]

Chand took her case to the Court of Arbitration for Sport, challenging World Athletics' rules directly. And she won. In its judgement, CAS ruled that World Athletics' policy was not justified. "While the evidence indicates that higher levels of naturally occurring testosterone may increase athletic performance, the Panel is not satisfied that the degree of that advantage is more significant than the advantage derived from the numerous other variables which the parties acknowledge also affect female athletic performance: for example, nutrition, access to specialist training facilities and coaching, and other genetic and biological variations," the ruling said.[5]

The 2015 ruling gave World Athletics two years to provide evidence that testosterone gave women a significant advantage. World Athletics later informed the court it would rescind the regulations challenged by Chand and institute new policies.

It was a victory not just for Chand, but also for Semenya. Following the suspension of World Athletics' policy by CAS, the IOC said it would not impose its own testosterone guidelines for endogenous, naturally occurring, testosterone in women athletes (different from the injected synthetic hormone that is policed as an anabolic steroid). That decision meant that Semenya and Chand could both participate in the 2016 Olympics without testosterone suppression, along with other athletes with differences of sex development (DSDs) that were unknown at that point.

Chand competed in the 100m at the Rio Olympics, but she did not advance to the semifinals. Semenya shined in Rio. During the final of the 800m, Semenya darted out of the blocks at the sound of the gun. Semenya ran in the third lane. After the first turn, Semenya eased her way to the front of the pack. She fell into second place down the first straight of the final lap, but once the runners hit the last turn, Semenya kicked her way back into first. She triumphantly strode toward the finish line, crossing first in 1:55.29 to win her first Olympic gold medal outright. The following year, Semenya won gold again in the

800m at the World Championships in London. She also took the bronze medal in the 1500m.

But Semenya's victories would be short-lived. After its defeat at CAS with Chand, World Athletics began working on proving that elevated levels of naturally occurring testosterone had an outsize impact on athletic performance in women athletes. In April 2018, World Athletics announced a new hyperandrogenism policy that effectively sidelined Semenya and other athletes like her indefinitely, possibly forever. Under this new policy, athletes with DSDs would be required to suppress their testosterone to under 5 nmol/L, half of the previous accepted level of 10 nmol/L.[6] World Athletics argued that athletes who are found to have specifically higher levels of naturally occurring testosterone have a significant advantage over others and therefore need to be regulated to ensure fair competition. DSD is a catchall description applying to a variety of sex differences, but in this case World Athletics argued to address only "46 XY DSD," or those individuals who have the typical number of chromosomes (46, or 23 pairs), but also have XY chromosomes and want to compete in the female category. These athletes would have likely been assigned female at birth. In Semenya's case, she has stated publicly that she was assigned female at birth, has always identified as a woman, and continues to do so.

The kicker was that these rules applied only to the 400m, 800m, and 1500m races. In other words, the races that Semenya would enter. Unlike what happened following Berlin, Semenya was not quiet. She openly refused to medically reduce her testosterone, and like Dutee Chand before her, she took World Athletics to the Court of Arbitration for Sport.

Semenya argued that the proposed regulations unfairly discriminate because they target only female athletes and only those with specific physiological traits. She also argued that the rules are unnecessary and could cause serious harm through medical treatments and resulting side effects from attempting to lower naturally occurring levels of testosterone. World Athletics argued that 46 XY DSD athletes have an advantage because they are comparable to cisgender men. While the athletes in question may, in fact, have testosterone levels akin to the levels in the typical male range, the science of the advantage of testosterone is not as straightforward as we would assume it to be. I want to underscore that medical information is private and each athlete is their own, individual case. We don't know Semenya's testosterone levels, so I'm speaking broadly here. Athletes like Semenya, however, don't process testosterone the way someone assigned male at birth does. If that were the case, there wouldn't be a difference of sex development in the first place.

World Athletics also argued that 46 XY DSD athletes were overrepresented in elite women's track and field. Since the conclusion of the Rio Olympics, the entire podium of the 800m (including Semenya) has said publicly that they would be affected by the World Athletics policy. By a two-to-one margin, the CAS dismissed Semenya's claim, arguing that "such discrimination is a necessary, reasonable and proportionate means of achieving World Athletics' aim of preserving the integrity of female athletics in the Restricted Events."[7] Semenya appealed and lost. Unless she medically lowered her testosterone, she wouldn't be eligible to compete in her preferred events at the Tokyo Olympic Games.

It's worth pointing out that the restricted events named in the ruling are the ones that Semenya runs. Though her Olympic medals are in the 800, Semenya has competed in the 400 and the 1500 professionally. The regulations do not include sprinting events, like the 100m and 200m, which is notable because Chand won her 2015 case against World Athletics after the organization tried to force her to limit her testosterone levels.

In the process of instituting these new policies that Semenya was challenging, World Athletics also released a report that sought to underpin the organization's argument that endogenous testosterone in 46 XY DSD athletes conferred a competitive advantage in women's track and field. The report, published in the *British Journal of Sports Medicine,* argued that in specific events, higher levels of testosterone gave athletes like Semenya an advantage.[8] That research was funded by World Athletics and was the sole scientific analysis justifying the organization's hyperandrogenism policy. Four years after the paper was published, however, and in the middle of the Tokyo Olympics, the journal issued a correction. That correction stated that "there is no confirmatory evidence for causality in the observed relationships reported."[9] Essentially the journal said that the causal relationship between testosterone and performance argued by World Athletics didn't exist in the data.

That correction, however, came far too late for Semenya. CAS had already ruled. The World Athletics policy was still operational despite the fatal blow to its scientific justification. The South African runner missed the Tokyo Olympics. She was still speaking out against the policy, but her path forward was no longer necessarily tied to getting back on the track.

IN THE INTRODUCTION, I discussed the episode of *The Good Fight* that talked about transgender athletes. There was a lot of lawyering (because it's a show about lawyers), but eventually the cisgender woman who sued because a transgender woman took her spot in the Olympics lost her case because "rules are rules," and she sued again over another athlete who had too high testosterone levels (because she was androgen insensitive), and *that* athlete—Piper Vega—lost her spot because her testosterone levels disqualified her. I told you we'd come back to this, and we're there.

Piper Vega isn't Caster Semenya, but she's not *not* Caster Semenya either. Technically, I suppose she would be more of a stand-in for a Patiño-like athlete. Regardless of who Piper Vega is supposed to represent, however, in the show they communicate that she is insensitive to androgen, so under the World Athletics policy, she would have been able to compete, and the other young woman suing would have been relegated to being off the team.

The presence of this story line, however, speaks to the power of Semenya's legacy. Prior to Semenya's case, the general public was not aware of the long history of sex verification in women's sports, nor was there much awareness about the science of testosterone and the units of measurement for such things. In some ways, the case turned everyone into an armchair expert. I'll be the first to say that's not exactly the best outcome. But Semenya opened the door to discussion on what we know about the science of sex, testosterone, and athletic performance. I don't think it's a coincidence that when discussing these topics, most people I run into bring up Semenya in one way or another. Her case was not only groundbreaking, but also instructive of our own failings to fully grapple with and understand these issues.

We don't know what we think we do.

5.

IT'S BIOLOGY, AND WE CAN'T CHANGE THAT

THE FOX TELEVISION show *Pitch* told the fictional story of Ginny Baker, the first woman to pitch in Major League Baseball. Ginny was prepared for her moment in the spotlight by her dad, Bill, who tried getting his older son into baseball, but Ginny was the one interested instead. So, they grinded through the club system and, after her father died, Ginny grinded through the farm system until she was called up for her opportunity with the fictional version of the MLB's San Diego Padres. The show lasted only ten episodes, but in the pilot episode, there was a sequence of two scenes that I think about a lot.

In a flashback, Bill took a teenaged Ginny to a local baseball diamond to have her try out for a local Little League team. He sauntered up to the coach and said, "My kid wants to try out." The coach tried to blow him off, but Bill insisted he let Ginny "throw a few." She did, and with a single throw, she impressed. The coach's skepticism was clearly about whether girls could throw a baseball, let alone throw one well. Bill just looked up at him. "You okay?"

While sitting on the front porch steps with his daughter after the tryout, Bill poured out a basket of nectarines. He picked one up with his right hand and delicately cradled it with his fingers. "You're never going to have the arm to get you to the majors," he said. "A girl will never be able to throw hard enough to compete with boys, not as they start growing. It's biology, and we can't change that."

What Bill is saying here is true. Ginny would never be able to throw a 98-mph fastball, just as no woman has ever run 100 meters in under ten seconds. And it's something of a cultural fascination. In the years I've spent covering and researching issues of gender in sport, especially transgender athletes, the argument I hear most often is that those assigned male at birth are better athletes than those assigned female at birth *because* of biology—that biology limits the ability of those assigned female at birth to compete against those assigned male at birth *in all circumstances*. That's why the coach looked at Bill like Bill was wasting everyone's time. And why Bill asked if the coach was okay. His worldview, that core assumption, had been shattered.

Of course, there are examples of instances where this assumption doesn't hold. The fictional Ginny Baker invokes images of the true story of Mo'ne Davis, who pitched a shutout in the Little League World Series in 2014. In 2021 Ella Bruning started as catcher for the Texas team competing in the Little League World Series.

It's this colloquial use of "biology" that drives snide remarks such as that a junior varsity high school boys' basketball team would wipe the floor with the University of Connecticut women's basketball team or a WNBA team—the inference being that bigger, faster, stronger amateur boys are still better than full-grown professional women when playing head-to-head.

This is important because our understanding of the differences between and within sexes drives policy governing participation in elite sports, which trickles down to all ages. And the focus of such policy is almost exclusively on women's sports, because that is viewed as the "vulnerable" category. This is especially true for intersex and transgender athletes.

But here's the thing. As with everything in this discussion, it's complicated. And the science doesn't say what anyone wants it to.

WHEN IT COMES to the science of sex in sports, the focus of the debate has shifted over time. But one thing has held the most influence over the conversation: testosterone. As a hormone, testosterone is present within all of us, though it is commonly referred to as "the male hormone." Similarly, estrogen is referred to as "the female hormone." This is so ingrained culturally that if a group of men are gathered together doing "manly" things like, I don't know, chopping wood, commenting about the "level of testosterone" in that space wouldn't be culturally strange. That's a thing people say. All the time. We do the same thing with estrogen. How many times has a half-hour sitcom on network television made a joke about the husband in the family being surrounded by women, saying he's around "too much estrogen"? We use these hormones as stand-in terminology to refer to masculinity and femininity, and the references are everywhere.

In the classic 2006 film *John Tucker Must Die,* Kate (Brittany Snow) plays a prank on John Tucker (Jesse Metcalf), spiking his protein powder with estrogen. Predictably, the effect is that Tucker begins having unexplained feminine mood swings—his nipples hurt and he gets more emotional. This culminates in him throwing a temper tantrum in the middle of a basketball game. His peers boo him and laugh as he stomps off the court. Sexist tropes aside, this is one example of how hormones are used as a stand-in for gender, something that is more cultural than scientific.

"The problem is most people have not been taught about some of the complexity of these issues," Katrina Karkazis said to me. Karkazis is a cultural anthropologist working at the intersection of science and technology studies, theories of gender and race, social studies of medicine, and bioethics. She is the coauthor of the book *Testosterone: An Unauthorized Biography*. "They started to sort of echo this folk wisdom that makes sense to a lot of people; chromosomes are your sex, or testosterone is this miracle molecule of athleticism. And people don't need to know the science, or have studied any of it, because just intuitively, they think they know."

Aside from the notion of testosterone as a "miracle molecule," there is also the differing understanding of gender versus sex. Colloquially, we use those words to describe the same thing, but they aren't the same. Gender has become more accepted as a social construct; it can be more malleable and flexible. But even as attitudes about gender have shifted in recent years, the prevailing notion of sex is that it's more fixed and rigid. Sex isn't about feelings; it's about biology and science. It's chromosomes and hormones. Over the past fifty years, gender has increasingly become seen as something that is fluid and complex, as more people challenge gender norms. It's not a fixed, immovable identity for many people, even if it is still seen that way by broad swaths of the public. There are more identities available—vocabulary is constantly expanding. But sex is still very much viewed as a cleaner, more clinical discussion.

You're either male or female or intersex. Except that's not exactly how it works.

"It's knotty," Karkazis said. "I feel like we're just at the point where feminists failed on this, too. They did a lot of work around gender, but not so much about the way understanding biological sex is affected by cultural ideas."

The notion that science and interpretation of science are affected by culture isn't a new concept. Scientific racism provided legitimacy for racist policies throughout the nineteenth and twentieth centuries, as scientists attempted to codify so-called racial characteristics as inherited, biologic traits. Black people's bodies were measured and categorized in order to claim that they were biologically different from white people, while other scientific research, for diseases, medicine, and pioneering procedures, was conducted with white men as the central focus. Most of our scientific data are still rooted in the study of cisgender white men. We know considerably less about every other demographic. That bias is present in our medicine, our understanding of the human body, and even in our artificial intelligence. It's not a wild idea that perhaps if that has happened—and continues to happen—with regard to race, maybe our understanding of sex could also be fundamentally flawed, or at least not as clearly understood as we think it is.

Our sex is made up of a number of traits: chromosomes, hormones, internal reproductive organs, genitalia, and secondary sex characteristics. All of those things work in concert to determine our sex. For the majority of people, those characteristics are within a typical variation of either male or female sex. But that's not how we think about it. We cherry-pick each of those characteristics to singularly refer to sex at any given time. "Your biologic sex is the interplay and the collective of your sex chromosomes, sex hormones, your internal reproductive structures, and what gonads you have, and your external genitalia," a pediatric endocrinologist said to me. "It's biologically false to say that it's any one of those things." An example of that is how we use the binary of testosterone and estrogen to indicate sex; we do the same thing with each of the other sex characteristics—treating them as if they are individually determinative. Do you have a penis or a vagina? Are you XX or XY? Do you have boobs or not? We often treat the answer to each of these questions—even if the answers are different for each question—as if your chromosomes *or* genitals *or* secondary sex characteristics *or* hormones determine your sex. But this is an *and* situation.

In sports, today's preferred international determination is testosterone. As discussed in previous chapters, this hasn't always been the case. The nude parades from earlier Olympic Games and gender passports with chromosome information are examples of using individual sex characteristics to determine eligibility. The use of testosterone as a marker is a similar practice. "If testosterone wasn't gendered, we wouldn't have this as a possible trait to demarcate people," Karkazis said. "It's precisely because it's understood widely as a male sex hormone, and responsible for all things masculine, that people are able to draw on it. If it didn't have that sort of frame around it, they wouldn't be able to use it in the way that it's getting pulled on right now."

I don't entirely agree with Karkazis on the point that testosterone is being used only because it's commonly referred to as the male sex hormone. There's some logic as to why testosterone has emerged as the proverbial line in the sand when it comes to determining eligibility for the women's category in elite competition. Sha'Carri Richardson, the fastest woman in the United States, won the U.S. 2021 Olympic Trials in the 100m with a time of 10.86.[1] Her 10.72 time from April 2021 was the sixth-fastest time in history for women. Jason Lorent from Shelton High School in Shelton, Connecticut, won the boys' 100m at the 2021 Connecticut State Open with a 10.69.[2] That time wasn't even close to the fastest among high school boys that year. No matter what a person believes about physiology and testosterone, those times are not disputable. The men's world record for the 100m sprint is 0.9 seconds faster than the women's world record. That is a lifetime in the world of sprinting, and the women's world record has stood since 1988. The generally accepted gap between elite women's and elite men's performance is 10–12 percent. The discrepancy has a lot to do with testosterone.

The testosterone levels of those who are assigned female at birth and those who are assigned male at birth are different. And that difference is of an order of magnitude that no endocrinologist I've ever spoken with has said doesn't exist. "The differences are really pretty broad," endocrinologist Dr. Myron Genel told me. "The lower level of men is five to six times higher than the upper level in women." The exact numbers vary from endocrinologist to endocrinologist, but for most people assigned female at birth, the typical testosterone level is under 3 nmol/L. For people assigned male at birth, that number is typically between 12–25 nmol/L. I want to be very clear and argue that there are exceptions to this. Caster Semenya and other athletes with differences of sex development fall into that category. People who have polycystic ovarian syndrome (PCOS) also have higher than typical levels of testosterone. There are also situations where a person assigned male at birth may have lower than typical levels of testosterone. It's not always as simple as we would like to believe, or as it is often presented.

I first spoke with Dr. Genel back in 2018, when I was reporting my first story on high school–aged transgender athletes. Genel joined the faculty at Yale School of Medicine in 1971. He specializes in pediatric endocrinology, and he has been a medical consultant to World Athletics and the IOC. He's retired now but still consults on these issues and studies them. I've heard he can still be found in the halls of Yale's medical school with regularity. The first time I called him, he changed how I think about this issue. When talking about testosterone, he said, "There is an appalling lack of actual physiologic data that compares performance in any sort of authoritative way that relates to sex hormones. Not that there isn't some demonstrated effect of testosterone, but applying it to demonstrated performance—there's very little data."[3]

To have a doctor who specializes in this field say this out loud to me was stunning, not because it wasn't true, but because it went against everything I thought I knew at the time. In 2018, I was twenty-seven years old. I had taken a genetics class in college. I was reasonably competent when it came to science, but I was floored when Genel said that. I was familiar with the "demonstrated effect" of testosterone that Genel mentioned. It's likely that you are too. We know a lot about how testosterone affects the body. For those who experience testosterone-driven puberty (mostly those who are assigned male at birth), there are a number of physiological and metabolic benefits conferred from the hormone: larger muscle mass, greater bone density, a greater capacity to process more oxygen during exercise (commonly referred to as VO_2 max), etc. Basically, people who experience testosterone-driven puberty are, on average, faster, stronger, and able to jump higher. There's a reason that testosterone is a banned substance when it comes to doping regulations in sports: it's athletically helpful. What those advantages mean in terms of athletic performance and how that should dictate policy is the open question.

However, the fact that testosterone is a banned substance is often construed to mean that there is definitive science on the effects of testosterone on athletic performance. This is more of what Karkazis was getting at when talking about how testosterone is misused in policy making. She often refers to these misunderstandings of testosterone as the hormone being treated as "jet fuel for athletes," or, in this case, a "miracle molecule." That is not true in the way many people think it is. This is partially what makes examining policies that govern sex separation in sport, particularly those that regulate the women's category, a tall task. Generally speaking, it's understood that men are "better athletes" because of the typically higher levels of testosterone. As discussed in the first chapters of this book, that core assumption undergirds the entire purpose for creating two primary categories for sports: men's and women's. The question of whether that assumption is true is a little trickier. Scientists can also disagree about both small and big things. If the scientific community agreed, and the science was as settled as is often presented, then policy would be much clearer.

Speaking with Dr. Genel illuminated how complicated scientific understanding is of this subject, because data can be vastly different depending on the circumstances of its collection. "Part of the problem in interpreting the results is it's not always clear when the blood was drawn," Genel said.

Apparently, testosterone levels in people assigned male at birth are highest in the morning and dip after exercise, which

I did not expect. The technique of the measurement also matters. "The most accurate measurement is by mass spectrometry," Genel said. "Some of the older measurements that have been reported that are so much more variable were done by radioimmunoassay. So how the testosterone is measured also becomes significant."

I know, I know. What does all of that mean? Basically, it means that when looking at a study that measures testosterone, it's important to consider all of the factors that produced that study, and not just the conclusions of that study. This is true with all medical studies, but I would argue that it's especially true in this case, due to the influence on our cultural understanding of testosterone.

A study often cited in pushing back against the use of testosterone as the primary marker of sex was published in Britain in 2014, titled "Endocrine Profiles in 693 Elite Athletes in the Postcompetition Setting." This study argued that the findings showed "complete overlap of the sexes" as it pertained to testosterone, which was quite the departure from the status quo as Genel outlined earlier. The study sampled 693 elite athletes in a post-competition setting. All participants were volunteers, and the samples were collected within two hours of competing at a major national or international competition. The results of the study were that 16.5 percent of men had low testosterone levels, 13.7 percent of women had high levels compared to their respective averages, and, of course, the levels overlapped between sexes.[4] But a closer look at the data shows vast gaps between the average levels of testosterone for the male group (16.7 nmol/L) and the female group (2.7 nmol/L). In looking at the data plots of the levels of serum (the amount of testosterone in the blood) measured, there is a bell curve of serum levels for the male group. In the female group, the dots skewed heavily toward the side of the chart representing 1–3 nmol/L, with some dots scattered into the higher levels. Notably, the mean level of testosterone found in this sampling of elite female athletes was double that of a nonathletic population. The study used radioimmunoassay and measured testosterone levels in a window close to completed exercise, generating results that showed many lower-than-expected testosterone levels within the male group.

So once again, what does all of this mean? Basically, the testosterone levels between elite male and elite female athletes are clear and distinct groupings at either end of a spectrum with *some* variance and *some* overlap. But that variance is interesting when it comes to both male athletes and female athletes, because testosterone levels *do* vary between and within sexes. Those testosterone levels, however, do not overlap in overwhelming numbers. Furthermore, a person's testosterone level does not determine athletic outcomes. The athlete in women's sports with the highest testosterone level isn't guaranteed a victory, and the same is true for athletes in men's sports. Despite the reality that typical testosterone levels differ significantly between those assigned female at birth and those assigned male at birth, it's still an imperfect measurement when it comes to determining sex, and a worse measurement for pinpointing any sort of advantage for the general public. I want to underscore that when it comes to sports, this level of scrutiny is being placed on elite athletes and often extrapolated into popular consciousness as applicable to the rest of us. For those of us who are not elite athletes, most don't know their hormone levels at all.

Let's use the example of my brother, who at twenty-six years old went to the emergency room because of swelling in his eye.

Turns out, he had a severe infection. To make sure that the infection had not spread to his brain, he received a CT scan. He did not have a bacterial infection in his brain, but he did have a tumor on his pituitary gland. This tumor, which he likely has had since he was in high school, is secreting prolactin. Prolactin is the hormone responsible for lactation, though it is present in small quantities in all of us. My brother's prolactin level was eighty-four times the level it should have been, and it was also suppressing his testosterone. His doctors said that his testosterone level should be between 10.4 nmol/L and 34.7 nmol/L but instead was hovering around 3.95 nmol/L. My brother is a man who, currently, has a hormone imbalance. Does that make him less of a man? I ask this question because testosterone is often presented as a line in the sand. On one side, you're female, and on the other side, you're male. Of course, this framing also leaves out the many intersex people or those with differences of sex development. It also overly simplifies something that is incredibly complex.

Questionable science and overly broad conclusions happen on all sides of this debate. Interestingly enough, the study used by World Athletics to justify changing its testosterone regulations to oust Caster Semenya from competition has since seen a correction. The correction was published on August 17, 2021—well after Semenya could have used it to become eligible for the Tokyo Olympics—and called those results "misleading" and "exploratory."[5] The making of policy based on science continues to be fraught, but there are some trying to take on this issue to seek a better understanding of what meaningful competition in sports could look like.

• • •

JOANNA HARPER, A Ph.D. student at Loughborough University, spoke with deliberateness and specificity in our Zoom room. Harper's research focused on the science of transgender athletes, particularly transgender women in girls' and women's sports. Harper is a transgender woman herself, and has been one of the primary voices shaping the scientific discussion about the inclusion of transgender athletes.

"I'm often reminded of the Harrison Ford line from *Raiders of the Lost Ark,* where he says, 'I'm working this out as I go along,'" Harper said to me.

Harper's journey to this moment began in Parry Sound, Canada, a town of around 5,000 people 100 miles from Toronto. Growing up, Harper participated in many different sports, but distance running became her best one. "Distance running was the first sport I was able to beat my father in," Harper said. "So that certainly, at whatever I was, fourteen or fifteen at the time, to be able to beat my father, who I considered to be this great athlete at something, was pretty good."

Harper continued running in college and into adulthood. In 2004, she decided to medically and socially transition. When she started hormone therapy in August of that year, she began to see her times slow quickly, which came as a bit of a surprise. "I knew that testosterone suppression would make me a slower runner, but I thought it'd become a gradual process and it wouldn't be all that big a difference," Harper said. "But within weeks I was noticeably running slow, and after nine months of hormone therapy, I was running twelve percent slower. And that's the difference between serious male and serious female distance runners. So I had lost my complete male advantage with nine months of hormone therapy.

"As a scientist, I was intrigued," she added.

Because of her personal experience, Harper began to study endocrinology and exercise physiology, and in 2005 and 2006, she began to reach out to other transgender women who were distance runners and gather data. It was a side gig; Harper worked as a medical physicist in the United States during this time. It would take seven years of data collection to have enough for a paper. The result was a small, published study analyzing the race times of eight transgender women, including Harper. In that study, Harper found that, physiologically, transgender women after undergoing hormone therapy were more athletically similar to cisgender women than cisgender men. This was reflected in hormone levels, hemoglobin levels, and in the race times themselves.[6] When the paper was published, "my life goes berserk," Harper said.

Everyone was calling. International sports federations, the media, even the International Olympic Committee. "In 2015, I had more data than all the universities throughout [the] world combined," Harper said.

It was the first study published that specifically examined the performance of transgender athletes. One person I spoke with referred to it as "anecdotal," but, as of this writing, there has yet to be a second study that also studies the athletic performance of transgender athletes. There have been other studies examining the effects of hormone therapy on transgender people's (mostly women's) ability to perform athletic tasks, such as push-ups or sit-ups, and how hormone therapy affects muscle mass loss and retention. And those studies have been illuminating in their own right. One such study examined the effects of hormone therapy on the ability of transgender men and women to perform push-ups, sit-ups, and run 1.5 miles.[7] Prior to hormone therapy, transgender men performed 41 percent fewer push-ups, and their 1.5-mile time was 21 percent slower compared to cisgender men. After one year of hormone therapy with testosterone, those differences disappeared. For transgender women, the results were more mixed. Before hormone therapy, transgender women performed 31 percent more push-ups, 15 percent more sit-ups, and ran 1.5 miles 21 percent faster than cisgender women. After two years of hormone therapy, the gap in push-ups and sit-ups disappeared, but transgender women were still 12 percent faster in the 1.5-mile run.

Another study examined the effects of hormone therapy on muscle loss and retention in transgender women and the inverse in transgender men.[8] Over the course of one year of hormone therapy, transgender men saw increases in their strength and muscle size, whereas transgender women saw modest decreases in muscle size and strength. It is worth noting that both of these studies examine results in transgender adults who, while in some cases they are performing athletic tasks, are not "athletes" in the ways we understand that term, meaning they don't train specifically for athletic performance. Another study out of Brazil by lead author Leonardo Azevedo Mobilia Alvarez examined the long-term effect of testosterone suppression and estrogen hormone therapy on the VO_2 max, among other attributes, of transgender women compared to cisgender women and cisgender men.[9] It was a small study with fifteen transgender women, thirteen cisgender women, and fourteen cisgender men, but an interesting one. The researchers on the study hypothesized that transgender women who have had androgen exposure—or gone through testosterone-driven puberty—would have different results in muscle strength and cardiopulmonary capacity (VO_2 max) than both transgender women and transgender men. This study specifically looked at transgender women who started blockers after age twelve, and at the time of their participation in the study, they ranged in age from twenty-five to forty-five and had been on hormone therapy for an average of 14.4 years. The transgender women and cisgender women had comparable levels of testosterone, with an average of 0.624 nmol/L (range: 0.4161–22.0858) and 0.658 nmol/L (range: 0.4161–1.3903) respectively. Cisgender men had an average testosterone level of 18.1784 nmol/L. Note that the original data were given in ng/dl, which I converted to nmol/L by a rate of 1 nmol/L to 28.842 ng/dl.

The results affirmed the researchers' hypothesis: transgender women performed differently from both cisgender men and cisgender women. The study upheld the average difference in peak cardiopulmonary capacity between cisgender men and cisgender women at 25 to 35 percent, and transgender women fell between those two points. The results were comparable in measuring grip strength, percentage of body fat, and hemoglobin levels as well. Notably, when adjusting for fat-free mass or bodyweight, the study concluded there was "no difference in relative VO$_2$ peak or strength between [transgender women] or [cisgender women.]" This small study gives an excellent window into how transgender women who have undergone hormone therapy for extended periods of time compare physiologically with cisgender men and cisgender women, underscoring that all three groups are different from one another, and that physiological assumptions made about transgender women do not always apply.

When transgender women are referred to as "biological males," the implication is that physiologically, transgender women and cisgender men are the same. That is not the case. Nuance is important here. The Alvares study showed that transgender women have some metabolic and physiological advantages diminished but not negated by long-term hormone therapy. But how does that diminished physiological advantage translate to a performance advantage? That's the core question that science needs to begin to answer.

These studies have been published within the last five years and are often cited to argue for more restrictions for transgender athletes at all levels, not just elite sports. They are important studies when it comes to furthering our understanding of hormone therapy and its effects on the body. But there's still so much to learn, in terms of both information gathering and discovering the limits of the application of that data. Having a data point that says transgender women exhibit, on average, more grip strength than cisgender women has nothing to do with basketball skill, but could be important knowledge for rock climbing. Both conclusions are speculation because there is very little data on how the existence of a possible physiological advantage translates to a performance advantage.

In the middle of all those numbers, however, there is a considerable amount we do know. To answer the question "What does the science say?" I can safely answer that the science is unsettled and evolving, but we do know a few things. We know that typical testosterone levels are considerably different for those assigned male at birth and those assigned female at birth, with some exceptions. We know that the reason for that difference, generally, is testosterone-driven puberty. We know that prior to puberty, the athletic differences between sexes is negligible. We know that some transgender people never go through endogenous puberty due to transitioning at younger ages and taking puberty blockers. We know that hormone therapy after puberty is effective for transgender men in raising athletic outputs. And we know that while, after two years of hormone therapy, transgender women do see their athletic outputs decrease, some physiological advantages do remain.

It must be said, however, that the studies mentioned in this chapter measure changes in adults, ranging from their twenties to their forties. There are currently no studies available that measure athletic performance in transgender teenagers or children. And while we are beginning to know more about the effects of testosterone suppression and hormone therapy after puberty, we know considerably less (read: almost nothing) about how hormone therapy affects athletic performance if administered before, during, or in the end stages of puberty. We have no idea if there is a difference in athletic performance among transgender women who begin hormone therapy at thirteen versus seventeen versus twenty versus thirty-five. The arguments for "science-based" policy in this regard—no matter what a person believes is the appropriate policy—are rooted in extrapolating the information we do have to apply to other, understudied populations within the same community. Or, in some cases, applying knowledge we have about the differences between cisgender men and cisgender women to transgender athletes, which is not just inappropriate from an identity perspective, but is also physiologically inappropriate.

For all that we do know about testosterone and the physiological advantages it confers upon athletes, we also know that just as it is difficult to pick a single trait to determine a person's sex, it's impossible to select an attribute as determinative for athletic success in any sport. A tall person isn't immediately good at basketball or swimming, though height is certainly an advantage in both sports. What makes someone fast is a combination of factors, including strength and size (or lack thereof in some cases). There will always be physiological advantages and disadvantages in sports; that's a reality in athletics. Michael Phelps is often held up as an example of someone who is perfectly engineered physiologically for his sport; his body has a mythology all its own. Phelps' wingspan is wider than his height; he is reportedly double-jointed and has incredible flexibility in his ankles; he also reportedly produces significantly less lactic acid than most athletes, allowing him to swim longer without as much fatigue. Those quirks are celebrated. Phelps is an extreme example, but when looking at elite athletes, most cases are extreme. These are athletes at the very apex of achievement; they are the best examples of the distillation of pure athleticism that we have. Focusing on hormones and joints and physiology to explain achievement, however, papers over the greatest barrier to progressing in athletics to begin with.

When Lionel Messi signed with Barcelona FC at thirteen years old, part of the deal was that the club would pay for his medical treatments. The Argentine had growth hormone deficiency. Though Messi is listed at 170 cm—roughly five foot six—on the current Paris St. Germain roster, he was reportedly just four foot two when he was eleven. He needed human growth hormone to spur his growth, and that treatment was expensive. Messi has said that Barcelona was the only club who wanted to sign him that offered to pay for those treatments.[10] Messi, who has gone on to become one of the greatest soccer players to ever touch a ball, was so naturally gifted at soccer that he was able to secure funding for his medical treatments as well as the resources to nurture his talent. It is a beautiful story with a happy ending, but I find myself asking how many Messis could be out there who never had an equivalent opportunity.

Sport is physical, so we often focus on the physical to explain the incredible talent on display: Phelps' flexible ankles, Messi's speed and dribbling skill, Diana Taurasi's ability to sink three-point shots from anywhere on the floor, etc. But to get to the Olympics or the Champions League or the WNBA, you have to first be able to access, and pay for, sports in the first place. In a review of studies published between 2011 and 2021, the Canadian Centre for Ethics in Sport found that biomedical studies are overvalued in sport policy development for transgender athlete participation in elite sport while diminishing the impact of sociological ones.[11] That myopic inquiry, however, belies all the other factors that create successful athletes, including perhaps the biggest advantage of them all: money.

Sports cost money. Some more than others, but generally speaking, the financial cost of sports is considerable. There's the equipment and the uniforms. But then there's also the travel. The space rental. The private coaching and instruction. The club team fees. It all adds up to enormous sums. And no, sports don't *have* to be so expensive. One of the best things about the school sports system in the United States is that public schools field sports teams. It's the core reason why Title IX has had the impact it has. Sports is an education program in the United States. But elementary schools aren't always fielding sports teams, so parents supplement what is publicly available with other options. I experienced this myself.

When I was eight years old, my parents enrolled me in the co-ed indoor soccer and basketball leagues at the Boys and Girls Club in Plymouth, Indiana. It was my first time playing competitive sports, and my parents had to take me to the next town over to make it happen. Culver, my hometown, is tiny. The speed limit in town is 20 mph. There's one grocery store, a CVS, a Family Dollar, and a Subway. To this day, my mom still drives an hour once every 4–6 weeks to go to Target and Costco.

Competitive sports opportunities were just as thin as the shopping options, especially for younger kids. I'd played some T-ball and soccer, but that was specific to the spring and summer. And I loved sports; I wanted to play all the time. Basketball was the sport I loved the most, and it was probably my best too. But in my town, there were no opportunities for girls to play until sixth-grade school ball (my dad has reminded me that my brother was playing in a local rec league in third or fourth grade). So my parents decided to have me try out this league at a Boys and Girls Club twenty minutes away. It was a relatively cheap option that allowed me to play against real competition. It also happened to be co-ed, which I loved.

This was the experience that I credit with giving me the foundation to be a competitive basketball player in high school. I learned to dribble and shoot, first on a nine-foot rim and then on a ten-foot one. And as I developed into a better basketball player, opportunities to play in more competitive environments presented themselves. There were summer camps, and then elite camps, and the ever-looming option of competitive travel basketball through the Amateur Athletic Union (AAU).

My parents are teachers at a private school. They raised three children on those salaries. We never went hungry or wanted for any essentials, but for most of my life, we were middle class. When it came to my burgeoning passion for basketball, they made a decision early: I wouldn't be participating in travel basketball until I was in seventh grade. Most of my eventual teammates had been traveling since they were nine years old. Once I started traveling, my parents paid team fees, tournament fees, hotel fees, gas costs, gear costs, etc. According to my parents, all of those fees totaled to about $1,000 a month in mid-2000s dollars. At one of the programs I played for, we were expected to pay for private workouts to "demonstrate my commitment."

And basketball is a cheap sport! It's worth noting that basketball is one of the most accessible sports we have. A study looked at demographic data of Olympians in Canada, the United States, Australia, and Great Britain and found that 94.9 percent of winter athletes were white and 30.3 percent were privately educated.[12] For summer athletes, those numbers were 81.7 percent white and 32.7 percent privately educated. The results were averaged to create a combined race socioeconomic access index (CAI), with a number of 1.0 being a representative distribution of race and type of education for that country. The United States' CAI for summer athletes was a 1.13, but for winter athletes, it was 0.42. Those data make sense, considering sports like basketball and track and field are summer Olympic sports, and winter Olympic sports are much less likely to be accessible. (How does one get into luge? Or curling? Or skeleton? Or biathlon? You get the point.) The influence of socioeconomic status on sports isn't restricted to just elite sports; it affects youth participation too. Middle school children from affluent families were three times as likely to meet physical activity recommendations.[13] At the high school level, youth from affluent families were three times as likely to have ever played sports at all. One of the common barriers reported by youth from lower levels of affluence: affordability. Youth sports have become big business. *The Washington Post* reported youth sport revenue increasing by 55 percent to $19 billion from 2010 to 2017.[14] This phenomenon has only been compounded by the explosion of sneaker brands in youth basketball, specialization, and the advent of name, image, and likeness (NIL) rules allowing some high school–aged athletes (and all college athletes) to make money from social media, autographs, and brand deals. The stakes for youth sports continue to climb for many families, something that I'm pretty unconvinced is a good thing. "If we can't tolerate inclusion because our high school sports have gotten too commodified, then we need to change high school sport," Western New England University law professor Erin Buzuvis said.

The ability to pay for sports and private instruction is an accepted advantage, just as having lower levels of lactic acid production is an accepted advantage (looking at you, Michael Phelps). But blurring the physiological lines of sex separation is not accepted. That's seen as unfair, and science is often cherry-picked to make that argument. Looked at holistically, however, it's not scientifically supported to completely ban transgender girls and women from girls' and women's sports, or to root out athletes in women's sports with intersex variations. Yet that hasn't stopped people from trying.

What is accepted, however, is that testosterone is athletically helpful, which is why it's a banned substance. That's the primary reason for most policies not allowing for transgender men to take testosterone to medically transition and still compete in women's sports. There is a case, however, where that did happen. Outside of Dallas, in a suburb named Euless, a transgender boy won a girls' wrestling championship. And all hell broke loose.

6.

THE WRESTLER

WHEN THE REFEREE blew his whistle, Mack Beggs knew exactly what to do. In a flurry of movement, he locked up his opponent, Chelsea Sanchez, and went to work. He twisted and lunged and stretched and pulled and rolled. Each movement was designed to put points on the board. Get ahead. And stay ahead.

It had been a long day. Beggs was up early to get over to the arena from his hotel. His headphones had stayed glued to his ears in an effort to tune out the noise, which was considerable. Since he had qualified for the state championship tournament after his district opponent forfeited, cameras were everywhere. He'd never seen so many. Growing up in Euless, Texas, in a small, unassuming home with his grandmother, Nancy, there'd never been cameras around him. He was just a kid who loved to wrestle.

But the cameras came to Houston with him. When he walked into the arena, they were there. When he stretched before matches, they were there—in a semicircle, pushing their lenses into his face. He'd put up the hood on his sweatshirt to try to block them from view, to try to feel like the typical kid he knew himself to be and escape the gawking. His coach finally started taking him into the hallway just to get him away from the limelight.

Even now, as he escaped from a Sanchez takedown to score two more points, he knew the cameras were trained on him. Of course they were. He's a transgender boy competing in the girls' wrestling state championship. If the past week was any indication, the whole country was interested in that story.

A whistle blew, but it wasn't the one Beggs desperately wanted. The referee pulled him off Sanchez's back. Beggs could see a few droplets of blood on her skin. It was quickly wiped off, and Beggs realized that he was the one bleeding. He must have taken a shot to the nose. Somehow, because of the angle, the blood was running up his face.

"Ugh, that is *nasty,*" a teammate said from the side of the mat.

With a plug up his right nostril, Beggs resumed scrapping with Sanchez. His arms flew to the sides of her head, trying to get her into a clinch. Time favored him, though, so he began to put space between them. As the seconds ticked off the clock, Beggs outstretched his arms to bat Sanchez away and stay out of her reach. He was up 11–2, and in a few more seconds, he'd claim his first state championship.

The referee blew the whistle to end the match. Beggs put his arms in the air in triumph before covering his face with his hands, incredulous that he'd pulled it off. An undefeated season with a state championship win.

Beggs fell to his knees on the blue mat, while a mixture of cheers and boos rained on him from the stands of the arena. It was so much noise. He couldn't decipher any of it. After getting up, he looped an arm around Sanchez to tell her good job.

Emotional, she rushed off the mat. The referee raised Beggs' arm in victory. In a matter of seconds, his coach took him back into the hallway. There was no basking, no confetti, no hugging his parents or his grandmother. He was rushed out of view, to a place the cameras couldn't follow.

In the documentary *Mack Wrestles*, Beggs said of the experience, "It didn't even feel like a celebration."

MACK BEGGS BECAME a household name during an otherwise innocuous February weekend in 2017. *The Dallas Morning News* published an article just after he won his regional meet by forfeit, and the story blew up. News trucks had camped out on his lawn, and not just from Texas. He did a couple of TV interviews and had been featured in magazines. Ellen even called. And all because he was a boy who won a girls' wrestling state championship. Actually, two state championships. In back-to-back undefeated seasons. But that comes later.

Once the news of Mack's district championship became public, a former family friend, Jim Baudhuin, filed a lawsuit on behalf of another parent to try to bar Beggs from state competition. As a transgender boy who had been taking small dosages of testosterone under the care of a doctor since his sophomore year, he was labeled a danger by parents and segments of the media. His life became an object of intense intrigue for local and national media. Why was this boy wrestling girls?

Beggs ended up in the middle of a perfect storm that allowed for his story to have maximum cultural impact. Texas is one of only a handful of states that separates wrestling into girls' and boys' categories. Most states have one unified wrestling sport. Girls are allowed to participate, but the sport caters to boys. Sort of like football. Texas also operates with a rule—which has since become law—that uses the sex indicated on a student's birth certificate as the appropriate sex for athletic competition. Those two things together forced Beggs into a situation where he was wrestling against girls (and winning). The third factor was that Beggs was taking testosterone as a means of medically transitioning. Some members of the public took that information to mean that Beggs was "doping," like professional athletes or, worse, East German women. "Mack shouldn't have been wrestling against the girls any more than the East German women shouldn't [sic] been showing up at competitions with chest hair and deep voices," Jim Baudhuin, Mack's former family friend, said to *The Washington Times*.[1]

The Texas policy that created this quagmire didn't consider that a transgender boy might be competing, or that he might have wanted to compete in the boys' category. The policy was designed to continue the lineage of protecting women's sports from an incursion by men. The irony, of course, is that—in many people's eyes—it did the opposite.

The birth certificate policy was voted on in the summer of 2016 by Texas school district superintendents. The University Interscholastic League (UIL), the organization that governed Texas high school sports, said that such a policy was already being used informally. The rule change in the handbook was just formally recognizing common practice. That policy passed with 586 of 620 superintendents voting in favor of the measure. It went into effect on August 1, 2016, just as Beggs was about to begin his junior year in school. Beggs had begun hormone therapy the fall of his sophomore season. He was public about that process on his social media accounts.

Beggs' story was intriguing on its own merits, but a big reason why the story exploded wasn't just the headline of a transgender boy taking testosterone and winning girls' wrestling championships. It was that Beggs lived in Texas. And Texas was already embroiled in a fight with the federal government over transgender inclusion in schools.

By 2016, THE Department of Education's Office for Civil Rights (OCR) had been responding to questions for years from parents, educators, students, and school administrators alike about the fundamental issue of how Title IX applied to transgender students. These questions ranged from pronouns to bathrooms to athletics to academics. And it wasn't just a matter of how schools should handle these questions; reports were also coming into the office from families of transgender children of difficulties accessing services and support in their local schools. The question needed to be answered.

Answering the question would accelerate an asymmetric culture clash across the country, but no one really knew that at the time. The Obama administration had quietly been codifying an expansion of the definition of sex through policy memos for nearly five years. With Congress deadlocked, and yet another version of the Employment Non-Discrimination Act (ENDA) stalled—leaving federal LGBTQ+ inclusive civil rights legislation still unpassed—the executive branch embarked on a remarkably aggressive expansion of government protections in the spheres it controlled.

Further elaborating on a Dear Colleague Letter from 2011—that established sexual violence as a Title IX issue that schools and higher education institutions needed to pay attention to—OCR wrote in 2014, "Title IX's sex discrimination prohibition extends to claims of discrimination based on gender identity or failure to conform to stereotypical notions of masculinity or femininity and OCR accepts such complaints for investigation."[2]

That definition of sex discrimination—rooted in the Supreme Court decision on *Price Waterhouse v. Hopkins* (1989)—served as the foundation for what would follow in the coming years. In May 2016, OCR issued a Dear Colleague Letter[3] to specifically address the question of transgender youth in schools. The primary power of Title IX is that the Department of Education can remove federal funds if a school is found to be not in compliance with the law. In this Dear Colleague Letter, the Obama administration made it perfectly clear that being in compliance required schools to affirm a student's gender identity regardless of their sex assigned at birth, in all matters of educational and school activities. That meant bathrooms, sports, dress codes, everything.

The guidance kicked off a firestorm, especially in Texas. The UIL was in the process of voting on a policy that would restrict transgender athletic competition by defining sex as being what was on a student's birth certificate, the same policy that forced Mack Beggs to wrestle against girls. Houston was in the middle of a ballot box battle over the city's transgender-inclusive nondiscrimination policy. The state did not have statewide protections for LGBTQ+ people and had no intention of expanding nondiscrimination protections. Just days before the Dear Colleague Letter was released, Lieutenant Governor Dan Patrick called on the Fort Worth ISD superintendent to resign *because* the school district adopted a transgender-inclusive policy.[4]

What does a state do in response to a transgender-inclusive federal mandate if that state's government is dominated by those who question the validity of transgender people? Well, in this case, they sue the federal government.

Texas Attorney General Ken Paxton tested the waters on a bathroom policy directly at odds with the new guidance from the Obama administration with at least two school districts, Wichita Falls and Harrold.[5] Ultimately, Harrold's school board adopted the proposed policy, and Paxton used that as grounds to sue the federal government. Led by Texas, an eventual twenty-three states filed a lawsuit to challenge the guidance, arguing that the federal government had "conspired to turn workplaces and educational settings into laboratories for a massive social experiment, flouting the democratic process, and running roughshod over common-sense policies protecting children and basic privacy rights."[6]

One of the Texas lawmakers particularly upset with the way the Obama administration handled this issue was State Senator Lois Kolkhorst. Kolkhorst is a self-avowed fifth-generation Texan who grew up in Brenham, Texas, a town that sits an hour northwest of Houston with a population that hovers around 15,000. She is an alumna of Texas Christian University, where she played on the college's golf team. She regularly cited protecting Title IX as a reason for sponsoring and cosponsoring the legislation she did during the 2017 regular and special sessions.

When Donald Trump ascended to the presidency, he focused on undoing many of the previous administration's policies, including the guidance on transgender students in schools. The same week Beggs won his first state championship, the Departments of Justice and Education rescinded the Dear Colleague Letter issued under Obama. The lawsuits were dropped, and the door was open for bills like Kolkhorst's. The move was just the opening salvo in the battle to come.

Kolkhorst, a committed conservative, became gravely concerned following the guidance issued by the Obama administration, the victory of Mack Beggs in Texas, and the emergence of another athlete, Andraya Yearwood, in Connecticut. "We're here today because Texas has a history of taking care of these issues and not being dictated to by the federal government," she said at the Texas Senate Committee on State Affairs hearing of her bill SB 3. She characterized the Obama-era guidance as directing public schools to "remove all privacy barriers between genders and any division between boys and girls—in essence, a rewriting of Title IX without a vote of Congress."

In that hearing, she also confronted the issue of transgender girls competing in girls' sports. "Ask a female athlete after she's spent her lifetime trying to compete in a sport if it's fair for a boy to decide to play in her sport," she said.

OF COURSE, THERE already was a boy playing girls' sports. As Beggs entered late elementary and middle school, he struggled internally. He didn't have the words to explain the tension he felt, or what exactly was going on. But in a car ride with her child, Angela McNew turned to Mack and asked, "Are you transgender?"

As she explained what she meant to Beggs, something clicked. That was the word he'd been looking for. He didn't socially or medically transition right away, but that moment began a yearslong process of Beggs living the life he wanted as the person he is, rather than the person others thought him to be.

Wrestling became part of that process. After seeing a poster calling for tryouts as a freshman, Beggs went to his first practice and fell in love with it. He came home smelling like the mats he'd been rolling on all afternoon. His grandmother and legal guardian, Nancy, fanned her nose when he finally made it through the front door, asking him what he'd gotten himself into. "Wrestling," Mack answered with a smile.

Mack began living with Nancy when he was ten years old. He moved in with her, seeking some stability, as he and his mom (along with his sister) had moved around a lot during his childhood. Nancy put a roof over his head every night for nearly a decade: an unassuming brick home with a cement patio porch and a small backyard, room enough for multiple dogs and a lot of love. When he came home after that first practice, he was late. Nancy gave him hell for that.

The discipline of the sport offered Mack a much-needed outlet. He'd been struggling with his mental health as he processed his gender identity, beginning to cut himself in middle school. When he started to wrestle, the cutting stopped. Nancy credits wrestling with saving his life.

Just like every other freshman who'd never wrestled before, Mack wasn't dominant when he started. In his first season, he finished in fourth place in his region. His second season, he did make it to the state championships but didn't place. His junior year went a bit differently.

That season, Beggs went undefeated. As he racked up wins, his social media garnered more attention. Suddenly people cared about his medical transition, which he'd been documenting for more than a year at this point. Heading into the regional competition, which qualifies wrestlers for the state championships, Beggs figured he had a good shot to win. The wrestler who had won for the last two years, and beat him regularly, had graduated. A week and a half prior to the tournament, though, Jim Baudhuin filed his lawsuit to attempt to block Beggs from competition. When a wrestler from that same district was slated to wrestle Beggs in the final, she forfeited, handing Beggs the title. The news exploded.

For the next week, news trucks followed the Beggs family everywhere. Reporters showed up to the house, to his school. People were calling the house and trying to get into wrestling practice. His social media blew up. It seemed as if everyone wanted a piece of him.

The cameras followed him all the way to Cypress for that championship he won. Of course, not everyone was happy about it. Parents of his rivals and of wrestlers he'd never competed against spoke to reporters. He was constantly misgendered. Even now, years after it happened, people encountering the story mistake Beggs for a transgender girl. The hostility shown toward Beggs following his junior year state championship run in 2017 was just beginning. Disgruntled fans and parents passed the baton to state lawmakers, who were quick to run the next leg of the race. And Lois Kolkhorst was out in front.

PUTTING HER CONCERN about Title IX into action, Kolkhorst authored SB 6, the Texas version of what came to be known as a "bathroom bill." A year prior, in 2016, the North Carolina legislature had passed a law, the infamous HB 2, that overruled the transgender-inclusive nondiscrimination city ordinance enacted by Charlotte earlier that year. The public response to HB 2 was unlike anything previously seen: concerts cancelled; championships moved; conventions relocated. It was a full-court press of public pressure, including—perhaps most famously—the 2017 NBA All-Star Game being relocated from Charlotte. Despite North Carolina experiencing that level of pushback, Kolkhorst still filed SB 6.

Modeled after the North Carolina law, SB 6 not only directly rebuked the guidance from the Obama administration regarding transgender youth in schools, but also sought to invalidate local municipalities' existing nondiscrimination protections for the entirety of the LGBTQ+ community. In Texas, five cities with populations over 100,000 had such nondiscrimination policies in place, including El Paso and San Antonio.[7] In addition to overturning local ordinances, like HB 2 did in North Carolina, SB 6 also barred transgender people from accessing bathrooms and locker rooms in accordance with their gender identity. SB 6 easily passed the Texas Senate less than a month following Beggs' state championship victory.

Kolkhorst went even further, though. She cosponsored a bill written by State Senator Bob Hall, SB 2095, that critics argued targeted Mack Beggs directly. At the core of the issue with Beggs—outside of the fact that he's transgender—was the impression that he was "using steroids" in the form of medically prescribed testosterone. The UIL explicitly banned steroid use because of the competitive advantage of doping, which is a fair position to take. In the Texas education code, however, there is an explicit exemption for those drugs that are medically administered which would otherwise be considered performance-enhancing drugs (PEDs), likely not written to be inclusive of transgender youth, but the impact was the UIL felt hamstrung by the law as it stood. The UIL also contended that the organization had no authority to ban those who were found to be using PEDs. The organization had only the authority to test, but that funding had ceased following a lack of positive results. SB 2095 would have allowed the UIL to form a medical commission to evaluate the cases of those being administered testosterone medically to determine eligibility.

None of this would theoretically be harmful or discriminatory. Athletes shouldn't dope; most people agree on that. If a high school association wants greater authority over the activities it sanctions for the purpose of addressing cheating, theoretically, that wouldn't be an issue. But in this instance, the legislation was seen as closing a loophole that allowed Beggs to wrestle at all. Under Texas policy at the time, he still had to wrestle in the girls' category; this legislation wouldn't change that. This is an important point. The storm that Beggs and Texas were caught up in was of Texas' own making. If Beggs had lived in Indiana, where I grew up, there would have been no separate girls' wrestling category. Even with a highly restrictive policy toward transgender athletes, he probably would have been able to participate. His participation likely would have been controversial, but that controversy would have been quite different. That's not to say that separate girls' wrestling categories are bad; I tend to think they're good for the sport. But the policy decision to enforce a birth certificate requirement as a means of rigidly enforcing a binary in school sports allowed for something like this to happen. The proposed solution to close the loophole had the effect of putting a young person in the crosshairs of the state government. To also empower the UIL to disqualify athletes who were taking testosterone, even for medical purposes, would have put Beggs' remaining year of eligibility in jeopardy.

During the forty-five-minute floor debate on SB 2095, state legislators mentioned Beggs twenty-seven times, and though the bill passed the Senate, it ultimately was never voted on by the Texas House of Representatives. At that point in time, Beggs was the only publicly known transgender person competing in UIL sports. For all the hullabaloo about transgender girls and women being "men in bathrooms" and the sanctity of women's intimate spaces, policies that restrict transgender people from accessing bathroom and locker room space in accordance with their gender identities puts young men like Beggs into women's spaces. The hysteria around Beggs in Texas, as reflected in this bill and in subsequent debate, also foreshadowed the extreme burdens that would be felt by a small number of transgender young people over the next half decade. Beggs' lonely experience as the only publicly known trans athlete in his state was not an aberration; it's the norm. As of this writing, more than five years later, there hasn't been a wave of transgender kids dominating school sports in Texas. To the best of my knowledge, there hasn't been another transgender person to win a state championship in the state since Beggs graduated.

In the summer of 2017, Beggs was the grand marshal for the San Antonio Pride Parade. He received an award from Athlete Ally, which took him to New York for the first time in the fall. Athlete Ally is one of the few organizations that works at the specific intersection of sports and LGBTQ+ equality. It was founded in 2011 by Hudson Taylor, a former all-American collegiate wrestler who is not a member of the LGBTQ+ community. As a senior at the University of Maryland, Taylor wrestled with a Human Rights Campaign equality sticker on his headgear as a way to show his solidarity with the LGBTQ+ community. The response he received from LGBTQ+ athletes, families with LGBTQ+ kids, and other advocates encouraged him to create an organization that sought to harness the power of athlete voices, queer or not, to fight against homophobia and transphobia in sports.

It was in the lobby of Beggs' hotel where I first met him. He was disheveled and late due to a subway snafu. (Who among us has not been late in New York because of the subway?) I was struck by how small he was, which makes sense considering that he was the champion in the 110 lb weight class. He couldn't have been more than five feet two. Sitting in the lobby in the fall of 2017, I could see the exhaustion etched onto his face. And he still had one more season to go.

RIDING IN A van coming home from the 2018 state championships during his senior year, Beggs was trying to sleep. He'd just defeated Chelsea Sanchez—the same competitor as the year before—with a score of 15–3. There weren't as many cameras present as the year prior, but in 2017, Beggs and his family had felt like the cheers in the stands ultimately outweighed the boos, even with all the negativity. This year, the referee raised his arm as attendees rained boos on him from above. Not exactly how he'd dreamed winning two state championships would feel.

As soon as the tires started rolling from the parking lot at the Berry Center, the adults in the van, parents of his teammates, immediately started in on him.

"You need to let them wrestle with the boys," they said, using the wrong pronoun for Mack.

"You shouldn't have done this," they said.

"You cheated," they said.

Nancy leaned over to Mack and urged him to go to sleep to block it out. Nancy, for her part, was completely flummoxed. She'd been sitting next to these people in the stands for *years*, thinking they were all on the same page, that these folks supported her grandson. Instead, trapped in this van for a four-hour drive, she had to listen to the extent to which they in fact did not support her grandson.

The lack of support never made sense to Nancy. It's not like she was liberal. "I'm a hard-core Republican," she said to me. What she and Mack were asking for was respect. When I talked to her on her porch in January of 2018 for the first story I ever wrote about Mack, Nancy talked about how members of her family didn't quite understand what it meant to be transgender. "You don't have to get it," she said. "You just have to go along with it."

For all the love and support Mack received from Nancy, they didn't see eye to eye on politics at all. Their general motto was "agree to disagree." Mack was actively talking about racism on social media during his later high school years, especially police brutality. Nancy was a cop; she'd been a cop for Mack's whole life. She didn't work on the street anymore; instead, she worked in courthouses. Their disagreements usually took the form of memes and videos texted between the two of them, showing their opposing viewpoints. "No one would believe it, but we get into it quite a bit," Nancy said to me. "You wouldn't think we would still be able to laugh about it and get along, being the total political opposite. Being around us is entertaining sometimes."

In Texas, the legislators targeting Mack were members of the GOP, Nancy's party of choice. The legislators pushing back against anti-LGBTQ+ legislation, including policies that would have affected Mack directly, were Democrats. It was an odd spot for Nancy to be in from where I sat, but she didn't exactly see it that way. "The thing is, the Republicans I know and that I deal with on a regular basis, the LGBT movement is not a problem for them," Nancy said to me. "The thing is, we have the freedom to make our choices. Even if you don't believe in Mack, Mack has a freedom to make his choice."

That's how Nancy was; she sought understanding from those around her. Even when someone challenged many of her core political beliefs, like Mack often did, Nancy had deep wells of patience and compassion, even as they vehemently disagreed. Nancy didn't see how it would be different with anyone else, and certainly not in the form of being verbally ambushed in a van.

That drive home was a precursor to a spring and summer that would continue the difficulties Beggs faced. The previous summer, Beggs had received outsize attention, much of it negative, including from the state legislature. Since the legislature was only in session every other year, he'd had a reprieve from being targeted by the government. But this year, Beggs was preparing to make a run at qualifying for USA Nationals in Fargo. In the boys' category.

USA Wrestling adopted a transgender inclusion policy that more closely mirrored recognized standards—transgender boys and men taking testosterone had to wrestle in the boys' category, while transgender girls and women needed to have completed at least a year of HRT to compete in the girls' category. The NCAA and IOC have similar policies, as do a number of United States governing bodies. Following the public revelations of Beggs medically transitioning, USA Wrestling vacated all of his wins in the girls' category retroactive to the date he started HRT in October 2015. After receiving a therapeutic use exemption (TUE), Beggs was cleared to wrestle in USA Wrestling events in the boys' category while continuing his testosterone dosage.

In the summer of 2018, Mack Beggs finally got to wrestle against the boys. It's what he had publicly said he wanted. It's what parents in Texas said should have happened. It's what the media had been saying should have happened for the past two years. But when he got out on the mat and scored his first victories, the parents of his competitors were pissed. At one point, Mack turned to his grandmother and said, "What do they want? Why is there such anger now?" And of course, the cameras and news coverage had long gone. There's no sensationalism in covering a boy wrestling other boys.

It's hard not to look at Beggs' story and assume that folks in Texas never had any intention of letting him wrestle in peace. The public was angry when he wrestled against girls, and they were still angry when he wrestled boys. But Beggs defied everyone's expectations and made it onto the Texas team that would go to Nationals in Fargo, North Dakota. He was looking forward to making the trip, and making history, but from the moment he made that team, his new teammates and coaches made it clear that he was unwelcome.

Beggs began to lose interest. The kid who loved wrestling suddenly didn't want to go to practice. He blew off meetings and team commitments and didn't listen to his coaches. The day before he was supposed to leave for Fargo, one of the coaches called him and told him he was off the team. Beggs slammed the phone down. "I don't care," he said. "It's not important anymore."

IN THE FALL of 2018, Mack Beggs packed up his car and drove the 800 miles from his hometown of Euless, Texas, and the house he'd shared with his grandmother—also with him in the car—to Life University in Marietta, Georgia.

Life University offered a reprieve, a place where he could introduce himself without the immediate recognition and suspicion. No one calling him "Hollywood" in the hallways or stirring the pot on Snapchat. He could finally breathe fresh air instead of being the poster boy for all the ways transgender athletes threaten women's sports. But even as he was preparing to move on from the identifier and attention of being a transgender athlete, the country had just begun to focus its attention on transgender people playing sports.

Following the defeat of her bills in the 2017 legislative session, Kolkhorst resurrected SB 6 during the special session that summer. She refiled SB 6 as SB 3, and this time, there was a provision that would have codified the UIL's birth certificate policy into law. On the floor of the Texas Senate, Kolkhorst again made mention of the existence of another transgender athlete—the one running in Connecticut. If the dustup in Texas about Mack Beggs was a preview, the battle that was swirling around Andraya Yearwood in Connecticut was the whole ball game. And the heat was about to get turned up.

7.

THE RUNNERS IN CONNECTICUT

WITH BRICK BUILDINGS towering above, Andraya Yearwood walked across campus at North Carolina Central University in the fall of 2020. She pushed her braids over her shoulder as her fingers curled around the book she held in her hand. The feeling of being a college student was still exciting, even if it wasn't exactly the freshman fall she thought she'd have. The ongoing COVID-19 pandemic truncated her senior year of high school, and she thought things with the virus would have improved when it came time for her to start college.

Though that hadn't happened, Yearwood was determined to enjoy her first year of school away from home. North Carolina Central University is a historically Black university, something she intentionally chose. Most people had no idea who she was beyond what she shared with them, except for that one professor who referred to her as a celebrity in one of her first classes. It was flattering and awkward. But mostly awkward.

An NCCU athlete jogged by her, the school letters emblazoned on the student's clothes. Yearwood couldn't help but feel a pang of longing. She'd love to be wearing school colors and competing. "It makes me miss being on a team," she said. "I miss running."

But she didn't miss everything that came with it. At all.

Of all the attention she received as a high school athlete, little paid much beyond lip service to who she was as an athlete—a kid at a small school who ran in her free time. Her parents required all of their children to play sports, preferably one per season. Track was Yearwood's spring sport in middle school, and that continued naturally into high school.

On its face, her choice was a simple one—a kid deciding to run track. But it hadn't been about that for a long time.

Yearwood first told the public that she was transgender in spring 2017 when she was fourteen years old. Outdoor track and field season was just kicking off, and the local paper, the *Hartford Courant*, published an article about her. It was one of Yearwood's first races of the season, as well as one of her first in the girls' category. She had competed against boys the year prior, even as she began to socially transition, which was awkward for her, and not particularly affirming. Moving to high school offered the opportunity to participate in girls' sports, so she took it. She posted an unofficial time of 11.99 seconds in the 100m—a time she'd never again beat in her high school career—to win easily. She won her class state championship— the one for small schools—and then lost against all the larger schools in the State Open. The whole season happened largely without incident. The attention paid to transgender people by most media outlets at the time was minimal, and Texas had sucked up all of the oxygen in spring and summer 2017, writing about Mack Beggs and the Texas bathroom bill. As a result, mainstream media outlets barely paid attention to Yearwood.

When Lois Kolkhorst amended her bathroom bill in Texas to include a passage about protecting women's sports, it didn't seem like a huge deal. The bill was unlikely to pass the Texas House and become law. High-profile businesses had come out against it, and Texas is all about business. But when Kolkhorst went onto the floor of the Texas Senate and referred to Yearwood as a "young man competing in Connecticut," it became apparent that what seemed like a fleeting mention of a kid more than 1,000 miles away was not a red herring, but instead a harbinger of things to come.

Mack Beggs may have lit the match in Texas, but it was Andraya Yearwood whose story would roil the country, engulfing each "concerned" state in a culture war fireball. Yearwood has been pointed to in bill after bill after bill as the reason why restricting access to sports for transgender kids is necessary. The references to her often take race results out of context. I've been on panels where proponents of transgender inclusion have said that transgender athletes in the state have won only "a couple of races," and I've been in rooms where those opposed to transgender inclusion hold up the number of championships won by Yearwood and fellow transgender competitor Terry Miller as an indication of unfettered dominance, without providing full context. Neither approach is correct.

Yearwood and Miller won a lot of races and a lot of championships. They're also different athletes, and they weren't unbeatable, especially later in their high school careers. What happened in Connecticut is complex, but it is the single most consequential example of transgender girls competing and winning at the high school level. It's messy and nuanced, but it necessitates discussion. So here are the facts, and the context. All of it.

• • •

THE ORIGINAL ARTICLE that first introduced Yearwood to the wider public appeared in the *Hartford Courant,* dated April 7, 2017. The story revealed that Yearwood, who was a freshman in high school at the time, hadn't started hormone therapy.[1] She was allowed to compete because the Connecticut Interscholastic Athletic Conference (CIAC) policy did not require medical or legal intervention for transgender athletes to compete in the sport category that matches their gender identity, one of nearly twenty states that had such a policy at that time. There was no requirement for name change, birth certificate amendments, hormones, or surgery. School districts decided where their athletes would compete, and the state reminded them that they could not discriminate based on gender identity as a matter of state law.

"We've always been grounded in an inclusion approach," said former CIAC executive director Karissa Niehoff. Niehoff now leads the National Federation of State High School Associations, an organization akin to the NCAA that organizes high school associations across the United States, as its executive director. "School-based programming should be inclusive to all."

At fourteen, Yearwood hadn't yet begun hormone replacement therapy (HRT). That's not unusual; kids begin to medically transition at all ages. Some kids who realize they're transgender at a young age and have supportive parents are able to begin puberty blockers and never go through the puberty associated with their sex assigned at birth—also known as endogenous puberty. Others begin hormone therapy in their early teens, some transition in their late teens and in adulthood, and some transgender people never medically transition—whether by choice or due to lack of access to gender-affirming health care. It's not a uniform process, which makes the policy-making process difficult.

"Part of the issue is that we are looking for a one-size-fits-all solution for an incredibly complex conversation about inclusion," said Anne Lieberman.

It was the spring of 2017, Yearwood's freshman year in high school, when I first met her. I remember sitting with her in her bedroom at her mom's house. We were on the floor, and she had her legs stretched out on the carpet. She ate chicken fingers with BBQ sauce, promising her mom that she wouldn't spill anything on the floor. The next day was the State Open, where she'd be competing against runners from schools of all sizes, many of which were much larger than her own.

Yearwood wasn't favored to win the next day. After all, she was just a freshman. The week prior, she did win state championships in Class M, winning both the 100m and 200m races. But at the State Open, she ended up placing third and eighth in the 100m and 200m, respectively. I remember standing in the bleachers next to her and her mom before the 200m final. She looked so tired. She didn't want to run; she just wanted the season to be over.

Having grown up playing sports myself, I understood some of that feeling. At the end of every season, I was ready to be done. I was tired of my teammates, tired of practice. But what I saw on Yearwood's face that afternoon was different. There was a weariness resting on her shoulders that I'd never felt.

As a kid growing up in Cromwell, Connecticut, Andraya was pushed into sports by her parents. Her father, Rahsaan, played collegiate football at Macalester, a Division III school in Minnesota. Her mother, Ngozi Nnaji, runs her own personal fitness business. Sports were never going to be an option for their kids—they were a requirement. So Andraya played football and baseball and soccer and ran around the neighborhood like every other kid her age. "Sports was very much a positive thing in my life," she said. "It gave me an outlet to do things that I love."

But sports also complicated how she saw herself. When she was six or seven years old, Yearwood dressed as Cinderella for Halloween. As she stood next to her brothers, the long, bright dress glowed against her darker skin. She looked like a princess, just like the one on the backpack she wore to school every morning. "I don't think I ever really saw myself as a girl until I put on that costume," Yearwood said. That fleeting moment of affirmation, however, didn't spur an epiphany.

The oldest of her parents' four children together—they divorced when Yearwood was twelve, and her father has had two additional kids since remarrying—Yearwood always gravitated toward more feminine things, even telling her parents at one point that she wanted to be a girl. "But I don't think they thought anything of it," Yearwood said.

And because of sports, she pushed down her own feelings about her gender. "Being on the boys' team, I felt like I had to conform to those acts of masculinity, especially when I played soccer or football," Yearwood said. As a kid, Yearwood didn't have the language to express her dysphoric feelings. She liked Cinderella dresses and wore a princess backpack to school and played with dolls and wondered if she was a girl, but boys' sports demanded different things of her. "I don't want to say I was intentionally hiding myself," she said. "I guess I followed sheep or whatever, and did what everybody else was doing."

Sitting on the bleachers on that cloudy afternoon of her freshman year in June 2017, Yearwood once again wanted desperately to do what everyone else was doing: be a typical teenager. No one else ran with the weight she did. No one else endured the whispers floating through the stands. No one else was bullied in right-wing media. That was a burden that belonged to her alone, at least for the time being.

KARISSA NIEHOFF ENTERED the CIAC's Cheshire, Connecticut, office, steeling herself against the oncoming tidal wave she was sure would materialize. It was early 2018, and she was about to host an information session about the CIAC's policy governing transgender participation. There wasn't a large-enough room for the conversation except for the atrium, with its white walls and matted red carpet. School administrators, track coaches, parents, and a handful of students crowded into the room to hear Niehoff's explanation of the CIAC's transgender-inclusive policy. Some wanted to show support, a few were curious, but many just wanted to yell.

Niehoff stood at the front of the room, accompanied by a lawyer, and took the onslaught. In communities around the state, few people were bold enough to say publicly what they thought about the policy, but the pressure was starting to mount. Niehoff was getting more emails and calls from people on both sides of the issue. Some felt the policy was an abomination, while others thought she was doing a good job by standing up for the transgender kids in her state. This meeting was attended by those who leaned more toward the abomination side.

As Niehoff explained the state's inclusion policy, as well as the Connecticut nondiscrimination statute, those in the room hurled criticisms and accusations.

"How dare you do this!"

"You were an athlete. You had a scholarship!"

"Why would you think like this?"

"You're destroying women's sports!"

Niehoff tried to take the temperature down in the room. She reminded everyone that they were discussing kids, not the Olympics. That she, herself, had been a Division I athlete and wasn't threatened by an inclusive policy at the high school level. She'd hoped that by opening the door to conversation, folks would feel like their voices were being heard on the issue. But it was becoming clear that there was a gulf between her organization and some it served, and it only grew larger each time Andraya Yearwood won a race.

"They would not admit that winning and losing were really the crux of the issue," Niehoff said. "It wasn't until somebody started winning that anybody really made a big deal with it. We had a policy in place for years."

To make matters worse, the simmering discontent Niehoff felt in that room was about to reach a boiling rage. Andraya Yearwood wasn't the only transgender girl who wanted to run, and the new girl was even faster.

AT BULKELEY HIGH School—one of three public high schools in Hartford—Terry Miller had made a consequential decision. Inspired in part by Yearwood, Miller decided that she, too, would run in the girls' category in the outdoor track and field season. In her first meet, a head-to-head between Bulkeley and Bloomfield High School, Miller posted a time of 12.21 seconds in the 100m. The second-place athlete ran a 14.07. That's an unbelievable time difference in track. But it was a dual meet—

meaning two local schools going head-to-head—it wasn't in any state-level championship. The next meet, however, was a different story.

Just three days later, Miller lined up on the blocks next to Yearwood for the first time. It was the 100m race at the Greater Bristol Outdoor Track and Field Invitational. The weather that Friday evening was cool. It had rained earlier in the day and the temperature never cracked 60 degrees. As the top seed, Miller settled into her blocks in lane five, the middle lane on the track. Also in that race were Chelsea Mitchell and Selina Soule, two cisgender girls who would later sue the CIAC over the participation of Miller and Yearwood. The four sophomores claimed the top four seeds for finals.

When the gun sounded and the runners took off down the track, Miller left no doubt as to the top competitor in the field. She won the race and clocked a time of 12.22 seconds. Yearwood took second, followed by Mitchell and Soule, respectively. These race results laid the foundation for the "inevitability of defeat" arguments that Mitchell and Soule would come to parrot—the idea that to be trans meant that a runner would win, no matter what. If a transgender girl runner was competing, then a cisgender girl shouldn't even bother to lace up her spikes because the result was predetermined. "Winning and losing has introduced a fogged, clouded-over perspective," Niehoff said. "Because, as you probably know, on Terry's team there was another transgender girl. Nobody talked about her because she wasn't winning."

When Niehoff told me that, it took everything I had not to jump out of my chair. I did not know there was another transgender athlete competing that season, let alone on the Bulkeley team. It just never came up before this conversation, and I'll admit, I was taken aback. I started asking myself all these questions: *Who was this person? Where is she now? How do I find her?*

Aryana Brown was a senior in the spring of 2018. At eighteen years old, she finally felt like she could take control of her life and live the way *she* wanted, instead of how everyone expected her to. Growing up, she didn't know what being transgender meant. She described herself as being flamboyant as a child. "I just always thought I was going to be a gay boy," Brown said. She began experimenting with drag, putting on wigs and her younger sister's clothes. Sometimes she'd make videos. And then she'd have to take it all off. "I would be so sad," Brown said. "It was just so out of place that I had to be a boy again. And it was just like, 'This is not working for me. I can't.'"

It was a discussion with her mom that led her to therapy, which helped her realize that she was a woman. And for her senior year, her first at Bulkeley, she came into the school registered as Aryana. She decided to go out for the track team. "Track was something I was always interested in," Brown said. "But it was never the right time."

She told people who needed to know that she was transgender, but, otherwise, it wasn't something that dominated her senior year. "I don't know if the [athletic director] knew, but I'm pretty sure he did because people talk," Brown said. "But it wasn't a big deal because I wasn't coming in first place and knocking down barriers."

It was Terry Miller, a sophomore that same season, whose winning sucked up all the attention because of her dominance. Brown ran in that same race Miller dominated against Bloomfield. Brown posted a time of 14.80, coming in sixth place. "It's okay when you lose, but the minute you start winning and breaking records, now it's 'She's a boy. It's not fair,'" Brown said.

Brown saw the work Miller put in every day. She watched her in warm-ups and in practice. She got beat by Miller over and over again. "You would have thought track was her job, like full-time job," Brown said. "It wasn't like she just got on the track and because she used to be a boy, she was the best. If that was the case, how come I didn't get out there and break a record? What was going on with me?"

Brown was right; Miller ran her way into the record books in 2018. She dominated the 2018 outdoor track and field season, winning class state championships in the 100m and 200m as well as overall state championships in those same races. Her time of 11.725 in the 100m set a Connecticut Open record. At the New England championships, Miller again swept the 100m and 200m races.

Yearwood finished second in the 100m at her sophomore state open, and seventh in the 200m race. The latter result is almost always forgotten.

THOUGH NOT MUCH national media attention was originally paid to Yearwood and Miller, by the 2019 season that had changed considerably. The change was spurred by Yearwood and Miller's 1–2 finish in the 55m at the State Open Indoor, with their times qualifying both of them for national competition. Coupled with the 1–2 finish at the previous season's State Open Outdoor, the media frenzy officially began. Selina Soule, who finished sixth at the 2018 outdoor meet and missed qualifying for the 55m final by one spot in 2019, took to television to make her case. She appeared on *Fox & Friends* and *The Ingraham Angle,* both Fox News programs, in February 2019.

"I'm very happy for these athletes and fully support them for being true to themselves," Soule said in her appearance on *The Ingraham Angle*.[2] "But in athletics it's a different situation. It's scientifically proven that males are built to be stronger than females. It's unfair to put someone who is biologically male, who has not undergone hormone therapy, against cisgender girls."

This viewpoint was consistent with what Soule and her mother, Bianca Stanescu, had been stating publicly since Miller began competing in the girls' category in 2018. That year, Stanescu circulated a petition trying to ban Miller and Yearwood from competition. Local news outlet WWLP reported that Stanescu's position at the time was to require testosterone suppression and implement a wait time "like they do in the Olympics."[3]

It was true that the CIAC did not require hormone therapy to begin competing in the girls' category, and it was true, as stated above, that in her freshman season, Yearwood had not yet begun hormone therapy. The public divulgence of that piece of information continues to influence how Yearwood is understood. Because she wasn't on hormone therapy at the beginning of her high school career, Yearwood was often talked about as if she never began testosterone suppression. As Soule was talking during the local news segment, the images shown looping under her words were of Yearwood. Miller's hormone status was unknown at the time.

The thing is that Yearwood had absolutely begun HRT by that point in 2019. This is a clear fact because Yearwood competed at the New Balance Nationals meet in the girls' category, which employs a policy that mirrored the NCAA's at that time. Transgender girls and women wishing to compete in the girls' category must have been engaged in testosterone suppression for at least one year. Yearwood placed thirtieth in the 55m at that meet. Miller did not compete and has not publicly disclosed the reason.

This was where the conflict heated up in Connecticut. In the summer of 2019, Selina Soule was a named complainant—the only one of the three complainants on the case—in a Title IX complaint filed with the Department of Education on her behalf by Alliance Defending Freedom (ADF), a conservative legal firm. ADF is categorized as an anti-LGBTQ+ hate group by the Southern Poverty Law Center, a designation it refutes. ADF has argued multiple cases in front of the Supreme Court on anti-LGBTQ+ grounds, including for a baker's right to not bake a cake for a same-sex wedding. They won that case.

Christiana Holcomb, the ADF lawyer representing Soule, announced the complaint filing alongside Soule on *Tucker Carlson Tonight*. The basis of the complaint was that transgender girls are biological males, therefore stripping cisgender girls of athletic opportunities and creating a culture of unfairness. "Unfortunately for complainants and other girls in Connecticut, those dreams and goals—those opportunities for participation, recruitment, and scholarships—are now being directly and negatively impacted by a new policy that is permitting boys who are male in every biological and physiological respect—including unaltered male hormone levels and musculature—to compete in girls' athletic competitions if they claim a female gender identity," the complaint reads. Left out of the argument is anything inconvenient, including Yearwood's seventh-place finish in the 2018 200m. Also omitted from the results table is the 2019 100m State Open race. Ahead of the race, Miller false started and was disqualified. Chelsea Mitchell—a plaintiff in the eventual federal lawsuit—won the

100m championship, clocking a time of 11.67 seconds, which was faster than Miller's State Open record (though it wouldn't be entered into the record books because it was wind assisted). Alanna Smith—another complainant and plaintiff—placed third. Yearwood took fourth. According to the Title IX complaint, it's as if that race never happened.

In the middle of this brewing legal drama, Yearwood was trying to figure out where she was going to attend college. A 2019 documentary, *Changing the Game*, featuring her story during the 2018 outdoor track and field season, premiered at the Tribeca Film Festival, and she would regularly speak about the film at events across the country. On one such trip to Baltimore, she made a special trip to visit Howard University. "Her eyes lit up," her mother, Ngozi Nnaji, said.

"I've always gone to predominantly white schools," Yearwood said. "I wanted something different. I wanted a change." And though Yearwood might have been looking ahead as 2019 turned into 2020, thinking that with high school coming to a close, the drama would soon dissipate—she would soon learn that the past refused to stay put.

STANDING ON THE steps of the Connecticut State Capitol in Hartford on February 12, 2020, Holcomb announced that ADF would be suing the CIAC over its policy governing transgender participation in athletics. She was flanked by the three plaintiffs—Soule, Mitchell, and Smith—along with their families, some of whom held pink signs that read "protect women's sports" in white cursive font. The lawsuit was an escalation of the Title IX complaint, but the argument was the same. In addition to listing all of the ways in which those assigned male at birth have "a powerful physiological advantage over females," the lawsuit enumerated the relief sought by plaintiffs.[4] In other words, Mitchell, Soule, and Smith thought the CIAC policy was inappropriate, so their lawsuit asked for injunctive relief to prevent Miller and Yearwood from racing against Mitchell at the Class S state meet that Friday, on the basis that should Yearwood compete in the 55m and Miller in the 55m and 300m against Mitchell, it would "deprive Chelsea of a victory position that she has earned in the Class S Championship."[5] Mitchell was seeded second in the 55m and first in the 300m. Yearwood was seeded first in the 55m. Miller was seeded third in the 55m and tenth in the 300m.

It's hard to overstate just how inflammatory the language used in the lawsuit is. Throughout the complaint, Miller and Yearwood were referred to as boys and males. Sex was defined by chromosome—girls as XX and boys as XY. "That's a test that most trans people can never meet," American Civil Liberties Union (ACLU) lawyer Chase Strangio said to me. "You can't change your chromosomes."[6]

The ACLU intervened on behalf of Miller and Yearwood in the federal suit, elevating what started as a local debate about a high school policy to a full-blown culture war in the middle of the indoor track post season. Three of these teenagers, Miller, Mitchell, and Yearwood, all had to share a track two days later.

To SAY THE atmosphere was tense at the Floyd Little Athletic Center on Valentine's Day 2020 would not be doing it justice. When I walked into the field house for the Class S indoor track and field state championships, the girls' 4x200 relay, the first event of the evening, was just kicking off. Indoor track was run on a 200m oval, which made everything feel just a bit faster.

Cromwell, Yearwood's school, trailed for much of the race, falling back into fifth place at one point. Then Yearwood was handed the baton. She took off, and in all the races I've seen her run, this was one of her best. She passed every uniform in front of her except for the orange uniform worn by Miller—anchoring Bloomfield, where she'd transferred after her sophomore season—who was almost half a lap ahead. Yearwood was running hard. Though she would always tell me that she didn't care about the haters, that she had nothing to prove, that she was ambivalent about track most days, I watched her try to outrun everything trying to hold her back in that one lap around the track.

The 55m didn't go as planned, at least for Yearwood. Lined up in the blocks, with Miller standing on the back to hold them down, almost guarding her, Yearwood jumped early. She false started—the first time in her career. That meant she was disqualified, which meant no championship, no State Open, and no Nationals.

Without Yearwood on the track, the marquee matchup in the 55m was between Mitchell and Miller. I stood at the end of the track and watched them barrel toward me, matching each other's stride the whole way. When they crossed the finish line, the times flashed on the screen—Miller at 7.20 and Mitchell at 7.18. It was the first time the crowd roared all night.

For all the fireworks in the 55m, though, the 300m was anti-climactic. Miller placed sixteenth, with a time of 46.01. Mitchell earned her second championship of the night, crossing the line in 40.98 seconds. Neither Yearwood nor Miller are running in college. Both Mitchell and Soule received Division I scholarships. Alanna Smith, the best athlete of all of them, signed to compete for the University of Tennessee, a prominent program in the Southeastern Conference and one of the best in the country.

It was an anticlimactic end to a tumultuous three years, but it's hard to overstate just how important this case has become in the discourse about transgender athletes nationwide. The federal lawsuit was heard by the Second Circuit Court of Appeals on September 29, 2022. When it comes to considering the application of Title IX and transgender youth in school sports, this case is the one often discussed. It has dragged on for years. Yearwood, who was fourteen when I first met her in 2017, will graduate from college in May 2024. Though Yearwood and Miller have been held up in state Houses as examples of the threat transgender girls pose to women's sports, neither of them ever stepped foot on a track again after February 2020. At the 2022 Class S outdoor state championships, an athlete broke Miller's class record in the 100m. Sydney Segalla was a senior who was heading to college on a soccer scholarship, but she'd always wanted to run track. She came out of nowhere to break one of Miller's records and went on to win the 200m and 400m championships at the 2022 State Open, besting Smith in the process. Segalla is cisgender. It is worth noting that Yearwood holds no track and field records.

This case has proved to be consequential, but it is also gravely misunderstood. ADF cherry-picks race results to fit its narrative of Miller and Yearwood's unfettered dominance, leaving out anything that casts doubt on that perspective, while progressive groups will often downplay Miller and Yearwood's accomplishments and/or the importance of high school sports to many people. If I've learned anything from following Yearwood's story for more than half a decade, it's that this issue has become incredibly emotional for many people, and emotions often defy logic. We now know that Miller and Yearwood weren't the only transgender girls competing in track and field during their time in high school, but no one cared about Aryana Brown because she wasn't winning. That should tell us something about how transgender girls are treated in this discussion.

The emotions felt by the teenagers in Connecticut and their families shaped this debate in more ways than just the obvious. There was the national attention in the media and state Houses, but the issues brought up in these communities spilled over into unexpected places. And that would have disastrous consequences.

8.

THE BREAKUP IN WOMEN'S SPORTS

PAT GRIFFIN AND her wife, Kathy, pulled into the parking lot of Tavern on the Hill—an understated, casual restaurant in Easthampton, Massachusetts—unsure of what to expect. She was meeting Donna Lopiano and Felice Duffy for dinner to talk about transgender athletes. Griffin had received a call from Lopiano, a fellow women's sports advocate and respected colleague, and been asked to meet for dinner on April 3, 2019. Griffin lived right up the road and always had time to talk about important issues such as this one.

A New England native, Lopiano loved Tavern on the Hill, and she appreciated the excuse to make the drive to Western Massachusetts for some of her favorite food. On this occasion, Lopiano was playing matchmaker. Felice Duffy, a lawyer from Connecticut, had questions about transgender athletes because of the ongoing controversy in the state with Andraya Yearwood and Terry Miller. Lopiano didn't have the answers, but she knew someone who would: Pat Griffin.

Griffin and her wife—who competed against Lopiano in

softball in the 1970s—took a seat at the window-facing table along with Lopiano. They were joined by Duffy shortly after. Duffy was trying to will herself to feel less sick from the severe head cold that plagued her. She almost hadn't come, but she decided the trip up I-91 was worth it to sit at the big kids' table. As a lawyer with a focus on Title IX and gender equity in sports, Duffy knew of Lopiano, and they'd shared conversations, but they'd never met. She'd seen photos of Lopiano but had no idea who Griffin was and was unfamiliar with her despite their shared commitment to women's sports. Duffy had played soccer at the University of Connecticut in the late 1970s after filing a Title IX complaint to compel the school to create one. She was named a first team All-American and selected to the first U.S. Women's National Team, before coaching at Yale for a decade.

Duffy had heard that a cisgender girl in Connecticut was considering a lawsuit challenging the existing CIAC transgender athlete policy that allowed Andraya Yearwood and Terry Miller to compete in the girls' category regardless of whether they'd begun hormone replacement therapy. Duffy didn't know much about the topic, but she was a prominent Title IX lawyer in the state and this felt like a question she should have an answer to, especially as the topic kept coming up as it pertained to Title IX enforcement. Lopiano was similarly unfamiliar with the topic of transgender athletes. Griffin, however, had helped draft the existing NCAA guidelines for transgender inclusion back in 2011.

Griffin explained the existing policy in Connecticut—that transgender athletes may compete in the category that is consistent with their gender identity without requiring legal or medical intervention—and that she agreed with that policy. Duffy explained her opinion that both cisgender and transgender women were covered by Title IX, and also that she "didn't believe a cisgender woman should lose opportunities because of the empirically supported physiological differences that make cis men more superior in some areas." In addition to a law degree, Duffy also has a Ph.D. in education and sports psychology and a masters in exercise physiology. From her perspective, there was merit to having some concern about a policy that doesn't require testosterone suppression for teenagers competing in high school sports, especially a sport like track, which relies heavily on speed, power, and strength. But that didn't mean that transgender girls weren't entitled to protection under the law, or that they should be required to undergo hormone therapy to participate. Duffy was working through her opinion on the issue in real time, grappling with her own cognitive dissonance and lack of familiarity with transgender people at that point. Lopiano was also asking questions. Lots of them. They were all feeling one another out and trying to get on the same page, but for Griffin and Lopiano, it became clear that they were definitively not in agreement on this issue.

As Duffy was talking, trying to work through unfamiliar language, she could feel the tension rising. "I just felt a wave of resistance from Pat," Duffy said. "Her whole body language changed."

Griffin sat uneasily, listening to Lopiano and Duffy struggle with their questions and processing the gulf forming between herself and Lopiano. Griffin had been working on LGBTQ+ equality in sports for decades, and she'd already thought about these topics; she knew where she stood on transgender athletes participating in school sports: they should be allowed with as few restrictions as possible. Lopiano and Duffy were new to this discussion and came to it from a different lens. Cisgender girls were their primary concern, and Connecticut's policy seemed to pose a threat to them. Griffin was being grilled about the fairness of a policy that allowed "biological males" into girls' sports. The language was all wrong to her—borderline offensive in some moments. Griffin knew Lopiano was familiar with her work, had followed her career in the space of LGBTQ+ education and advocacy in sports. But it was also clear that Lopiano didn't quite understand the work that Griffin did or the issues already being discussed when it came to transgender athletes. "If there had been a transgender person at the table, they probably would've left," Griffin said about the experience.

Lopiano had sat down at that dinner just looking to help a friend get answers to some questions, while having an excuse to enjoy one of her favorite meals. But as the conversation continued, Lopiano got further sucked into the issue. And what she learned was difficult for her to swallow. The policy supported by Griffin—a person whom she respected deeply—allowed for athletes assigned male at birth to participate in girls' sports without any sort of medical requirements. Those athletes could win races and championships. It was already happening just across the Massachusetts border. Lopiano thought to herself, "This is a sticky wicket."

Lopiano had worked to gain equality for girls' and women's sports since she was a kid yearning to play baseball. She'd spent her entire professional life fighting for equality. When she left dinner, it seemed to her as if everything for which she'd fought was up for debate.

DONNA LOPIANO HAD been advocating for women's sports for the overwhelming majority of her life. As a kid growing up in

Stamford, Connecticut, in the 1950s, she wanted to play Little League Baseball. "I was a baseball nut," Lopiano said.

She tried out, and she did so well that she was picked first. She was about to go pick out her uniform when an administrator brought out the rule book and read the section that stated girls were ineligible for Little League. "This was, like, twenty years before the court case that gave women Little League," Lopiano said.

Well, it was more like fifteen years, but the point stands. In 1972, the same year as the passage of Title IX, twelve-year-old Maria Pepe was forced off of her Hoboken, New Jersey, Little League team because she was deemed ineligible. With the support of the National Organization for Women (NOW), she sued, and the court ruled in her favor, opening Little League Baseball for girls. Without Maria Pepe's lawsuit, Mo'ne Davis may not have ever pitched a Little League game.

That relief wasn't available for Lopiano; she had to wait until she was sixteen to try out for a corporate-sponsored softball team thirty minutes up the road in Stratford. The Raybestos Brakettes was the preeminent softball club in the United States, and Lopiano scored a tryout because her dad cajoled an old army buddy—and current scout for the Pittsburgh Pirates—into calling in a favor as he fed him Italian food and poured a bottle of Chianti.

But the army buddy—his name was Sal—kept his word. Lopiano rode with him up to Stratford with her glove and ball. He'd never seen her play and had no idea what he'd just signed up for. Luckily for everyone, Lopiano was good.

Sal was standing over by the third base fence, watching Lopiano crush the tryout. The Brakettes' manager, Lee Devin, came over and asked him where he'd found her. "To this day,

I think he found me at the bottom of a [bottle of] Chianti," Lopiano said.

Lopiano played for the Brakettes from 1963 to 1972 and is a member of the organization's hall of fame, as well as a member of the National Softball Hall of Fame. After her athletic career, she entered athletics administration. In 1975, she was hired as the first director of women's athletics at the University of Texas, a position she held for seventeen years. She has since dedicated her entire professional life to advocating for women's sports. She was the CEO of the Women's Sports Foundation from 1992 to 2007 and continues to consult on Title IX matters across the country as well as give expert testimony in relevant lawsuits.

It was through that work that Lopiano met Griffin. Griffin also grew up in the 1950s, but she spent her childhood in Maryland. An excellent athlete, she competed in field hockey and basketball, and she swam at the University of Maryland. She was hired as a swimming and diving coach at the University of Massachusetts Amherst in 1971, a year before Title IX passed. Though she wasn't out to many people prior to her arrival at UMass, Griffin found Western Massachusetts—now commonly known to be a haven for queer women—to be welcoming. After coaching for five years, Griffin transitioned into teaching at the university. It was through conversations with various LGBTQ+ athletes in the 1970s and 1980s that Griffin realized not much had changed since she'd competed. Almost everyone was still in the closet, and students were afraid of possible consequences, such as losing a scholarship, if they came out. Additionally, the women's sports equality movement was nearly silent on the issue. So Griffin began speaking up, and, in 1987, she publicly shared her sexual orientation for the first time.

It was at a conference, and she was sitting on a panel about homophobia in sports during the last session of the event, the spot where a presentation was almost guaranteed to not have any attendees. And yet, the room was full. Griffin looked out into the rows of chairs in the bland conference ballroom and saw friendly faces staring back at her. It gave her the courage to say what she'd been holding back for so much of her life. "It was just amazing," Griffin said. "We were like sheroes afterward."

Subsequently, Griffin focused her advocacy on women's sports and LGBTQ+ inclusion in athletics. She led initiatives for the Women's Sports Foundation and the Gay, Lesbian, and Straight Education Network (GLSEN), among others. She also helped write the 2011 NCAA transgender inclusion guidelines alongside representatives from the National Center for Lesbian Rights (NCLR). "I'm so happy we did that, but at the time, no one was talking about those issues, or cared about them," said NCLR legal director Shannon Minter. "It just wasn't on the radar of the movement yet either. A lot of the foundational work got done a decade ago."

After the initial dinner between Griffin, Duffy, and Lopiano, Griffin and Lopiano continued the conversation they'd started. Griffin brought in former NCLR sports director Helen Carroll, with whom she'd collaborated on these issues for the better part of a decade, to help facilitate and be another transgender-affirming voice. The two of them had worked together on the existing NCAA guidelines governing transgender participation in sports and regularly presented together at conferences. Griffin, seventy-six, and Carroll, seventy-one, were of a similar generation to Lopiano. Their perspectives were different as lesbian women, but they intimately understood where Lopiano was coming from as they all began this conversation. Lopiano brought in Nancy Hogshead-Makar, a three-time Olympic gold medalist turned women's sports advocate. Hogshead-Makar, fifty-nine, had worked with the Women's Sports Foundation in various capacities for three decades, and her legal advocacy for women athletes around the topics of sexual assault and abuse has been transformative. Through Lopiano and Hogshead-Makar, Doriane Coleman was added to the conversation. Coleman was also a former elite athlete, and a law professor at Duke—also where Hogshead-Makar received her law degree—who had written extensively about sex and sports.

This core group met once a month, sometimes twice, beginning in April 2019, to talk about transgender inclusion in sports specifically. "They were very collegial," Carroll said of the conversations. "Not saying we didn't get a little hot-tempered disagreeing with each other, but it was never enough to stop conversations."

Those disagreements centered on high school competition, or rather the discussion about high school students exacerbated fundamental differences within the group. At the center was the question of what to do about a situation like the one in Connecticut. There was tension building nationally due to the successes of Andraya Yearwood and Terry Miller, and that tension existed in this group as well. Yearwood and Miller winning championships brought new scrutiny to the question of whether they should be allowed to participate in the girls' category and under what conditions. That was the question that had started all of this in the first place—a phone call from Duffy to Lopiano is what led to the original dinner in Western Massachusetts, after all. This was a small, albeit powerful group of women, who were all respected by major organizations pushing for equality for girls and women in sports, law, and education. They were on different pages when it came to transgender athletes, but if they could settle their disagreements, that would go a long way toward being able to work on messaging, talking points, and policy and unite the sports feminist movement on the issue. Settled for now were the regulations that Griffin and Carroll had helped draft for the NCAA. At the time, those rules stipulated that transgender women needed to be engaged in hormone therapy for one year to compete in the women's category, and that transgender men could compete in either men's or women's sports, but once they began hormone therapy, they must compete in men's sports. These guidelines were not binding for each member school, but they were the governing policy for every NCAA championship. The Olympic/IOC policy was basically the same, though it added an additional hormone threshold requirement stipulating that a transgender woman's testosterone level may not exceed 10 nmol/L (World Athletics, which governs track and field, has that number at 5 nmol/L).

The goal of these conversations was to identify a uniform policy that the group could advocate for together, and hopefully bring additional stakeholders along with them. But they were already too late; the poison pill had been taken before Griffin and Lopiano had even sat down to dinner.

ON APRIL 2, 2019, Doriane Coleman took her seat in the crowded House Judiciary Committee Hearing room on Capitol Hill. She found herself in a somewhat unfamiliar position: arguing for exclusion in service of feminism. Coleman considered herself to be liberal, but she was at this committee hearing at the invitation of Republicans because she believed the Equality Act as written would undercut sex separation in sports and, as she saw it, the integrity of the female category. Coleman sat near the end of the long table before the members of Congress waiting to hear the day's testimony.

With her black hair pulled tightly back into a bun, and a string of pearls looping across her chest, Coleman passionately defended her position that women's sports were under threat if the Equality Act codified discrimination on the basis of gender identity as a form of sex-based discrimination. Prior to this moment, Coleman wasn't perceived to be a prominent player in this space, but she'd been involved in sports and law for much of her professional life.

Coleman's path to this table began on a track in New York in the 1960s. Short and slight, she'd wanted to be a gymnast, but her family couldn't afford it. Track, however, required nothing but a decent pair of shoes and a willingness to show up. "I was faster than the boys," she said to me over Zoom with a smirk.

She began her collegiate running career at Villanova—where she set the indoor 600m world record as a freshman—one of the first women to receive a sports scholarship from the university, before transferring to Cornell for her sophomore season. By the time she graduated from Cornell in 1982, Coleman had etched her name all over the school's record books in middle-distance races. She then raced on the international level in the 1980s—before there was any kind of anti-doping system in place, such as those that have become commonplace in the decades since.

"I was competing in a period in which other athletes like me, who were not going to take drugs, made very intentional, thoughtful choices about whether to continue to compete or not," Coleman said. "Because you kind of knew that you weren't going to make the podium ever, and so why do it at that level? A lot of people walked off the track who were as good as and better than me. I chose to stay because I had invested so much time that I just wanted to see how fast I could go."

Coleman was on the track in Munich in 1983 when Jarmila Kratochvílová set the world record in the women's 800m at 1:53.28. It's a record that has stood for forty years, with only one person coming within one second of it during that time. It's a controversial record, and undoubtedly a suspicious one when it comes to possible doping. Kratochvílová, however, has maintained throughout her career and retirement that she never took performance-enhancing drugs, and there has yet to be proof to the contrary.

Coleman's experience of unfairness throughout her running career led her to participate in the drafting of documents that ultimately aided in the creation of the World Anti-Doping Agency (WADA). She continued working in the anti-doping space until the mid-nineties. "The result is that I know a lot about androgens," Coleman said. "I know a lot about female bodies on androgens, and that women's sport at the elite level can't achieve the goals I think it has if we don't police androgens." Androgens, like testosterone, for example, are hormones commonly linked to regulating sex, though they provide other essential functions.

It was androgens, or, more specifically, testosterone, that knitted together Coleman's journey to sitting in front of the U.S. House Judiciary Committee. When Caster Semenya won the gold medal in the 800m at the 2009 World Championships in Berlin, Coleman decided that she would reenter the arena. She had received a law degree in 1988 from Georgetown Law and her professional law career centers on sex and the law. "And so everything converges for me," Coleman said.

She testified twice in support of the World Athletics policies that regulate testosterone levels for athletes competing in the women's category, and wrote an academic article that was published in 2017 in *Law and Contemporary Problems*, "Sex in Sport," arguing for the necessity of retaining sex segregation in sports. "Sport is committed to this approach on the view that to ensure females' equal opportunity to compete and the institution's ability to promote female empowerment, it is both necessary and lawful to set aside money, coaching, facilities, and events for them only," she wrote.[1]

This article was the basis for her invitation to this hearing, albeit not from the group she would have preferred. That became clear as they all mingled before walking into the hearing. Everyone was perfectly nice, but Coleman was not a Republican. "I was not in the right locker room," she said. "It didn't feel like that was my team."

As she sat in her chair, it became increasingly clear that she was there for the GOP to score points on television and in the transcript—that the entire hearing was just political theater. The Democrats had the votes, and here was Coleman, steadfastly raining on their parade in cahoots with their political enemies. It was like asking a question that delays an early dismissal on the last day before summer break. The Democrats, in Coleman's estimation, weren't answering any of the questions she wanted to raise. "I didn't know any of that going in," Coleman said. "I could have. If I had taken the time to do more homework I would have realized that, but I didn't. And so that felt odd as well, in part because I do support the Equality Act and to be in the way is hard, was hard then, and it remains hard.

"So here were the options, and they're the options for anyone who stands in my shoes, who is committed to sex equality the way I define sex equality in competitive sport. We either take advantage of opportunities Republicans give us to speak, or our voice is not heard, our positions are not heard, because there is an absolute lockstep, unbreakable wall on the [Democrat] side."

NANCY HOGSHEAD-MAKAR USED to agree with her former colleagues at the Women's Sports Foundation. She was the advocacy director when she published a position paper on behalf of WSF alongside fellow Title IX expert Erin Buzuvis that argued for the full inclusion of intersex athletes in women's sports.[2] "I'm pretty sure it's still up there," she said to me over Zoom from her fuchsia-walled study. "But I felt a little uncomfortable because those of us who have been involved in elite sports know how big the gap is between boys and girls, men and women."

The gap she was referring to in this case was the often cited 10 to 12 percent performance gap between elite male and elite female athletes, which is seen as a direct result of testosterone-driven puberty, which gives those assigned male at birth considerable advantages in terms of speed and strength. It was a gap Hogshead-Makar said she witnessed herself in the years she spent in the pool as an elite athlete growing up in Florida. She became world class at the age of fourteen and by eighteen had qualified for the 1980 Olympics, though she never competed due to the United States' boycott of the games. She did compete in the 1984 Olympics in Los Angeles, where she became the most decorated swimmer at the games, with three gold medals and one silver. She spent hours in the pool and often was the only woman. "In my whole career, I probably only trained with maybe three or four women," Hogshead-Makar said. "I was between ten and fourteen percent slower than my male competitors. I had a phenomenal diet. I had excellent coaching. I had access to weight rooms. I had everything the male athletes had, and I was still much slower than they were, starting in high school."

Coleman agreed. "Those of us who are athletes know that the separation on the basis of sex is necessary to achieve equality in this space." There is an uncomfortable kernel of truth to Hogshead-Makar's and Coleman's positions. That doesn't mean that they're the only thing that matters. In Hogshead-Makar's experience as an elite athlete in the 1980s, getting outswum by boys with less relative talent was essential to the perspective she brought to her work as a lawyer fighting for the equal treatment of women under Title IX. That experience is also something Hogshead-Makar regularly cited as a driving force behind her advocacy of protecting women's sports from transgender women competing with what she saw as an unfair advantage. For those who disagree with the policy positions of Hogshead-Makar and Coleman, the lens through which they view the topic of transgender inclusion in sports and Title IX is different. Instead of approaching it through an elite competitive lens, they look at it through one driven more by participation. "[The debate about transgender athletes] seems to really bring up a lot of emotions and personal experiences for some Olympic athletes who have dealt with other situations," National Women's Law Center General Counsel Neena Chaudhry said.

"Elite athletes are locked into this mentality of zero-sum game, and my victory comes at your expense and your victory comes at my expense," another person said to me. "And I'm not at all surprised that someone who is as steeped in that mentality as I know [Hogshead-Makar] still is would want to create policies, even whether she means to or not, with an elite sport focus in mind."

• • •

No ONE WAS quite sure how or why everything fell apart. Some remembered a conference call that didn't go well; others thought it was a few email exchanges that went awry. Others contended that no one would meet with them. In every conversation I had with members of the community of advocates talking about transgender inclusion in sports, I got a different take on the moment at which it all officially went to hell. This intracommunity fracture was a painful experience for everyone I spoke with about this. "Heartbreaking" was the most common response when I asked about the breakdown in these conversations.

That heartbreak was something I shared. One of the beautiful things about writing this book has been spending hours in conversation with folks who have varying perspectives on these issues; it's also been one of the hardest parts of it. There is no doubt in my mind that many of the sporting experiences of my youth wouldn't have happened without the advocacy of Lopiano and Hogshead-Makar. They have been incredibly influential in the enforcement of Title IX in the United States. Martina Navratilova, who would later join the organization cofounded by Lopiano, Hogshead-Makar, and Coleman, was one of the first queer athletes about whom I learned. Coleman is someone with whom I connect deeply on an emotional and intellectual level. And yet, there have been moments in working on this book when I am reminded of just how big our otherwise small differences are. I wonder as they talk about transgender women participating in sports if they see me, a nonbinary person, for who I am, or if that's even a valid expression in their eyes.

Part of reporting on these topics, I believe, is having your assumptions challenged. Nowhere was I more challenged than sitting in this space with the voices of Lopiano, Hogshead-Makar,

Coleman, Mosier, Lieberman, Buzuvis, Strangio, and others wrestling one another in my head. I could hear it coming out of my mouth during interviews, reflecting my internal struggle as I processed what everyone was going through. These are hard conversations that weigh on people because the stakes are high. They become further complicated when the allies you thought you had turn out to be in stark disagreement with you on an issue you think is important. That disappointment and heartbreak was felt on both sides of the canyon that emerged.

While the original group of five—Griffin, Helen Carroll from NCLR, Lopiano, Hogshead-Makar, and Coleman—tried to work through their differences, a broader coalition of advocates and organizations was invited into the conversation.

The group of people engaged in that process was disparate, with policy goals ranging from sports and LGBTQ+ identity, specifically, to women's sports advocacy to civil rights advocacy to LGBTQ+ rights, all trying to align on a policy and messaging about transgender athletes. In addition to the original five, there was now Chase Strangio at the ACLU, elite transgender athlete and pioneering advocate Chris Mosier, Anne Lieberman and Hudson Taylor from Athlete Ally, Shannon Minter from NCLR, Jennifer Fry from GLAD, and Neena Chaudhry from the National Women's Law Center (NWLC), among others. This group, while not household names, was a collection of serious advocates who carried influence in their respective areas. But outside of Athlete Ally and Mosier, there were few folks who were familiar with Coleman, Hogshead-Makar, and Lopiano. Chaudhry, whose work for NWLC focused on education, had crossed paths with almost everyone, including a working relationship with Lopiano that spanned multiple decades.

This group of people had not worked together before. Some

individuals knew other individuals, including some with long-standing working and personal relationships, but other relationships were brand new. There was no collective trust; they barely knew one another.

Coleman's Equality Act testimony had the unfortunate impact of poisoning the ability for the broader group to have any productive conversation. Even if some trust could have been built through an in-person convening, those hopes were all but dashed by the publication of an op-ed by Coleman, Sanya Richards-Ross, and Martina Navratilova in *The Washington Post* under the headline "Pass the Equality Act, but Don't Abandon Title IX" on April 29, 2019. The article was a distillation of Coleman's testimony at the Equality Act hearing a few weeks prior, arguing that the Equality Act would "redefine 'sex' to include 'gender identity'" and that sports was in need of an exception because "sex segregation is the only way to achieve equality for girls and women in competitive athletics."[3]

This article was a betrayal for some. While conference calls and cordial emails could paper over some differences, this op-ed was an inflection point that many simply couldn't see past. It put in print all the ways in which they disagreed, the differences in their respective views and values. That was only further exacerbated when the Court of Arbitration for Sport (CAS) ruled against Caster Semenya the very next day. In an email written to the group, Athlete Ally executive director Hudson Taylor wrote the following:

Yesterday, Doriane and others published an opinion piece in *The Washington Post* about Title IX. I'm not sure why we are all in conversation together privately if Doriane and others will publish whatever they want publicly. I can't underscore enough how dangerous it is and how the far right—the very people we fight against every day—have and will continue to use these arguments about sport to perpetrate further violence against trans people and LGBTQ people as a whole.

These "good faith" conversations don't feel like they are really in good faith when what is being said and done publicly is counter to the purpose of our private dialogue.

Put succinctly, whatever they were trying to accomplish together was going nowhere. It was over. Things didn't immediately dissolve; it was more of a slow decay. Coleman responded and offered to remove herself from the group. She was rebuffed by Lopiano. "Sorry to interject, but no one gets to quit," Lopiano wrote. "There are huge stakes here for all women."

And that was the rub. It was unclear to the advocates in the room if "all women" included transgender women. "I think, fundamentally, they don't see transgender women as women," Griffin said. "I think they see them as men." The "they" referred to was Lopiano, Coleman, and Hogshead-Makar.

As this group went back and forth on an email chain, trying to figure out how they could all meet in person and have some kind of summit, it became clear behind the scenes that such an idea was untenable. There was just no way all of these folks were going to get into a room together, especially not when the people who were transgender felt completely invalidated. "There were several people, mostly the trans folks, who were like, 'I'm not going to put myself in a room with people who fundamentally deny my rights and existence,'" Lieberman said. "We all understood the importance of trying to have conversations, but also it is challenging and assaulting to have to defend your fundamental right to dignity and to play sports."

To make matters more complicated, the conservative law firm ADF filed its Title IX complaint in the summer of 2019. It was a clear warning shot of what was to come. This wasn't some small-time law firm stirring up trouble; it was ADF. Suddenly, the time for theoretical discussions about best practice policies had passed. The unbreakable wall Coleman had observed added a moat, one that continued to widen and deepen.

On February 2, 2021, Lopiano, Coleman, and Hogshead-Makar launched the Women's Sports Policy Working Group, alongside two-time Olympic gold medalist and WSF cofounder Donna de Varona, Martina Navratilova, and former Olympic coach Tracy Sundlun, officially taking what was once a private dispute public. It had been a year since the conversations between advocate groups ground to a halt. There never was a summit; there were no more conference calls or email chains. Even the original group of Lopiano, Coleman, Hogshead-Makar, Griffin, and Carroll didn't talk anymore. "Pat and I knew nothing about the women's working group until we read it in the news," Carroll said.

Throughout the COVID-19 pandemic, the Working Group advanced toward launch. On a Zoom press call that featured each of its founding members, the group calmly delivered prepared remarks to describe their collective position. The Working Group argued for splitting up transgender athletes into multiple categories. Transgender boys and men should be able to compete in the men's category without restriction before hormone therapy, and must do so when beginning hormone therapy. Transgender girls and women were a bit more complicated. For transgender girls who began puberty blockers and never went through endogenous puberty, they should be allowed to compete in the women's category without restriction. If a transgender woman had gone through endogenous puberty, then she needed to "mitigate that sex-linked advantage," Coleman said.

In plain English, a transgender woman who had gone through (or begun) puberty would need to be on hormone therapy for a year—or whatever the length of time is determined to be appropriate for her sport—before competing in the women's category. And if an athlete didn't wish to begin hormone therapy or didn't have access to hormones, then she could run with the girls, but her scores shouldn't count. If she played a team sport, then instead of competing on her high school's girls' basketball team, she could join the district or county or regional transgender girls' basketball team. And these rules would extend into K–12 sports. "It's analogous to what we do in adaptive sports," Lopiano said. "For instance, if you wanted a wheelchair basketball team. To have a school district team as opposed to an institution team."

The Working Group stated their goal was to find middle ground between the perceived extremes. On one side was ADF, advocating for permanent bans on transgender girls competing in scholastic girls' sports. On the other was the coalition of the ACLU, the National Women's Law Center, WSF, Athlete Ally, and the Human Rights Campaign (HRC), among others—basically the whole broader progressive movement—arguing for what the Working Group said was a gender identity–based policy that would allow for transgender girls and women to compete at all levels of sport, including elite levels, without medical intervention. In other words, the policy that allowed Andraya Yearwood and Terry Miller to run in Connecticut would be applied at the collegiate level and beyond. "When it comes to sports, we want to preserve sex segregation based on science and biology, not based on identity," Hogshead-Makar said. "They want to dictate the terms of the conversation. They want to erase biology. They want to say that you're a transphobe if you want to talk about the science of sex."

It is worth noting that those arguing for transgender inclusion in sports are not arguing for an identity-based policy at elite collegiate and Olympic levels. The policy landscape is shifting but, as of this writing, it was not a mainstream position to be advocating for the complete removal of restrictions at all levels of athletics. The reality was that when distilled to policy recommendations, the stated positions of the Working Group and the progressive movement at that time were not all that dissimilar. Most everyone was in agreement on about 90 percent of the discussion—that restrictions for children shouldn't happen, and reasonable restrictions like testosterone suppression for elite athletics made sense. But the gap that once appeared to be small might as well have been an ocean by February 2021. And it was fueled by complete and utter distrust, disappointment, and bitterness. The announcement of the Working Group brought all of that baggage into the public square. Former WSF presidents and board members took a position directly at odds with the organization. Lawyers who had once sat on the same side, arguing for Title IX protections for women athletes, now stood on opposing sides. "There was a hope that we could try to figure something out without having this public fight," Chaudhry said. "But that ship has sailed."

It all happened in the middle of what would be a catastrophic legislative session for transgender Americans, especially transgender youth. It was deeply personal, and there was no room for error or negotiation. "There are threats to women's sports that have nothing to do with trans people," Lieberman said. "I just don't understand why this is their cause right now in this current political moment."

The hardening sides were compounded by the nature of the political moment Lieberman alluded to. Even though nearly all the bills targeting transgender youth in sports flew in the face of the Working Group's espoused policy recommendations, the group had rarely come out and vigorously opposed them. They didn't join up with ADF, but they haven't forcefully denounced the bills proposed by the organization either, even as Coleman's work, for example, was cited in many of the bills, including Idaho's HB 500. Hogshead-Makar defended the group's work. "Not everything we do is public," Hogshead-Makar said. "I've said over and over that people are using these state bills in order to shame transgender people. They are using them specifically as part of the culture war. It has nothing to do with women's sports."

Hogshead-Makar did testify in South Carolina. Coleman placed op-eds in local papers, criticizing lawmakers for misrepresenting her work. She wrote letters to legislators, urging them to not vote for these bills and not use her writing as a means to support them. But for some organizers, they didn't go nearly far enough.

"I can't stress enough how utterly politically naïve they are," one person working in the movement told me. "They're not taking the initiative in doing anything. They do it when asked. It's just like they've set off this political bomb, and then they're just like, 'Oh, we don't want to be political. We just want to have a science-based policy.' It's just very naïve."

The consequence of not successfully coming to a settlement of sorts behind the scenes was not limited to the personal disappointment and devastation of either side of the schism. These were powerful people doing hard advocacy work behind the scenes, and that power bloc was fractured. In the coming years, Hogshead-Makar emerged as one of the loudest critics of Pennsylvania swimmer Lia Thomas, her voice undoubtedly influencing the development of policies within aquatics that ultimately restricted transgender women's ability to participate in the women's category. Coleman also helped shape that policy, which will be explored more later. The distrust that festered between these groups of people who, at one point, publicly shared a lot of the same values became clearer over time.

The situation in early 2021 was bleak for advocates of transgender inclusion. There was dissent and disagreement among those who wielded tremendous power in policy circles. It wasn't just among those who advocate in women's spaces; the entire LGBTQ+ equality movement was unprepared for the avalanche that awaited them.

THE QUEST TO SAVE WOMEN'S SPORTS

LATE ON A Sunday evening in the winter of 2018, Idaho State Representative Barbara Ehardt walked along a path down by the Snake River not far from her home in Idaho Falls. She breathed in the fresh Idaho air as she considered the thoughts weighing heavily on her mind. Ehardt had seen the news of Andraya Yearwood's and Terry Miller's track success all year. "They came from the boys' side and absolutely started to dominate and annihilate the women," Ehardt said. "This was incredibly frustrating."

This felt personal to Ehardt. She grew up around sports. Born in 1964, she spent most of her life in Idaho Falls. She loved to play and much preferred the boys' toys to the ones she typically ended up with—think the Johnny West GI Joe set over the tea party set. "We had pictures of me crying because Santa Claus didn't quite understand how to shop for me," Ehardt said.

When presented with questions about what she wanted to do when she grew up, Ehardt didn't see many options. Her mom was a beautician, and she knew that career certainly wasn't her calling. She'd seen airline stewardesses, but that career didn't fit her either. Neither did being a secretary. What she wanted to do was play sports. "I was told that's not what girls do," Ehardt said.

She had dreams of playing basketball. Every recess, she'd be out on the blacktop playing with the boys. And while she was never picked last, it was always made clear to her that her future in sports was murky. In fourth grade, a classmate showed her photos of older girls playing three-on-three half-court basketball. Girls and women weren't allowed to run up and down the court in those days, so they played six-on-six, three players from each team on each half of the floor. Title IX's passage changed that. Ehardt was eight when it passed, and by the time she reached junior high school, she was playing five-on-five basketball just like the boys. After graduating, she got into coaching, spending fifteen years as a Division I coach in the 1990s and early 2000s before returning to Idaho Falls.

She had been appointed to a seat in the Idaho House early in 2018 and had yet to make an impact. She was juggling the election—which she had just won—for pretty much the entirety of her term. But this issue in Connecticut remained stuck at the front of her mind. Ehardt started posting about it on Facebook in the spring. She shared links with her followers highlighting the story she saw in Connecticut and the threat she believed Miller and Yearwood posed. Her followers responded with vigor. Many of them agreed with her. And they seemed to care just like she did.

Ehardt knew what she wanted to do. She decided to write a bill—her first—and she even knew what to call it. The Fairness in Women's Sports Act.

• • •

THE TEA LEAVES began to point to transgender youth competing in sports as the next culture war battleground all the way back in 2015. South Dakota State Representative Roger Hunt commented to local papers that he was considering filing legislation to void the South Dakota High School Activities Association (SDHSAA) policy adopted a year prior. That policy created a pathway to participation for transgender athletes in a manner consistent with their gender identity.[1] Hunt's proposal would establish birth certificate checks, and possible "visual inspections," as the means of determining gender for athletes rather than the stated identities of the students themselves. "This is South Dakota," Hunt said to the *Rapid City Journal*.[2] "We haven't adopted the East Coast culture. We haven't adopted the West Coast culture. We maintain our own culture."

The eventual 2016 bill sponsored by Hunt did not include the visual inspections provision but did seek to get rid of the SDHSAA policy. Though the bill failed to pass, it was a clear warning shot. The problem for the LGBTQ+ equality movement was that in 2016, legislative attacks against the LGBTQ+ community were lobbed from multiple angles. North Carolina's so-called bathroom bill—HB 2—passed that March to an avalanche of public criticism. There was also concern about Religious Freedom Restoration Act bills—legislation that proponents of LGBTQ+ equality saw as granting broad exemptions for adhering to anti-discrimination law in public accommodations that mirrored Indiana's 2015 law, seen by LGBTQ+ inclusion advocates as a law that created loopholes for discrimination. So a little dustup in South Dakota about an issue that didn't seem to be of national importance drew little attention. "You have to remember how much this was about bathrooms and locker rooms," said former GLSEN executive director Eliza Byard.

When Ehardt decided that she wanted to write a bill to confront what she saw as a pressing issue in women's sports, the conservative organizations she reached out to, including Alliance Defending Freedom, had no model legislation at the time. "I'm calling ten different pro-family groups," Ehardt said. "No one has anything. And these [groups] are throughout the country."

All through the fall of 2018 and into 2019, Ehardt tried to figure out a way to write her legislation and get a vote on it. The organizations she'd been in touch with told Ehardt that such legislation would be tricky because "you'd be entering into a private business, which would be the Idaho High School Activities Association, and the state legislature probably can't interject themselves into that," Ehardt said. In most states, including Idaho, the state high school association is not a state agency; it's a private membership organization that sets its own rules. Those rules do affect public schools, and the association is also subject to state law.

Matt Sharp at ADF found a loophole. He found an instance in 2012 where the Idaho legislature had previously enacted legislation affecting the state's high school association. It was a concussion law.[3] But ADF didn't have any legislation, so Ehardt continued working on her own. After coming up with draft legislation with help from one of the other organizations she'd consulted, she sent it over to Sharp at ADF.

ADF also started working on their own legislation, and Sharp offered the organization's take on the issue to Ehardt. She decided to use the draft legislation. Unlike other proposals and policies, this bill would have nothing to do with birth certificates. In the intervening years between the first South Dakota bill and the drafting of Ehardt's bill, a few more legislative proposals had been kicked around state Houses, but none stuck. South Dakota tried to pass HB 1225 in 2019, which would have codified the use of birth certificates when determining the appropriate gender-based sports category for high school students. A handful of states had already filed bills by the time Ehardt introduced hers, but they all differed from hers in structure and language. Alabama's HB 20 repeatedly referred to "biological gender";[4] Iowa's HF 2202 focused on "sex assigned at birth";[5] Kentucky's SB 114 focused on "biological sex" and would have placed restrictions around high school and collegiate athletics in the state.[6]

Ehardt's bill, HB 500, was unveiled by Ehardt on February 13, 2020,[7] the day after ADF announced its federal lawsuit in Connecticut to challenge the policy allowing Andraya Yearwood and Terry Miller to run girls' track. It cannot be overstated how momentous it was that Ehardt went to ADF for guidance and that the organization took up this issue. The entrance of ADF into this conversation escalated the issue from a conversation happening mostly on the fringes to the mainstream of conservatism. Ehardt was just one legislator in one state, but with ADF on board, and now with legislation in hand, suddenly more states could be in play to take up the mantle. The moment marked a new turn in the movement to restrict transgender athletes from participating in sports.

Idaho governor Brad Little signed HB 500 into law on March 30, 2020, saying that he thought "the issue [was] the girl's right to participate without having to be concerned about who they're competing with."[8]

"It was the first of its kind," Ehardt said. "I wanted it to be based on chromosomes, because I don't care how many hormones, or whatever you take, your chromosomes never change. You are what you are. Our mind's eye will paint a picture when we're talking about something based on the descriptive words we use. I want it to be very clear that when we talk about biological boys and men who identify as women, we are talking about biological male traits that never go away." This interpretation and use of the phrase "biological male," which is often parroted by those who, like Ehardt, supported HB 500 and legislation that followed it, is why many transgender inclusion advocates chafe at the usage. Ehardt used that phrase to conjure an image of a cisgender boy, someone who is assigned male at birth and identifies that way, running down the track alongside cisgender girls to win a championship. That's not who transgender girls are, either from an identity perspective or physiologically. But it's successful emotionally, because who is in favor of boys playing girls' sports? It is, however, a disingenuous argument, especially considering the scope of the legislation.

Ehardt wrote this legislation in response to Yearwood and Miller winning championships at the high school level, but HB 500 was written to establish sex testing for school sports beginning in elementary school. It even affected collegiate intramural competition. At Boise State, intramural competition is open to not just students, but also faculty, staff, spouses, and alumni of the university. There is a physiological discussion to be had about how puberty affects competition in high school, competitive college, and Olympic-level sport, but HB 500 went much further than that, attempting to prohibit transgender girls from playing fifth grade soccer and transgender women from playing on an intramural volleyball team while in college.

The other key component to HB 500 was codifying the ability to challenge a student's sex and putting in place a process for that student to establish that they were assigned female at birth. If a student's sex is disputed, then they can prove that they are eligible for girls' sports by having a physician provide proof of their chromosomes, endogenous testosterone levels, or internal reproductive organs. It's worth noting that an athlete who is completely insensitive to androgen but has XY chromosomes would also be affected by the law.

In August 2020, a federal judge blocked HB 500 from going into effect. Judge David Nye, who wrote the order in the case that granted the preliminary injunction, did so because "the Court finds Plaintiffs are likely to succeed in establishing the Act is unconstitutional as currently written . . ."[9]

Following the introduction of HB 500 and its eventual passage, the number of similar bills multiplied through the 2020 legislative session. And even though it was blocked in federal court, never going into effect, the true impact of HB 500 would be felt in 2021.

IN THE EARLY months of 2021, Anne Lieberman's phone kept buzzing. Every day there were more emails, more texts, more calls, because more bills were being filed across the country. Bills that looked like Idaho's HB 500. The wave was intense, and it didn't appear to be abating. Quite the opposite. "It felt like a new state was dropping an athlete ban every single day, or a medical care ban, or any other piece of really horrific anti-LGBTQ+ legislation," Lieberman said.

Lieberman joined the staff of Athlete Ally in January 2018. For most of her time on staff there, they've seen the landscape for LGBTQ+ youth, specifically transgender youth, worsen. The past few years had been a bit like playing Whac-A-Mole. Bathroom bills. Religious freedom bills. Locker room bills. And now, after a wave of fear stoked by anti-LGBTQ+ activists in response to a handful of high-profile stories like those of Yearwood, Miller, and Beggs, bills affecting sports and health care.

Lieberman grew up playing team sports to find community, and to also fit in a bit better, despite the fact that they weren't very good at playing team sports. At all. As a self-described chubby queer kid, they were relentlessly bullied by older students, but they found a sport community in Muay Thai as an adult that welcomed them. "I wanted to make sure that the environment I was creating as I was coaching was one where everybody felt included, no matter sexual orientation, gender identity, race, ability level, body type," Lieberman said.

That commitment to inclusion drove Lieberman's work as an advocate. It was why the barrage of calls and emails from states facing anti-transgender legislation each felt like Lieberman had gotten their ass kicked in a Muay Thai fight. If this legislative session was a combat sport, then transgender inclusion advocates were getting bloodied. Mostly because of Idaho's HB 500.

In 2021, thirty-six states filed legislation with the explicit purpose of restricting transgender athletes' ability to participate in sports. Supporters of these bills argue that the legislation does not ban transgender athletes from participating, it just requires them to do so in the category that matches their sex assigned at birth. Of the thirty-six states that filed legislation, seven states joined Idaho to pass laws, and South Dakota Governor Kristi Noem signed two executive orders seeking to impose similar restrictions. All of the laws that have been enacted employ similar language and structure to HB 500, which was not the case for the legislation filed in previous years.

"HB 500's influence on this legislative session was tremendous," Lieberman said. "You saw copycat legislation around the country in 2020, and then it just exploded in 2021. Even with an injunction, these legislators are still passing these laws."

Alabama, Arkansas, Florida, Mississippi, Montana, Tennessee, and West Virginia were the states that passed legislation mirroring Idaho's HB 500. All of these laws regulate sex segregation in sports from elementary schools to intramural collegiate competition, specifically prohibiting transgender girls from competing on the teams aligned with their gender identities. That means transgender girls are barred from competing in girls' and women's sports from fifth-grade girls' soccer to intramural women's flag football at Ole Miss. Alabama went one step further by also restricting who could play boys' and men's sports. In Alabama's law, young people assigned female at birth were prohibited from playing boys' and men's sports unless there was no equivalent girls' team. So, a transgender boy would likely be able to play football, but not a commonly sex-separated sport like soccer or track and field. Tennessee similarly restricted the participation of transgender boys. It is worth noting that the effect of laws like those in Alabama and Tennessee is to place boys and men onto girls' and women's teams. We've already seen that play out in Texas with Mack Beggs.

The legislative proposals governing transgender athletes often accompanied other proposals to restrict transgender youth. Thirty bills were filed in twenty states that sought to criminalize transgender young people receiving health care related to their medical transition. For example, treatment commonly referred to as puberty blockers would have been criminalized. Puberty blockers delay the onset of endogenous puberty and are reversible. Such legislation also would have criminalized the use of cross-hormone therapy for young people under eighteen. Driving the hysteria of this legislation is the idea of genital surgery happening on children, something that does not happen and is outside the standards of care. There are some older teens who may have surgery on their chests, but the approach to care for transgender youth is individualized. It is also inaccessible for many. Some families travel for hours to go to a children's hospital that provides gender-affirming care for transgender youth. These hospitals are now coming under intense scrutiny, with physicians and clinics being harassed and threatened with funding cuts.

Gender-affirming health care for transgender youth is endorsed by both the American Medical Association (AMA) and the American Academy of Pediatrics (AAP). The AMA wrote to the National Governors Association in 2021 to vehemently oppose proposed legislation popping up across the country. "We believe it is inappropriate and harmful for any state to legislatively dictate that certain transition-related services are never appropriate and limit the range of options physicians and families may consider when making decisions for pediatric patients," James Madara wrote on behalf of the organization.[10]

After signing a bill into law that restricted transgender athletes' ability to participate in sports, Arkansas Governor Asa Hutchinson vetoed a bill that would have restricted health care for transgender youth, saying that such a measure "puts a very vulnerable population in a more difficult position. It sends the wrong signal to them."[11] The Arkansas legislature overrode his veto, passing the "Save Adolescents from Experimentation Act" into law, though it was blocked in federal court in July 2021. It was the only one of the health-care bans to become law in 2021, but the fact that it passed alarmed LGBTQ+ equality activists. More states have joined Arkansas in the years since the state passed its ban on gender-affirming care for minors.

"Fundamentally, it's about erasing trans people from public life and keeping trans people from existing, without realizing or understanding that we have existed for generations and will continue to exist," Lieberman said.

The 2021 legislative session was an existential crisis. Many advocates described the onslaught as the worst in the nation's history when it comes to LGBTQ+ rights. For much of the American public, the issue of transgender kids playing sports may have felt like it came out of nowhere, but instead, it was like passing a baton in a relay. A series of small steps and then an explosion. So why weren't LGBTQ+ advocates more prepared?

No PERSON I talked to who works on LGBTQ+ advocacy thought the LGBTQ+ political organizations did a good job preparing for these attacks on transgender young people, even though there were multiple signs pointing to the emergence of a new wedge issue.

"I don't think that we're doing the best job," said Mosier. "I think that we are behind on the attacks. We worked ourselves in a position where we're defending ourselves as opposed to pro-actively making moves."

Some of the defensive position was understandable. Following Trump's inauguration, the secretary of education and attorney general—Betsy DeVos and Jeff Sessions, respectively—rescinded the formal guidance issued by the Obama administration that required inclusion of transgender students in all facets of school life, including bathrooms, locker rooms, and athletics. The action had immediate consequences. "The day after the rescission, they took [bathroom access] away," Byard said. "We had chapters calling us from Missouri, saying, 'Oh my god, [a student] had access to the right bathroom yesterday, and now they're telling him that they can't use it anymore.'"

The rescission of the transgender-inclusive guidance was just the first step from DeVos in the Department of Education (ED) and the Trump administration more broadly. Transgender people were soon banned from the military. Multiple judges with records of judgments against LGBTQ+ people were nominated and confirmed. There was early reporting that the Department of Health and Human Services would roll back inclusion of health care for transgender people offered by the Affordable Care Act—something that eventually happened in 2020.

By 2020, it had also become clear that the Departments of Justice and Education were taking increasingly aggressive steps in opposition to transgender inclusion in schools, particularly athletics. The Department of Justice filed a statement of interest in the ADF's lawsuit against the CIAC in Connecticut, *in favor of ADF's position*.[12] The statement of interest gave context to the ensuing moves from DeVos and the Department of Education, when the department also sided with the ADF in its Title IX complaint that had been filed in the summer of 2019, writing in a May 2020 Letter of Impending Enforcement that the CIAC "by permitting the participation of certain male student-athletes in girls' interscholastic track in the state of Connecticut, pursuant to the Revised Transgender Participation Policy, denied female student-athletes athletic benefits and opportunities . . ."[13] The "male student-athletes" in question were actually transgender girls, specifically Yearwood and Miller.

In a standoff in September 2020, DeVos and the Office for Civil Rights threatened to withhold grants totaling tens of millions of dollars from multiple Connecticut school districts unless those schools left the CIAC.[14] The specific issue was the CIAC's policy allowing transgender athletes to participate in a manner consistent with their gender identity. The funding had nothing to do with athletics; it was for desegregation programs. "It's effectively extortion," New Haven's mayor, Justin Elicker, said to *The New York Times.* "The federal government is trying to force us to take a side against transgender individuals." The grant money was eventually released without the schools in question leaving the CIAC.[15]

But the department did have success in forcing another institution to change its policy. In October 2020, Franklin Pierce University (FPU) in New Hampshire announced that it would change its policy governing competition eligibility for transgender athletes, following a letter from OCR stating that FPU's transgender inclusion policy violated Title IX.[16] After CeCé Telfer, a transgender woman competing for FPU, won an NCAA Division II championship in the 400m hurdles, Concerned Women for America filed a Title IX complaint against FPU with the Department of Education. Because the NCAA policy applies only to championships, many individual schools also put policies on the books, often mirroring the NCAA's approach. The FPU policy that allowed Telfer to compete closely mirrored the NCAA's guidelines, which requires transgender women to be on hormone therapy for at least twelve months prior to competing in the women's category. OCR determined that policy to be insufficient, writing that the department "has concerns that the Policy denies female student-athletes equal athletic benefits and opportunities by permitting transgender athletes to participate in women's intercollegiate athletic teams."[17]

The letter went on to say that this particular finding shouldn't be seen as OCR policy, but FPU heard the message loud and clear. The letter from OCR was dated October 16, 2020, and two days later, local press reported the change in FPU policy.[18]

All of this was happening weeks before an election that was considered to be a bellwether for LGBTQ+ people and organizations and amid the COVID-19 pandemic. Informal meetings and check-ins ground to a halt in early 2020. "We all went into lockdown," Byard said. "We couldn't meet with each other except over Zoom. There was no sort of go-down-and-do-a-trip-to-DC-and-go-say-hi-to-everybody because nobody was moving around, at all, and nobody was playing any sports and nobody was in school."

The movement for LGBTQ+ equality is comprised of a collection of organizations that do various slices of work, some slices bigger than others. And the organizations do that work with different levels of funding that they're often in competition with one another to receive. "Sometimes the fragmentation and competition of our movement means that we have serious tactical and strategic unforced errors that come back to haunt us," one advocate told me. "In the absence of a coordinated strategy, we have vulnerabilities collectively that are created individually. By one organization or another."

In the case of the anti-transgender sports bills, fragmentation took multiple forms. There were varying model policies floating around from different organizations. There was also the reality that different approaches to the specific questions posed by the sports bills hampered a unified and coordinated response. There were some folks who saw merit in having a conversation like the one proposed from the triumvirate of Donna Lopiano, Doriane Coleman, and Nancy Hogshead-Makar, who made up the eventual Women's Sports Policy Working Group. There were some folks who thought a carve-out for elite sports participation made sense, or the convening of some kind of commission. But some folks rejected those ideas entirely. Even as the missions of multiple organizations overlapped, the priorities differed at times. And communication was not always the best. "One of the things about a movement is that nobody's in charge, right?" one person said.

There was also the reality that, in addition to the disagreements about an approach to fighting the bills, there was also a disparity of sports knowledge or even the acknowledgment of the growing threat of anti-transgender sports bills at all. "There are a handful of us who have been talking about the sports angle for a really long time and were not taken seriously," Lieberman said. "That was really frustrating. On some level, we couldn't have prepared for the total onslaught, but there could have been some more prep around the sports conversation."

The structure of sports can be complicated to understand for those who are not enmeshed in it. As someone who lives and breathes sports, I often forget that how these organizations function may not be easily understood by all. It can be difficult to parse which organization governs which level of sport, and which policy applies to which organization, and so on and so forth. The experiences of LGBTQ+ people in sports have not always been positive, and some of the relationships to sports within the community are gendered. "I would go to my board and say, 'I want to do something on sports,'" Byard said. "And all the gay men would laugh. They were like, 'Of course you do. You're a lesbian. And all of us hated gym class.'"

Plus, Ehardt, ADF, and the Trump administration got to the issue first. Before Ehardt even filed her bill, Selina Soule and the other athletes who filed the Title IX complaint in Connecticut and the eventual lawsuit were on Fox News talking about how they lost opportunities to Andraya Yearwood and Terry Miller. This put LGBTQ+ organizations on their heels from the jump. "People have made their opinions based on the messaging they've seen first, which was messaging from people who think that we don't belong in sports," Mosier said. It is worth noting, however, that there was an eight-month gap between ADF filing the Title IX complaint in June 2019 and when ADF unveiled the federal lawsuit and Ehardt filed HB 500 in Idaho in February 2020.

The fractious nature of LGBTQ+ movement politics and lack of sports knowledge aside, there was also the simple fact that the real decision makers—the cisgender gay white men with the checkbooks—weren't writing checks to talk about transgender kids playing sports. In fact, many funders would rather that thorny issue not get brought up at all.

By 2022, no federal law that barred discrimination against the LGBTQ+ community had ever been enacted into law, though queer activists had been trying to address the topic for decades. Plus, there was always controversy. The most visceral modern example came in 2007 in the U.S. House of Representatives. There, politicians took a vote on the Employment Non-Discrimination Act (ENDA). It should have been a celebratory moment, but the bill had been stripped of protections for transgender people. The transgender community felt betrayed by the decision to essentially move forward without them. The outrage launched protests against the Human Rights Campaign (HRC) as well as former Massachusetts Representative Barney Frank. Frank was the first publicly out member of Congress, but he ignored the calls by the trans community to maintain specific protections for them in the bill, partly based on his belief that it would make the bill harder to pass, which angered the transgender community.[19]

I was sixteen at the time, but as I became more interested in LGBTQ+ advocacy in college, this incident came up over and over again. As of this writing, it is still one of the primary moments that undergirds the distrust of HRC within many parts of the LGBTQ+ community, especially among transgender people. Since that ugly moment more than a decade ago, the LGBTQ+ advocacy community would not entertain making such a maneuver again—if for no other reason than those in leadership valued their own employment.

The creation of a wedge issue around transgender youth playing sports threatened to upend that unity and make the passage of the Equality Act—the spiritual successor to ENDA—more politically fraught than it already was. The funders who were heavily invested in seeing the Equality Act passed didn't want to go near the issue of transgender kids playing sports. "[The Gill Foundation] wouldn't fund it, because they don't really care about trans issues," one advocate told me. "They were more so concerned with getting the Equality Act passed and not wanting trans issues to hurt that."

The Gill Foundation is one of the largest funders of LGBTQ+ equality advocacy in the country. Founded by Tim Gill, a philanthropist and gay man, the organization has invested more than

$390 million into programs and organizations across the country working on its priorities, including equality for transgender Americans. On its website, Gill highlights multiple priorities, including youth and family. In the past three years, the organization has given fifteen million dollars in support of transgender equality, including two million dollars dedicated to transgender athletes. Gill funds major LGBTQ+ organizations such as the National Center for Lesbian Rights (NCLR), GLBTQ Legal Advocates and Defenders (GLAD), and the Transgender Legal Defense and Education Fund (TLDEF). Gill pulled together many of the organizations it works with in January 2020 for a meeting on the issue of transgender athletes and messaging. Many advocates I spoke with who were in that room, however, left disillusioned and frustrated. The movement was not on the same page.

"There are a few major donors like the Gill Foundation, for example, who we felt did not take this seriously," Lieberman said. "Only now are they putting money into trans inclusion in sport through a media focus." Even after the 2021 legislative session, however, there was no mention of the sports and medical care bills as priorities on Gill's website.

But it wasn't just Gill who sat on the sidelines; almost everyone else did too. The funder most mentioned as having stepped up to marshal resources against the coming onslaught of anti-trans bills was the Wellspring Philanthropic Fund. Wellspring prioritizes human rights and social justice, including racial, gender, and economic justice. Wellspring funded a number of LGBTQ+ advocacy organizations around transgender inclusion work, but, frankly, the money available for LGBTQ+ organizations paled in comparison to what ADF brought to the table as these bills were filed all across the country. "You've got to remember, the Alliance Defending Freedom has a one-hundred-million-dollar associated attorney program that's always looking for test cases," Byard said. "What I love is how we manage to beat them."

In 2021, though, ADF was winning. Yes, the LGBTQ+ movement was fractured, unprepared, and under-resourced, but one of the biggest issues was that an important part of the coalition—one that had embraced marriage equality and other issues pertaining to the LGBTQ+ community—had stayed out of this fight almost entirely.

WHEN THEN–INDIANA GOVERNOR Mike Pence signed Indiana's Religious Freedom Restoration Act (RFRA) in March 2015 during a closed-door ceremony, the response was brutal and swift. Indiana's RFRA stated that a governmental entity could not "substantially burden" the free exercise of religion; it was a broad law that LGBTQ+ equality advocates argued provided a means for discrimination against LGBTQ+ people by companies, restaurants, hotels, etc. Prominent leaders in the Indianapolis business community spoke out against the law almost immediately, including Eli Lilly and Co. CEO John Lechleiter, Angie's List cofounder Bill Oesterle, and Salesforce CEO Marc Benioff.[20] The sports world joined corporate America to denounce the law as well, including the NCAA, the Indiana Pacers, and the Indiana Fever. The pressure was so intense that Pence amended the law within a week.

A similar coalition spoke out a year later when North Carolina passed their "bathroom bill"—HB 2—which required people to use public restrooms that corresponded with the sex listed on their birth certificate. It also barred local governments from enacting nondiscrimination legislation that protected classes of people not included in the state's law, which was a direct assault on the common practice within the LGBTQ+ movement of working with cities to protect LGBTQ+ people from discrimination even if the state government would not do so. HB 2 passed in response to Charlotte enacting such an ordinance.

Like in Indiana the year prior, the response was immediate from corporations, celebrities, and sports organizations. After Republican Governor Pat McCrory lost his reelection bid that fall, his successor, Democrat Roy Cooper, worked to repeal HB 2 and restore the large-scale sporting events, conferences, and concerts to the state. HB 2 was repealed and replaced by HB 142 in April 2017. On the surface, it looked like a win for LGBTQ+ equality and the effects of public pressure. But as with all things, the devil is in the details.

LGBTQ+ advocates felt betrayed by the deal that was struck between Cooper and the Republican legislature. The "bathroom" part of the bill was repealed, but the moratorium on local ordinances remained until 2020. The NBA and NCAA, however, touted the compromise and returned events to North Carolina. Charlotte was awarded the 2019 All-Star Game to make up for losing the 2017 game, and the state became eligible to send bids for NCAA championships.

Both Indiana and North Carolina were examples of large corporations and sports organizations standing alongside (for the most part) the broader LGBTQ+ community. But as the bills targeting transgender youth swept across the country in 2021, there was not the same level of engagement or outrage.

"Marriage equality was won, thanks, in part, to many companies and corporations standing in solidarity with LGBTQ+ activists and organizations," Athlete Ally founder Hudson Taylor said to me. "When it comes to the support of the trans community, either access to safe and affirming health care, or sports, corporate America has been, by and large, silent. I view this as being in this era of 'deeply concerned.'" Taylor's sardonic jibe at the end criticized the press releases from organizations and companies that don't outline action steps but instead say they are "deeply concerned" by the proposed legislation.

The NCAA was one of the organizations that had been "deeply concerned" by the continuous passage of the anti-transgender sports legislation. But the organization took no discernable action to stand against the legislation. After Idaho enacted HB 500, the NCAA declined to move championships from the state or bar them from being awarded. While state after state passed copycat legislation in 2021, the NCAA published multiple statements condemning the laws and reaffirming the organization's commitment to transgender inclusion. But the NCAA didn't *do* anything. And on August 3, 2021, the organization officially stated that it wouldn't be doing anything at all. No events would be moved from the states that passed laws affecting transgender athletes. On the eve of Texas enacting its own restrictions on transgender athletes in fall 2021, the NCAA stood by their August statement. In 2023, the Women's Final Four was held in Dallas, and the Men's Final Four was played in Houston.

Though the NCAA may have skirted the issue from a policy perspective during the 2021 legislative session, the success of another athlete would force the organization back into the arena. A swimmer from the University of Pennsylvania dove into the pool at the precise moment the issue of transgender athletes entered mainstream discussion. Her name is Lia Thomas.

10.

THE CASE OF LIA THOMAS

UNIVERSITY OF PENNSYLVANIA swimmer Lia Thomas dove into the pool at the University of Akron on December 3, 2021. As her body sliced through the water, to her it was just another meet, another race. The water was where she felt the most at home, and today was no different. Thomas' arms churned through the water, pushing it behind her. As she turned at the wall, her feet propelled her off the ceramic back in the other direction. She wasn't focused on any of the other swimmers. Her eyes stayed glued to the black line beneath her, guiding her strokes and pacing.

Her fingers touched the wall, stopping her time. Thomas turned around to gaze up at the board. She'd finished first. Again. In the first five meets of the 2021–22 swim season, Thomas hadn't lost a race. But the time that flashed on the board was a different category of fast. Thomas won the 500-yard freestyle in 4:34.06, setting meet and pool records as well as being the fastest time in the country at that point. The next day, she'd win the 200 freestyle in 1:41.93, which also set the meet and pool records and was the fastest time in the country so far that season. On the third day, Thomas would win the 1650 freestyle, beating second place by 38 seconds. The video of the gap in her third victory as well as her two best times in the nation began to stir controversy.

Lia Thomas wasn't just a senior having a record start to her final season in the pool; she was transgender. As the news of her performance and her gender identity leaked out from the Akron pool, it became clear that Thomas' life was about to change, and a sport often only paid attention to during Olympic years would become the next battleground over transgender athletes and women's sports.

When the name Lia Thomas began to appear in conservative news, the landscape around transgender athletes had changed considerably from when similar things happened to Mack Beggs and Andraya Yearwood. The 2020 and 2021 legislative sessions had been largely successful in terms of passing restrictive laws for transgender athletes. The days of the quiet hostility Andraya Yearwood faced as a freshman in 2017 had given way to a more virulent dissent. In the days following Thomas' performance at the Zippy Invitational, articles appeared in conservative outlets with anonymous quotes from disgruntled teammates.

Anti-transgender activists criticized the NCAA's existing policy governing transgender athletes that allowed Thomas to swim in the women's category. Transgender inclusion advocates were mostly quiet about Thomas specifically. I later found out from a number of people that she asked them to not mention her. She wasn't exactly seeking attention from this relatively unexpected national moment. While the controversy began to brew around her, Thomas remained silent. Outside of an interview with the *SwimSwam Podcast* and a later interview with *Sports Illustrated,* Thomas did not speak to media for the entire swim season, despite being asked repeatedly by a whole host of outlets.

Thomas' emergence onto the national scene struck a particular chord at a particular time. With the graduation of Andraya Yearwood and Terry Miller in 2020, they were no longer competing and therefore weren't in the news. The specter of their dominance and ongoing victory doesn't carry the same cultural influence in right-wing circles as it once did. It's sort of hard to argue the possibility of the world ending when Yearwood and Miller did not earn scholarships, but all of the cisgender athletes suing them did. Thomas offered a new opportunity in an even more politically charged moment.

Most conservative outlets printed Thomas' birth name—commonly referred to as a deadname within the transgender community—and some continued to use he/him pronouns. This is a common tactic by anti-trans activists, who use the deadnames of trans folk and/or the wrong pronouns to further emphasize publicly that the person has a different sex assigned at birth than their gender identity. At best, they do this because they are ignorant to the knowledge that they should do otherwise, and at worst, it's a simple but effective tactic for denying the rights and dignity of trans people. Names and pronouns are about basic respect, and *everyone* has them. If your name is John and you use he/him pronouns, I would imagine that it would be disrespectful to you if I called you Taylor and only used they/them pronouns for you because I believe that everyone should operate in a gender-neutral world and that binary gender is oppressive and dumb. While I personally *do* think that binary gender is oppressive, I don't go around imposing that particular worldview on everyone I meet. It's weird that somehow the basic tenet of human respect that many of us—especially those of us who grew up in Christian households—learned as children, the Golden Rule, just doesn't apply to transgender people. It's not political to refer to someone using their correct name and pronouns; it's accurate and respectful.

Thomas was not, and still is not, getting that respect in the early days after the Zippy Invitational. The timing of the meet was just before Penn's finals week and the end of the semester, so she wouldn't compete for almost another month. During that time, the headlines continued to swirl. "Transgender swimmer Lia Thomas smashes women's records, stokes outrage," wrote *The Washington Times*.[1] "It's impossible to beat her," said an anonymous teammate to the *Daily Mail*.[2] "Transgender swimmer Lia Thomas' [Penn] teammates considered boycotting final meet in protest," wrote the *New York Post*.[3] And on and on. As of this writing, hardly a day has gone by without a mention of Lia Thomas in the press since December 2021. I should know; I have Google Alerts.

The attention paid toward Thomas in these days was different from what Yearwood or Miller faced while in high school, or even Beggs while in Texas. And it was different from what other high-profile transgender women collegiate athletes faced as well, in that the deluge of coverage was constant and increasingly aggressive in tone. There were articles about the Penn locker room, about Thomas' body, about her motivations, all of which were anonymously sourced from teammates, with no way to discern how many teammates were speaking out or how often. The consequence of this sensationalist coverage was that the facts of Thomas' story were almost immediately lost, along with any semblance of her humanity.

Thomas grew up in Austin, Texas, with her parents and two older brothers. She started swimming at an early age because she followed her brothers to the neighborhood pool for swim lessons. The pool wasn't heated, but four-year-old Lia didn't want to get out. Teeth chattering and lips turning purple, she stayed in the water. "I just really enjoyed just splashing around in the water and being in the water," Thomas said to me.

Her middle brother didn't stick with it, but Wes, her oldest brother, did and went on to swim at Penn. Wes and Lia both still hold pool and club records for their former swim club in the Austin area. "For Wes and Lia, swimming just clicked for them," Lia's mom, Carrie, said to me. "They loved it."

Lia became a freestyle specialist almost by happenstance. She, like Wes, primarily swam breaststroke when she was a child. While training for a competitive meet in high school, however, the time she needed to qualify in breaststroke seemed to be a bit too far off, but the time in the 500 freestyle was doable. So she qualified in the 500 freestyle and never looked back.

Though she never overlapped with her brother, Thomas also decided to swim at Penn. She was an economics major and a classics minor. The reason she fell in love with classics is that she discovered Greek mythology through the Percy Jackson series by Rick Riordan. Thomas largely had successful freshman and sophomore seasons on the swim team. By her sophomore season, she'd staked her claim as an emerging force in distance swimming, placing runner-up at the Ivy League conference meet in the 500, 1000, and 1650 freestyle events as a sophomore. She set a Sheerr Pool record for the men's program in the 1000 free-style in 2018. As of this writing, it's a record she still holds.

Over the course of her first two seasons at Penn, Thomas was struggling with her gender identity. She'd first begun questioning her gender when she was in seventh grade, but at the time, she didn't have the language to piece together what she was feeling. "I just started to feel like something was off," Thomas said. "There was a disconnect, but I couldn't express it and just eventually chalked it up as 'I guess that's just how it is.'" Just before entering her freshman year at Penn, Thomas discovered the language that described the disconnect she'd been feeling since she was twelve. Thomas had heard the term "transgender" before but, in some ways, wasn't sure if she could be trans. "I don't know if I really knew what being trans meant," Thomas said. "In my mind, at that time, being trans was something I felt you were born knowing."

That summer, however, everything clicked for Thomas, and she entered into her first collegiate swim season knowing that she was transgender. But everything was new and disorienting. While she was internally exploring her identity, she was also starting her first year of college, halfway across the country from her parents, meeting new classmates and new teammates, and trying to figure out how to be a competitive swimmer at this higher level of competition. "It was kind of a mess," Thomas said. "Eventually my strategy was just to push it all back down."

By the end of her sophomore year, however, that was untenable for her. She'd told her parents the year before that she was trans, but she hadn't yet begun hormone therapy. That swim season was difficult for Thomas. During the first month, she contemplated quitting. "It felt like too much," she said. "Being in the water and in nothing but a Speedo for twenty hours a week was incredibly dysphoric." For hours in the pool, as she dragged her body through the water, looking down at the black line beneath her, she struggled to push the feelings she was having from her mind. "I did struggle with suicidal thoughts," she said.

During that season, however, she was runner-up in all three of her events at the Ivy League championships. She showed promise in the pool even as she was struggling within herself. Something had to give, and Thomas decided that she was going to transition even if it meant giving up swimming. That spring, she shared how she was feeling with her parents, Bob and Carrie. Her parents listened as Lia became more emotional than they'd ever seen her, becoming increasingly concerned as they realized the depth of her depression and despair. Lia is known for her stoicism, but she was breaking down. "It was very evident that she was suffering," Bob said to me. "When we saw that, we realized what she was going through. And it was just like, 'Okay, let's get you what you need to be happy.'" Lia began hormone therapy in May 2019.

The NCAA policy at that time allowed for transgender women to participate in women's sports after twelve months of testosterone suppression. After Thomas shared her identity with her coaches and teammates, she spent one season on the men's team while beginning hormone therapy. During the 2019–20 season, she competed on the men's team while wearing a women's bathing suit. It was communicated to the entirety of the Penn swimming and diving team that Thomas would join the women's team once she met the requirements to do so, which was expected to be during the 2020–21 season. The emergence of the COVID-19 pandemic, however, caused the Ivy League to cancel competition for all sports. During that year, Thomas took a break from school explicitly to ensure her eligibility for her senior season. When she entered the pool in the fall of 2021 on the women's team, she'd been on hormone therapy for twenty-nine months, more than double the time that was required of her under the NCAA policy.

THE NCAA'S POLICY on transgender athlete participation was published in 2011 and in effect for more than a decade. The policy governed all NCAA championships at the Division I, II, and III levels, and required the following: transgender men could compete in the men's or women's category, but must compete in the men's after beginning hormone therapy; transgender women could remain competing in the men's category without restriction, but to be eligible for competition in the women's category, they needed to undergo twelve months of testosterone suppression.

After the first IOC policy went into effect for the 2004 Olympics in Athens, Pat Griffin and Helen Carroll began talking about what an NCAA requirement could look like. Griffin was consulting with the Women's Sports Foundation, and Carroll worked at the National Center for Lesbian Rights (NCLR) as the coordinator for the organization's sports project. The two hosted a think tank at the NCAA in Indianapolis in October 2009 that included a handful of transgender student-athletes, medical experts, lawyers, and representatives from the NCAA and National Federation of State High School Associations (NFHS). When that meeting concluded, Griffin and Carroll wrote a report summarizing the discussion titled *On the Team: Equal Opportunities for Transgender Student Athletes*. The report asserted a need for national, uniform policies at both the high school and college levels and pushed back against the medical requirements the IOC had at that time, which included surgery.

The policy recommendations in that original report eventually became the NCAA policy guidelines approved by the Board of Governors in 2011. "High schools did not really pick up," Griffin said. "But Karen Morrison picked it up and started internally pushing the conversation in the NCAA. She had the political savvy and understanding of the issue to push it within the NCAA and get it approved by the Board of Governors, which, actually, to be honest, I was shocked that she was able to accomplish that."

Morrison was the director of inclusion at the NCAA from 2006 to 2014. As of this writing, she is the chief diversity officer at the University of Central Florida.

Even though individual schools were not required to adopt such policies, the NCAA's 2011 policy provided rules and a pathway to participation for transgender athletes. It also inadvertently provided a check on the notion that transgender girls playing high school sports would be able to "steal" scholarships from cisgender girls and women without medically transitioning, and then "detransitioning" after their "free" degree (plenty of people have made this argument to me). It should be noted that this idea is fear-based and has no factual basis. To date there has not been a single known transgender woman who came out publicly in high school and received a scholarship to compete on a collegiate women's team. But even though that hasn't yet happened, at some point it will. One goal of transgender inclusion advocates is for that future to happen, while those who advocate against trans inclusion policies would like that future to become impossible.

But, of course, there have been transgender athletes competing in the NCAA for years, even predating the policy. Most of the athletes who are publicly known have been competing in women's sports and are transgender men or nonbinary/genderfluid. In 2005, Keelin Godsey was among the first collegiate athletes to come out publicly as transgender, while he was competing at Division III Bates College in women's track and field. The first Division I athlete to come out publicly as transgender was Kye Allums, who played women's basketball at George Washington. Allums came out in 2010, garnering a lot of media attention. G Ryan, who is genderqueer, competed on the University of Michigan swim team from 2014 to 2018. Schuyler Bailar became the first transgender man to compete on a Division I men's team when he joined Harvard's men's swim team in 2017. Even among all the uproar about Lia Thomas, another transgender athlete was competing in the Ivy League. His name was Iszac Henig and he was swimming on the Yale women's team, sometimes against Thomas. The following season, he began competing on the men's team. I will go more in depth on transgender men in coming chapters, but I wanted to acknowledge them here as well.

The only publicly known instances of transgender women competing in the women's category while on scholarship are women who were originally recruited to compete as part of the men's team in their respective sports and transitioned while in college. And to be clear, the number of transgender women who fit that criteria is two: CeCé Telfer (Franklin Pierce University) and Juniper "June" Eastwood (University of Montana). Thomas doesn't fit that criteria because the Ivy League does not offer athletic scholarships. But if she is included, then three transgender women over a decade are known to have competed at the Division I and II levels.

I use the word "known" because there have surely been others who have flown under the radar, who were not deemed to be threats because they weren't winning, who played lesser scrutinized sports, etc. There have also been transgender men not mentioned above who competed in both men's and women's sports at the NCAA level. Not to mention nonbinary and genderqueer athletes. There have also likely been multiple athletes competing in Division III, but those schools don't offer scholarships. The media and public often respond to transgender girls or women *winning* in their respective sports, which creates the perception that transgender girls and women win all the time. All of the transgender women athletes that are familiar names in public consciousness became so on the backs of those athletes winning some sort of championship or having success in elite athletics. That narrative, however, is an incomplete one. Statistically, it's nearly impossible for just a handful of athletes to have been transgender in the history of the NCAA. For the entire history of this policy's existence, transgender athletes had been competing in the NCAA, largely without incident. In that sense, the policy was working. For some, however, the fact that Thomas was able to swim and to win races in the women's category meant the policy was broken. As that perspective began to take hold, it was more than just Thomas' teammates who were disgruntled. The displeasure in the swimming and diving community rippled through the Ivy League.

GRIFFIN MAXWELL BROOKS was a diver on the Princeton men's swimming and diving team during the 2021–22 season. They grew up in New Jersey and followed their sister to gymnastics in fourth grade, which is how they got into jumping and flipping.

For most of their childhood, diving was something they did during the summers at the community pool, and not a serious athletic pursuit. But in eighth grade, Brooks decided to get serious, joining a diving club team and giving up gymnastics. Brooks, however, wasn't always the most dedicated athlete. It took them getting kicked out of practice by their coach for not focusing to spur the dedication that would take them to the Ivy League. "I decided, from then on, that I was going to go in and work extra hard and not talk and, you know, prove to him that I was worthy," Brooks said. "And I saw such a drastic improvement that I was like, oh, like I guess we should probably keep doing this."

While a freshman at Princeton, Brooks began to realize that they did not feel connected with their male peers and started to question their own gender identity. They'd been out as gay to their parents since sixth grade, but this feeling was a bit different. The concept of gender fluidity resonated with them, but they weren't sure if it fit or if they were ready to share. But when the COVID-19 pandemic hit, Brooks was sent home along with everyone else. And it was in their parents' basement that they started to find themselves. "I had a lot of time to look in the mirror," Brooks said.

They also were trying on new outfits, or "playing dress-up," as Brooks put it. They started exploring their identity through fashion, and posting it on the internet, specifically TikTok. Brooks was watching other people's explorations too. It was exciting and liberating. And they wanted to go out and buy new clothes and try different things, pushing the boundaries of what they thought was possible with each new outfit they posted. "I started realizing that I didn't feel affixed to any gender norms and, by extension, gender labels," Brooks said.

When Brooks returned to the Princeton pool, they did so with a large social following, a confidence boost, and a new sense of self. The adjustment was difficult at first. The team that had felt more welcoming as a freshman was making jokes that Brooks would prefer not to be included in the group chat. "The men on the team were doing that thing where they pretend to have sex with each other because it's funny to pretend to be gay," Brooks said. "And that's not a joke. For me, that's my life. I remember having to sit down with the whole team and be like, 'Hey, this isn't okay,' which was very different from my presence on the team as a freshman."

But as a nonbinary person diving on an Ivy League team, they also found themselves in the middle of a brewing controversy. "And then things sort of devolved in the spring when Lia Thomas became a talking point," Brooks said.

When the news broke about Thomas swimming in the women's category, Brooks was taken aback by the level of vitriol they witnessed within their own program. They were all friends. Brooks hung out with the women's team a lot. And now they were opposed to a transgender woman competing against them. It felt to Brooks that maybe their teammates were also opposed to them. "It didn't occur to me until I spoke with one of the female divers on the women's team that they were so, like, vehemently against Lia Thomas swimming," Brooks said. "And it kind of came as a shock to me, because prior to that moment, I always went to the women's team for games instead of the men's team. I was always around the women's team in social spaces, because the men's team just never felt like a comfortable space for me."

From Brooks' perspective, they tried to set meetings and have a conversation with teammates and coaches as a member of this community they loved. The response was tepid at first, then there was no response. Brooks hung transgender flags around the pool when Harvard and Yale came for their annual meet. Brooks said their teammates on the women's team iced them out after that, congratulating every other diving competitor except for them. "I felt like I was being bullied in middle school," Brooks said.

Brooks didn't dive at Princeton in 2022–23, which would have been their senior season. The pool that used to be a joyful escape for them didn't feel that way anymore. "I didn't really feel safe at the pool," Brooks said. "It didn't feel like a place I could go to and do the thing that I love because I constantly feel all these eyes on me."

The strife Brooks felt in their own program mirrored what I heard was happening in the Ivy League when Thomas began swimming in the women's category. At the time, however, few people would talk about it. When I was reporting at the Ivy League championships in February 2022, every interview request I sent to Princeton athletics was declined. Same for Brown and Dartmouth and Harvard. Some swimmers were willing to do an interview if they weren't asked about Thomas, but even those opportunities were few and far between. It was expressed to me that behind the scenes swimmers were afraid to put their names out there or, in some cases, were told they couldn't by their athletic departments. But the lack of public on-the-record comments didn't mean there wasn't pressure for something to be done about Thomas competing against women. It wasn't long before the NCAA itself weighed in on the issue.

• • •

ON JANUARY 19, 2022, the NCAA announced a policy change for transgender athletes, specifically transgender women. Instead of the guidance of twelve-month testosterone suppression that applied to all sports, the NCAA would be enacting the transgender athlete policies of the national governing bodies of each respective sport. The NCAA said that this policy change was in line with the changes the IOC announced in November 2021, which empowered each sport's international federation to develop its own policy, along with providing a statement of values that the IOC said should inform that policy development that called for respect and equal treatment, etc. The IOC values statement and recommendations were not binding for international federations, however; they communicated a vision and a position that clearly valued transgender and intersex athletes. The IOC rollout made it clear that the direction in which the organization was going was not impulsive; it was carefully considered. In contrast, the NCAA's process seemed incredibly rushed. The NCAA did not provide an accompanying statement of values like the IOC had; instead, the NCAA shifted the policy responsibilities onto national governing bodies (NGBs) with no forewarning or planning, despite the fact that many of the NGBs were unprepared with their own policies *because* of the IOC policy shift. The sudden announcement of a policy change felt targeted to one particular athlete.

"It's clear to me that the publicity and the success that Lia [Thomas] has been having elevated this issue at the NCAA," Ivy League executive director Robin Harris said in an interview with ESPN.[4] "I do believe that the NCAA missed an opportunity to be a leader, and instead tried to avoid having the NCAA policy be the focus of the attention, because Lia has met the

NCAA policy that had been in existence for over a decade." In effect, the NCAA was passing the buck, delegating responsibility to a scattered range of governing bodies rather than setting the standard itself.

After the announcement by the NCAA, the question became "What is USA Swimming's policy?" USA Swimming is the swimming national governing body in the United States, and at the moment of the announcement by the NCAA, the organization did not have a transgender athlete inclusion policy for its elite athletes separate from the old IOC policy. World Aquatics, formerly known as the Fédération Internationale de Natation (FINA), was the international federation governing aquatic sports. The organization had not announced a new policy, so USA Swimming was using older standards and a process-oriented policy for non-elite youth that mostly governed name change. But on February 1, 2022, USA Swimming announced an updated policy that would apply to USA Swimming members, elite events (which, notably, did not include the NCAA Swimming and Diving Championships because USA Swimming did not sanction that event), and athletes who wanted to be eligible for American records. The new policy requires transgender women to undergo thirty-six months of testosterone suppression and be under 5 nmol/L and to appear before a three-person medical panel to prove they have no competitive advantage over their cisgender peers. There is no additional criteria listed in the policy to explain how an athlete proves they have no advantage. At the time it was released, it was the most restrictive policy for elite sports in the United States.

It would be up to the NCAA Committee on Competitive Safeguards and Medical Aspects of Sports (CSMAS) to decide how and if the new regulations applied to the NCAA Swimming and Diving Championships. When the CSMAS came out with its decision about eligibility for the NCAA championships, it seemed to reverse course. Instead of adopting the USA Swimming policy, which would have rendered Thomas ineligible, the committee decided that eligibility would be determined by compliance with the previous NCAA policy and a submission of a one-time testosterone level under 10 nmol/L.

In the middle of the policy drama, multiple letters and statements were published that both supported Thomas' participation and criticized it, many of them anonymously. First was Stanford's Brooke Forde, whose father is a prominent sportswriter at *Sports Illustrated*. He read her statement on his podcast, which was supportive of Thomas. It read, in part: "In 2020, I, along with most swimmers, experienced what it was like to have my chance to achieve my swimming goals taken away after years of hard work. I would not wish this experience on anyone, especially Lia, who has followed the rules required of her. I believe that treating people with respect and dignity is more important than any trophy or record will ever be, which is why I will not have a problem racing against Lia at NCAAs this year."[5]

A group of Thomas' teammates also supported her, albeit anonymously, through a statement released by Penn Athletics. Then, Nancy Hogshead-Makar sent a letter to the Ivy League on behalf of sixteen Penn swimmers and their families that strongly opposed Thomas' inclusion and asked the conference not to sue the NCAA if the USA Swimming rules were adopted. Then, Athlete Ally released a letter signed by 310 athletes, including five of Thomas' teammates. This time period was a back-and-forth of (mostly) anonymous comments from teammates in the press, while they all shared a pool for swim practice every day. "Imagine having that amount of hatred and showing up in practice, and still competing," former Harvard swimmer and transgender activist Schuyler Bailar said. "And, by the grace of her own resilience, somehow winning still. I don't think people really sit and think about that."

When the dust settled, Thomas would get to swim in both postseason meets: the Ivy League conference championships and the NCAA championships. She would do so against the backdrop of an aggressive anti-transgender legislative session.

WHILE THOMAS WAS making headlines around the country and the world, more legislative measures restricting the participation of transgender athletes in school sports were filed in state Houses across the nation. The bills varied slightly across the states, but in many of the hearings, representatives from ADF— the same organization Barbara Ehardt worked with in Idaho— testified in favor of their passage. And, boy, did they pass. South Dakota was first, in February, with Governor Noem signing a version of the legislation she'd vetoed the previous year. Then, Iowa. Governors signed bills into law in Oklahoma, Arizona, and South Carolina. The Utah, Indiana, and Kentucky legislatures all overrode governor vetoes. And in Louisiana, the governor didn't sign or veto the bill, allowing it to simply become law by default. Tennessee, which had already passed a law restricting access to high school sports for transgender athletes, then passed *another* law that affects college athletics. By June 2022, the total number of states with anti-transgender athlete laws on the books stood at eighteen. The overwhelming majority of this legislation targeted school sports, not elite or elite-feeding club sports, sometimes in response to a single transgender girl participating in girls' sports.

Fischer Wells was in seventh grade when she joined the nascent field hockey team at her school in Kentucky. "The coach came in and passed out fliers," she said. "And I was like, 'Hey, I'll do that.'" She was twelve years old when I talked to her. Wells loved all the running around she got to do as a field hockey player. When her coach's whistle didn't work, she'd make a noise to get everyone's attention. She played all the positions, but she liked midfield the best. "Because it's basically playing offense and defense," Fischer said.

Fischer got into sports as so many kids do: at the urging of her parents. She started with cross-country in fourth grade, which was rough at first. But the next year, she loved it. Because, well, Fischer likes to run. In sixth grade, she came out to her family as transgender but continued to play sports. But in 2022, a bill passed that threatened her ability to continue to participate. SB 83 expanded the existing law regulating schools and athletics in Kentucky to require all sports to be designated as boys, girls, or co-ed. The determination of sex would be made by the "original unedited birth certificate," or by a signed affidavit by the medical professional conducting the standard physical required for sports participation. SB 83 affects grades 6–12. Fischer went to the statehouse to testify against it. She was the only known transgender girl competing in girls' sports in the state.[6]

"My brain has gone through the stage of 'Oh my god, what the heck?' to almost morbid laughing because it's so funny how dumb it is," Fischer said. "They're making up fake numbers. I looked and looked and looked for the numbers they're talking about and I couldn't find them." The "they" is the legislature. And the numbers are the ones where people assigned male at birth have an athletic advantage over those assigned female at birth.

"It's appalling, and it's infuriating," said Brian Wells, Fischer's dad. "It's been a bad time."

Before the legislature overrode the governor's veto to enact SB 83, the Kentucky High School Athletic Association already had one of the most restrictive transgender athlete policies in the country. Students could participate in accordance with their gender identity if they could prove they'd transitioned prior to puberty. If they'd transitioned after the onset of puberty, then they had to have surgery or be on hormone therapy. The World Professional Association for Transgender Health (WPATH) standards of care for adolescents make note of the difficulty in pinpointing specific age requirements for courses of treatment, but it is generally accepted that hormone therapy treatments begin for teenagers who meet criteria. For surgery, some older teenagers may undergo chest masculinization, or "top surgery." Genital surgery is not recommended for or performed on minors.[7]

Fischer was not alone in being targeted by the lawmakers in her state. In Ohio, a seventeen-year-old named Ember played softball and was the only known transgender girl competing on a varsity team in the state. She was an average softball player on a team that *needed players*. There weren't even enough to field a junior varsity squad.[8] The state tried to ban her anyway. When Utah Governor Spencer Cox vetoed his state's legislation, he said that of the 75,000 students competing in high school sports, only four were known to be transgender. And of those four—the 0.005 percent of high school athletes in the state—just *one* was a transgender girl. The legislature overrode his veto anyway.

This complete onslaught in state legislatures across the

country put the LGBTQ+ equality movement further on its heels, creating holes in organizing and staffing. When I was in college and graduate school, I worked on two marriage equality campaigns, one in Minnesota and one in Indiana. During that time, it wasn't uncommon to run into organizers from national organizations like the LGBTQ+ Task Force or the Human Rights Campaign. Even as of this writing, however, there are states fighting anti-transgender bills that are not seeing that type of resource investment from national organizations. Likely because there are too many fronts right now. When I spoke with Chris Hartman, the executive director of the Fairness Campaign in Kentucky, the organization was fighting against an anti-transgender sports bill. There wasn't a single field organizer in the state from a national organization. This wasn't 2020 or 2021. This was happening in early 2022. The LGBTQ+ equality movement was spending resources and capital to fight the bills restricting health care for transgender youth, and I don't begrudge those decisions. However, it's also clear to me that those bills wouldn't have proliferated without the unmitigated success of the bills affecting sports in 2020 and 2021, when the national organizations and funders were mostly on the sidelines.

During the debate over high school and middle school (and sometimes elementary school) athletes, collegiate swimmer Lia Thomas' name was brought up more than once. In Arizona. In Indiana. In Kentucky. And onward. Her success embodied the very fear Republican lawmakers spent two years warning about. Naturally, then, it came as no surprise that when Thomas showed up to race at the NCAA championships, she did so amid protests and a chorus of boos.

• • •

THOUGH IT WASN'T explicitly clear until just a couple of weeks before the national championships, Thomas would be eligible to compete against her collegiate peers in the women's category for points and eligible to win trophies. Her participation, as it had been all year, was controversial. Her best event, the 500-yard freestyle, was also her first of the meet. She swam her best time since Zippy, the meet where all of this began, to earn a spot in the finals.

Outside the McAuley Aquatic Center at Georgia Tech in Atlanta, a few dozen protesters gathered. They were mostly from the organization Save Women's Sports, but Concerned Women for America joined them alongside other anti-trans activists including Linda Blade. They handed out stickers saying "Save Women's Sports" and chanted the slogan throughout the day to many fist bumps from passing family members of competing swimmers.

A few weeks prior, at the Ivy League championships at Harvard's Blodgett Pool, the vibe was clearly different. I know from talking to people off the record that there was quite a bit of dissent present on that pool deck, but there were also multiple visible signs of support. If I could characterize the environment at Blodgett as anything, it would be cordial. The NCAA championships were not that.

It was clear from the moment the first loud boo rang out from the crowd and the protesters began to show up outside that this meet would be different. It was tense. It wasn't overwhelmingly hostile, but there wasn't a lot of support for Thomas in the stands or on the pool deck beyond her own family and friends. That reality was noticeable in the whispers permeating the hallways, the exasperated sighs from spectators, and the noticeable dip in the number of claps when she was introduced as a finalist and stepped up to the blocks.

Diving into the water, her body slicing through the surface, Thomas moved with purpose. She churned her arms in front of her. Each time her fingertips broke the surface, her hands pulled the water behind her to propel her six-foot-two frame forward. Length after length, she swam. Each time she got to the wall, her feet kicked hard off the ceramic to send her toward the other side. When her hand touched the wall, Thomas turned around to look at the board. She finished first with a time of 4:33.24, nine seconds off of Olympic Gold medalist Katie Ledecky's record. Quite a significant time gap in swimming.

Thomas had just become the first known transgender athlete to win a Division I championship. She swam in two more finals in Atlanta, finishing tied for fifth in the 200 freestyle and finishing eighth in the 100 freestyle. She was far from the most dominant swimmer in the pool. That distinction belonged to a pair of swimmers from the University of Virginia: Kate Douglass and Alex Walsh, who both won three individual (the maximum) national championships. Douglass won three championships in three different strokes and set an American record in all three events. She also added four relay race championships, bringing her total haul to seven, not including the team national title UVA took home in dominant fashion. Lia Thomas had one really good swim and won a title, but she was competitive in a field full of Olympians, which was enough to make her presence unacceptable for some.

University of Kentucky swimmer Riley Gaines tied for fifth place with Thomas in the 200-yard freestyle. After the race, she was given the sixth-place trophy for the trophy ceremony while Thomas received the fifth-place trophy. The NCAA told Gaines she'd receive the correct trophy in the mail. This experience, plus what she witnessed at the NCAA championships, made

Gaines want to speak out publicly. As of this writing, Gaines remains one of the few swimmers who competed against Thomas to share their opinion in the media. "There was just kind of anger and frustration across the whole pool deck," Gaines said. "There was extreme discomfort in the locker room. And being on that pool deck and witnessing these things is when I finally came to the conclusion that this isn't something that is happening with no effect."

Gaines grew up in Nashville, Tennessee, and started swimming when she was four or five years old. She went to Kentucky to try to build a program that could challenge some of the top schools in the SEC. Like so many swimmers competing in Atlanta, Gaines worked for years for the opportunity to compete. And she did so successfully. What I think is interesting about Gaines' story is that after her competition career was over, she openly criticized Thomas, and far from being punished for taking that position, she has benefitted considerably. For all of the fear expressed to me from swimmers in the Ivy League and their representatives about how they would be punished for speaking out against Thomas, Gaines is proof that those fears were unfounded. Gaines has been criticized, but she's been a staple on Fox News talking about this issue. She was a speaker at the Conservative Political Action Coalition—a popular conservative conference—and was in an ad supporting Rand Paul's Senate reelection campaign. Meanwhile, Thomas faded from view after the NCAA championships. Thomas began law school in the fall of 2022. Despite claims to the contrary, the position that had the most public support when it came to views about Lia Thomas swimming in the women's category was to criticize her inclusion. Nowhere was that more evident than in Atlanta during the national championships.

The protests in Atlanta weren't huge, but their tenor underscored how politically charged this issue had become and who, exactly, was putting their thumbs on the scale. A couple of anti-transgender activists flew in from the United Kingdom, Barbara Ehardt came from Idaho, Save Women's Sports founder Beth Stelzer came from Minnesota, and Linda Blade was there as well. The group held a press conference, with one woman repeatedly referring to gender-affirming health care as child abuse. I spoke to a counterprotester who was a Georgia Tech student, and they were visibly shaken after an altercation with the group protesting Thomas. I did not see the incident myself, but I'll never forget the look on the person's face when they saw me: at once terrified and relieved to see a friendlier face. The fear was familiar; I'd been burying my own all week. The shouting and the anti-transgender vitriol from the protesters was intense, and every time I went outside to do an interview, I wondered internally if this was the moment that it would be turned on me. I felt protected because ESPN produced the event, my credentials said ESPN on them, and I was never farther than a few feet away from a colleague. But for the first time in my career, I was afraid while doing my job. A fellow journalist who is a transgender woman was harassed in the hallway by a small group of the protesters for using the women's bathroom. That altercation was recorded and posted on the internet. To put it mildly, it was an ugly scene.

When I think back on what I witnessed covering Thomas, it's clear that the "Lia Thomas controversy" was a radicalizing event. The hysteria over her being allowed to compete in the women's category defied most reason, and misinformation thrived. An example of that was a photo that went viral following the 500 freestyle final, the lone championship Thomas won. In the photo, Thomas stood on the first-place podium, while the second, third, and fourth place finishers posed for a photo. Many people used that photo as a meme to show that Thomas was taller than her competitors, but also that those finishers were upset that Thomas was allowed to compete. The reality was that Emma Weyant (second), Erica Sullivan (third), and Brooke Forde (fourth) were all Olympians. Forde and Sullivan had actually publicly voiced support for Thomas.

I'm not saying that there weren't reasonable questions to be asked regarding appropriate policy for transgender women competing in NCAA sports, but the media coverage whipped up a hysteria that muddied the facts of the story. Hogshead-Makar, who had been trying to work with LGBTQ+ inclusion advocates only three years prior, was now on television and social media calling for Thomas' ouster from women's swimming and using rhetoric about single-sex facilities that was of a completely different tenor than where she'd started. Her organization, Champion Women, alongside the Women's Sports Policy Working Group, released a position statement in January 2023 that called for women's locker rooms to be "restricted to female athletes" on the basis that "people born with male bodies, but believe themselves to be women, are not biologically female."

The statement went on to read: "Males have a right to identify as women, present as women, and ask others to refer to them as women. Males can modify their bodies via puberty blockers, estrogen, and 'gender-affirming' surgeries. Still, transwomen cannot transform themselves into females." This kind of language is similar as that used during conversations about bathrooms from 2015 to 2017, and demonstrates how much Hogshead-Makar's various positions on transgender rights outside of sports had shifted. For many transgender inclusion advocates, such a position on locker room and bathroom access is a non-starter.

The presence of activists from Britain in Atlanta talking about health care for transgender youth at a protest against Thomas showed the increasing scope of what was considered to be included in the debate. For those who support LGBTQ+ equality broadly, and transgender rights specifically, the public panic over Thomas put so much pressure on the transgender community, especially transgender youth and their families, that sports seemed so unimportant. And yet, sports continued to be the primary battleground.

One fact that wasn't discussed nearly as much was that Thomas wasn't the only transgender swimmer at the NCAA championships. When she swam in the 100 freestyle final, another transgender athlete joined her: Iszac Henig. When we talk about transgender athletes, however, most everyone is concerned about transgender women. But transgender men have been competing for decades, so why are they flying under the radar?

11.

WHY AREN'T WE TALKING ABOUT TRANSGENDER MEN?

WHEN ELITE DUATHLON competitor Chris Mosier decided to transition, he didn't know if he would be able to continue competing. Or at least, he was unsure if he would be able to do so at a high level. Raised in the Chicago area, he had been competing in women's sports for most of his life. He'd done martial arts, played softball and basketball. And as an adult, he'd become a successful triathlon athlete in the women's category. Problem was, he wasn't a woman. And now that he'd allowed himself to acknowledge that truth, he wasn't quite sure what to do. *Can I do this? Is this possible?*

He asked himself those questions because in 2009 and 2010, when he was confronting this truth about himself, the landscape looked completely different. Transgender identity had not entered public consciousness in the way it exists today. There weren't role models for Mosier—whose oft-repeated refrain is to be who he needed when he was younger—so the possibility of success wasn't so much unreachable as it was unknown.

"The overwhelming notion was that I'd be a middle-of-the-pack guy," Mosier said. "That I would not be competitive, not worth talking about. That was messaged to me in many direct and indirect ways."

The fact is, however, that Mosier *has* been competitive. He's qualified for multiple Duathlon World Championships, placing as high as ninth within his age group. He competed in the 2020 Olympic Trials for Race Walking. He was the first transgender athlete to be sponsored by Nike, the first transgender athlete in a Nike ad, and the first transgender athlete to appear in *ESPN* magazine's Body Issue. He represented his country on Team USA, the first known transgender athlete to do so in accordance with their gender identity. He was, without a doubt, the most successful transgender athlete in United States history. And he was a man.

Outside of Mosier, there are few known examples of transgender men competing in men's sports. Many of the athletes we know about on elite levels have competed in women's sports and have not medically transitioned. Kye Allums, the first transgender college athlete to come out publicly, did so in the fall of 2010. And he continued to play on the women's basketball team at George Washington University. Harrison Browne came out in 2016 and continued to play in the league that was then called the National Women's Hockey League (NWHL)—it has since been rebranded to the Premier Hockey Federation (PHF). Browne played in the NWHL for two seasons after sharing that he was transgender. But there have been some transgender men who have competed in the men's category. There's Mosier, of course, and Mack Beggs, who was able to wrestle in the men's category near the end of his career. Patricio Manuel boxes in the men's category. Schuyler Bailar swam on the men's team at Harvard. And there are other, lesser known stories as well. But transgender men are present and compete in both men's and women's sports.

Though not at the center of the debate around transgender athletes, many transgender athletes are transgender men. In my time reporting on transgender athletes competing at all levels of sport, I've come across more transgender boys and men competing in either women's or men's sports than transgender girls and women competing in either category. My experience is anecdotal—we have no reliable data on how many transgender athletes are competing—but even the successes (and existence) of transgender boys and men in this conversation often go unnoticed. "People don't think that someone assigned female at birth can be competitive with people assigned male at birth in many sports," Mosier said. "For that reason, we are just largely overlooked. Even if we do well, even if we succeed in our sport, we're just given a shrug and a 'good job.'"

What Mosier said about the core belief that someone assigned female at birth would be uncompetitive in an athletic setting among those assigned male at birth is key to understanding why transgender men have historically not been considered in policy making and also do not drive the conversation of transgender athletes competing in various levels of athletics. Transgender girls and women are viewed as threats to women's sports *because* of their sex assigned at birth and the perception of competitive advantage. It's the opposite for transgender boys and men. They aren't considered a threat at all *because* of their sex assigned at birth.

SCHUYLER BAILAR BEGAN swimming before he could walk. "Or at about the same time," Bailar said to me. He's not sure when he started swimming—he had no memories of lessons. For as long as he could remember, Bailar has been swimming. He relishes being underwater, the liquid swirling around him, grounding his otherwise weightless body. "There's a unique gravity in water," he said. "And I think that's something I adore."

Growing up outside of Washington, D.C., Bailar could usually be found in or around a pool. He was always at the public pool near his home, splashing and swimming. He was active and also usually alone except for his family. "I don't think I had a ton of friends around," Bailar said. His parents' research took him on the road with them, and by the time he was ten, Bailar was spending lots of time in the pool, training and swimming competitively.

It was also around this time that he started to present as a boy in public. The barber at his local shop presented him with a book of haircuts, and he chose a shorter look that was a "boy's cut." "My mom was, like, 'Okay, sure, whatever,'" Bailar said. He was also wearing clothes from the boys' section. "So I was immediately gendered as male by everybody," he said.

People who knew him didn't do that, but it was happening in public by those who didn't know him at all. His friends and family had strong reactions whenever someone used he/him pronouns with Bailar or referred to him as a boy, seeking to correct them on the spot. It's important to note that Bailar wasn't communicating his identity at this point. "Everybody thought they were protecting me," he said. "So I don't have hard feelings."

Though Bailar enjoyed the feeling of being perceived as a boy, he internalized that being seen as a boy was a bad thing because of the jump to correction from his friends and loved ones. "And so then I thought it was bad that I wanted that,"

Bailar said. When he was in high school, his mental health declined. Bailar struggled with an eating disorder and depression, and he was still swimming and trying to succeed in school. After he graduated, his therapist told him that he should delay going to college for a year because he needed to go to rehab. While there, he started examining his sense of self and gender. "And that's where I was finally able to say that I'm transgender," Bailar said.

Putting words to the feelings of disconnection he'd felt for so long, however, did not bring relief beyond the initial moments. Bailar knew he was transgender, but he was also a swimmer. But swimming on the women's team felt incongruent with his identity as a transgender man. He'd already been admitted to Harvard to swim on the women's team, and he had worked toward being a Division I swimmer his entire life. The two options he thought he had were to either swim on the women's team or quit swimming and transition. Either option meant losing part of his identity. The choice was terrifying and paralyzing. "There was just so much difficulty that I saw in this process that I had no desire to deal with," Bailar said.

It wasn't immediately clear that he could embrace his identity the way he wanted and still swim at all, let alone achieve the goals he'd set for himself—like making the NCAA championships and qualifying for Olympic Trials. But about halfway through his gap year, Bailar discovered that he was eligible to swim on the men's team under the NCAA policy at that time. The policy for transgender men was that they could compete in either the men's or the women's category and be immediately eligible, but if they began hormone therapy, they *must* compete in the men's category. So he could swim on the men's team if Harvard would be open to it, but he still didn't know if he wanted to. "I had all these very clear goals," he said. "And letting those go was massively disruptive to what I understood as 'success' in the world."

The tension felt between athletic success/career and medically transitioning is something felt by many transgender boys and men in sports, especially those who want to be competitive at elite levels and are considering a medical transition after puberty. Just as testosterone suppression for transgender women can mute some physiological traits that are athletically helpful and not others, taking testosterone for medical transition enhances some traits but not others. For example, starting testosterone will allow a person to build more muscle mass, but it doesn't make them grow considerably taller if started after a person's growth plates have closed. The effects of hormone changes also take time. It's not like once a person starts a medical transition they Hulk out or become Super Soldiers. That's not how it works. For transgender men like Bailar, there were very real trade-offs when evaluating possible athletic achievement over a four-year career. In the women's category, Bailar was looking at the possibility of competing for conference championships, swimming at the NCAA national championships, and maybe even making it to the Olympic Trials. By switching categories, Bailar would be starting in the men's category with only a few months of testosterone, compared to the other men on the team, who presumably had begun puberty six to nine years prior. Over time, that disadvantage would shrink because hormones take time to affect a person's body, but switching categories would likely mean sacrificing certain goals.

It was a conversation with his father that changed everything. He sat down next to Bailar and said, "Schuyler, you're hinging this decision on being a successful athlete and winning all these medals in the women's record book, but you've already done a lot of that. And where are you? Will it matter to you if you keep being successful in this way? You've told me that those accolades don't mean very much to you."

That conversation with his father allowed Bailar to see his path forward. He decided to swim at Harvard on the men's team. In making that choice, he knew that he also needed to reexamine what success meant for him. Prior to his transition, Bailar measured success through his grades and swimming output. While at Harvard, he poured himself into advocacy and also focused on building social connections. In the pool, he was successful in the ways that mattered to him. Bailar didn't set any records at Harvard. He didn't qualify for NCAA championships, never swam in a conference championship meet, and didn't make the Olympic Trials ahead of the Tokyo Olympics. But as his conversation with his father had reminded him, Schuyler's happiness and alignment were far more important markers of success than any medal ever was or could be.

"There are plenty of people who feel that it was okay to stay competing as the gender they were assigned at birth," Bailar said. "I don't think there's anything wrong with that. It just wasn't right for me."

Bailar's sport was ostensibly the same no matter what team he swam with. The times were different, but the 100 breaststroke was still the 100 breaststroke. In some cases, however, the sport itself is gendered. Being a boy in a girls' sport, not just on a girls' or women's team, can be something else completely.

• • •

LESLIE COATES REALIZED early on that his child, River, had a really good arm. The two of them used to throw a ball back and forth in the yard, and Leslie loved baseball. He wasn't into sports growing up, and had a degree in musical theater, but there was something about baseball that Leslie loved. And he'd always wanted to share that with his child. "I remember asking the doctor, 'Developmentally, at what age should a child be able to throw and/or catch?'" Leslie said. "I was so eager."

Leslie hung up a mini basketball hoop—one of the ones that hangs on the door. And they played a game of their own invention. Leslie would be on his knees and River, who was maybe four or five at the time, would drive on Leslie to try to score. "It was very physical," Leslie said. "It was kind of a strange version of rugby-basketball."

But Leslie still loved baseball. He brought home a Wiffle ball set to teach River the sport he'd been such a big fan of for most of his life. And one day, Leslie and his wife, Trish, sat on their porch, tossing little balls down to their kid. The first couple swings of the bat were misses. But on the third or fourth pitch, the ball cracked against the bat and came sailing back at them, flying between the two of them and smacking against the metal door.

"We all just stopped," Leslie said.

The story has become part of Coates family lore. River displayed other athletic traits throughout childhood, often throwing balls back and forth with Leslie, accompanying him on fishing trips ("and casting accurately at age five right from the boat," Leslie said), and joining both of his parents on bike rides. When the family moved to Kansas during River's childhood, a neighbor commented, "There goes the family on wheels," as they rode down the street one day. As a unit, they were often doing something, or rolling somewhere.

But River was also noticeably good at stick-and-ball sports, as evidenced by the day Leslie and Trish sat on the steps and watched a Wiffle ball sail between them. So River began to play softball like other kids his age who were assigned female at birth. He played catcher and he was good. All that throwing he'd done with his dad was put to good use every time he whipped the ball from behind the plate to throw out a base runner.

As River got a bit older, Leslie and Trish could sense that their child was different. One night in bed, they lay down just kind of looking up at the ceiling and Trish looked over at Leslie. "What if [River] is gay?" she asked.

Leslie scoffed. "What do you mean 'if'?"

River being transgender wasn't on their radar; they didn't know much about that as parents. But River being part of the queer community felt very much like a forgone conclusion. As he entered adolescence, River began to share with his parents more about how he saw his gender. He shared the name he wanted to use on a family trip. He originally communicated that he was nonbinary, though he would later say that he was a transgender boy and using he/him pronouns. These developments surprised Trish and Leslie. "We left all this space for sexuality," Leslie said to me. "But we didn't even know about the gender thing."

And the gender thing started to complicate softball for River. After that conversation the family began seeing a therapist together. River settled into his identity as a transgender boy, rather than being nonbinary. (It's worth noting that this identity movement isn't reflective of indecision or a lack of conviction in that identity. In a world that projects relative rigidity when it comes to gender, it's not always easy to decipher how a person deviates from that rigidity should they discover that they do.) He began using he/him pronouns, and he was still playing softball, which by definition was a sport for girls. That's not true everywhere—there are robust fast-pitch options for men in Australia, for example—but in the United States, fast-pitch softball is largely a girls' and women's sport.

River was reminded of that fact each time someone referred to the team as "girls" or "ladies." As he communicated his name change, River worried that someone would call out his old name as they threw the ball to him. "And I wouldn't respond and get hit in the head with a softball," River said to me.

Those feelings were further compounded as he and his teammates entered their teenage years. They used to just wear their uniforms to games. Now there were ponytails and ribbons and makeup. They wore dresses and talked about boys and River didn't. The more attuned River became to himself, the greater the distance between himself and his teammates and between himself and the sport he loved.

Leslie could see that distance too. River would often be by himself with his headphones plugged into his ears, sitting under a tree between games. This sport that Leslie and River had loved together wasn't quite the same. So when River's travel team disintegrated because of drama with the team, Leslie was preparing to scramble and find River a new place to play. But River said he didn't want to play in the fall. And then COVID-19 canceled softball for everyone in 2020 anyway. Once it became possible for River to play again, he decided not to. When offered a spot on a team, River said to his dad, "I was in some dark places trying to play that game and I'm not willing to go back to those places for my own health."

As of this writing, River is fifteen years old and retired from sports. He took up photography, something both of his parents had experimented with previously. "I like the way photography makes me look at the world," he said. "Everything can have beauty in it and it just takes finding the right angle." His softball gear stayed in a closet. He considered baseball, but ultimately didn't think it was for him. "It's not a community I feel safe in," he said. He'd even stopped throwing with his dad.

But one night during the summer of 2021, River and Leslie went to a Wichita Wind Surge game together with a group from their church. The Wind Surge are a Double-A feeder club for the Minnesota Twins. It was the first time River and Leslie had done anything related to sports since River shared that he was transgender and stopped playing softball. In the second inning, River leaned over to his dad and made a comment about the batter's hand placement. For the rest of the game River and Leslie discussed technical observations they were making about the play of the game, just chatting back and forth. After a year of a door being closed, it felt like it was starting to open again.

A couple of days later, Leslie was out mowing the lawn. It was a beautiful summer evening. After finishing up outside, Leslie walked in to find River. "Riv," he said, "do you want to play catch with me?"

"Yeah," River said. They each grabbed a glove and played catch in the backyard for the first time in almost two years. Trish sat outside and watched the two of them play together like they used to.

River wasn't sure if he'd ever play organized sports again, though he hadn't closed the door on something like track and field. But he has no regrets about leaving softball. "It was worth it," he said. "For a long time when I was playing softball, I didn't know whether it would be worth it to quit to pursue who I was, because softball was one of the only things that brought me joy and comfort. But looking back it was very worth it because I don't know if I could have survived playing softball the way I did."

I'm not sure that anything could have kept River playing softball, and it was clear from listening to him that wasn't his goal. But something River said to his dad made me think: he said he'd play again if it was an all-queer team. For me, that put in stark relief the importance of the disconnection and lack of belonging River felt in the softball community he was part of. Despite the cultural reputation softball has as a queer-friendly sport, it can create a conformist culture just like any other sport (hello, hair ribbons). River feeling ostracized wasn't due to purposeful mistreatment or malicious intent from River's teammates; River just didn't fit in. He was a boy on a girls' team in a girls' sport. And then there was the not small factor that once medical transition entered the picture, he wouldn't have been able to play softball anyway. Neither River nor Leslie brought that up, but it is a consideration for many transgender men at some point. Whereas policies for transgender women have mostly focused on testosterone suppression, policies for transgender men have been focused on the inverse: all about what happens when a transgender man starts taking testosterone, should they choose to do so. For transgender boys like River, that meant that eventually a path forward in a gendered sport like softball would be impossible.

When River did start testosterone in the summer of 2022, however, something unexpected happened. After hanging up his softball cleats after the fall 2019 season, River wanted to play baseball. The confidence he got from feeling more at home in his body and having his identity affirmed consistently by those around him opened River up to the idea that he should try out for his high school team in the spring. He started working with a hitting coach to retool his swing to be more suited for baseball. The coach had worked with both softball and baseball players, which River felt would help him switch from one sport to the other. But he doesn't want to put any pressure on himself. "We're just seeing where it goes, you know?" River said.

When River started testosterone, the biggest change in his life was confidence. He's taking harder classes and voluntarily doing extra work. He's not avoiding being around cisgender guys anymore. Before starting testosterone, being around cisgender boys made River feel uncomfortable. He was always comparing himself to them and felt like he stuck out. That self-consciousness led him to avoiding his cisgender peers most of the time. Testosterone has changed all of that, opening doors and possibilities for River in sports as well.

River had spent the summer of 2022 working as an umpire at the softball field down the road from his house, the same field he learned to play on when he was younger. As he watched the kids hit the ball and run around the bases, he felt a familiar itch. He wanted to play again. He got his old tee and set it up in the yard. River didn't have a lot of baseballs, but he knew there were some floating around the house and the backyard, so he went on a personal baseball hunt to round up the handful of balls he could find. And he had his softball bat. He put a ball on the tee and took a swing. Then, he took another. And another. "I felt at peace," River said.

So he traded in his softball bat for store credit to help him buy a new baseball bat. "It felt good, but weird," he said.

River's story represents the young people I often think about when I consider these issues. He's just a teenager in Kansas who loves swinging a bat and throwing out runners from behind home plate. He's not going to become a professional athlete and isn't in line for a college scholarship. He's someone who is going to try out for the baseball team because he thinks the sport is fun. "For three years, it felt impossible to even think about playing on a baseball team with a bunch of cis boys from Kansas," River said. "But it's doable. It's hard, but it's worth it. If you love the sport and this is something you want to do, then it's going to be worth it."

WHEN MOSIER QUALIFIED for the 2016 Duathlon World Championships, it was not immediately clear that he would be able to compete. The primary driver of policy for transgender people in sports has been the notion of keeping transgender women out rather than including transgender men. The IOC published a set of guidelines (commonly referred to as the Stockholm Consensus) ahead of the 2004 Olympics that set the parameters for transgender people to compete in accordance with their gender identities. Those guidelines required surgery (specifically a gonadectomy), legal documentation, and an unspecified length of hormone therapy.[1] These requirements did not consider transgender men at all, as transgender men do not typically receive gonadectomies as part of their care. Additionally, for the purposes of sports competition, surgery doesn't address the core concerns people have about competitive advantage; hormones and testosterone are the primary drivers there. Plus, surgery is a personal choice for transgender people. Surgical requirements for athletic eligibility are now seen as outdated, but some high school associations do still recommend surgery as an eligibility requirement, which, again, is outside the standards of care for minors.

In the updated 2015 consensus statement, the IOC changed course, allowing for transgender men to compete in the men's category "without restriction."[2] But there would still be restrictions on the women's category, including bans against doping. Transgender men taking testosterone in the women's category would technically qualify as doping. That had been the status quo, stemming from the 2015 IOC statement and the 2010 NCAA policy. But in 2021, that ground began to shift.

The National Women's Soccer League (NWSL) released a transgender athlete policy that multiple parties found to be upsetting. I'll come back to policy in a later chapter, but what's interesting for the purposes of discussing transgender men is that the NWSL was the first major professional league that adopted a policy that allowed transgender men (and also nonbinary athletes) to take testosterone as long as they kept their levels below 10 nmol/L.[3] In October 2021, the Premier Hockey Federation, formerly the National Women's Hockey League, updated its transgender athlete participation policy to something similar (but I'll go into more detail on that later). The PHF policy also allowed for transgender men to take testosterone and continue to play in the league if they received a therapeutic use exemption (TUE).[4] These types of policies remove a key barrier for transgender men on the elite level, resolving the tension between choosing their sport or their medical transition. Whether it's good policy is another question altogether. But for transgender men competing in gender-specific team sports, it has created opportunities for them to continue their professional careers as their authentic selves instead of needing to make a choice.

It's the opposite direction from what's happening in those states that chose to restrict transgender athletes under the law. The inclusion of transgender boys and men in some of these laws revealed the intentions of some lawmakers and the reality that maybe the controversy of transgender athletes wasn't just about science and protecting the category of women's sports, but rather placing restrictions on transgender people *because they're transgender.*

As we've discussed, much of the attention being paid to transgender athletes focuses on transgender women and girls, and often the argument for restrictive policies—sometimes laws—is that transgender girls and women have an unfair advantage in sports on account of being assigned male at birth. As we've seen, higher levels of testosterone do confer athletic and metabolic advantages, but the science isn't clear on whether transgender women have a clear advantage in competition. In the public fight about transgender athletes, transgender boys and men are barely brought up. But that doesn't mean they aren't targeted.

Multiple states that have passed laws banning transgender girls and women from women's sports also ban transgender boys and men from competing in men's sports. Tennessee's law requires eligibility for sports to be determined by a student's original birth certificate.[5] Texas took their law a step further. In 2021, Texas filed more bills targeting the LGBTQ+ community than any other state. Almost none of them passed into law, but one did, SB 25. Unlike similar pieces of legislation that have moved away from using birth certificates—Barbara Ehardt from Idaho said this was an explicit move of hers because birth certificates can be amended and chromosomes cannot—Texas leaned in to the existing birth certificate rule at the high school association level. The resulting law mirrored the policy that forced Mack Beggs to wrestle girls.

SB 25 codifies the existing UIL policy of using sex assigned at birth as the determinative factor for gender eligibility in sports, which forced Mack Beggs to wrestle in the girls' category, and it explicitly outlaws all transgender youth from playing sports in a manner consistent with their gender identity. "An interscholastic athletic team sponsored or authorized by a school district or open-enrollment charter school may not allow a student to compete in an interscholastic athletic competition sponsored or authorized by the district or school that is designated for the biological sex opposite to the student's biological sex as correctly stated on the student's official birth certificate," the law reads. The exception is if there is no team for girls, then someone assigned female at birth—regardless of gender identity—is eligible to play on that team. Like football.

These laws are indefensible from a scientific perspective. Even if I wholly accepted the premise of testosterone giving an advantage to transgender girls and women (which I do not), it would stand to reason that by the accepted logic, transgender boys and men would have no advantage. That's why the policy status quo allowed for transgender men to compete in the men's category without restriction. The whole argument hinged on the premise that people assigned female at birth were athletically inferior, so why do they need to be restricted from sports participation?

The only logical explanation was ideology and animus. Texas filed more anti-LGBTQ+ legislation during the 2021 legislative session than any other state by orders of magnitude. I'm all for engaging in good-faith discussion on these issues, but sometimes it's important just to call a spade a spade. The targeting of transgender men just doesn't hold water scientifically, especially if we're talking about young people.

I keep coming back to young people because that is where so much of this legislation lands, despite people saying they want to focus on elite sports. There are real questions and debates to be had on a policy level about who should be able to compete in the women's category under what circumstances. But we're having separate conversations simultaneously, and that creates confusion. It also obfuscates the heart of the matter, in my opinion. It's usually at this point when I'm asked to give my opinion, to answer the question: "What should we do?" I don't normally answer, but I think it's time that I do.

12.

THE ANSWERS TO THE QUESTIONS I'M ALWAYS ASKED

THERE COMES A moment in most interviews—whether I am the interviewer or the interviewee—when someone asks me the dreaded question: What do you think is fair? My typical answer is some word salad about how it's not my job to recommend policy (it isn't), and here are the various things to consider as you weigh your own position. But something happened during the course of reporting on Lia Thomas. Though my reporting approach did not change, I was being called biased for simply reporting all sides of the issue and also because of my own identity as a nonbinary person. More than one news outlet specifically noted my pronouns in copy when citing my reporting, as a means of casting doubt on my ability to report on and think about these issues. It was a sudden development of scrutiny that made me feel the political heat of the moment. My identity, the person I am, was suddenly a problem. I was always careful and measured in my reporting, but I can't change the person I am, nor do I think that's a reasonable criticism and expectation. But it did give me a window into what many of the transgender folks I'd spoken with over the years felt as their essence, not their actions, were vilified.

I've thought long and hard about how and why I would eventually answer the question of what I think. These are complex issues; if I could answer this question in three bullet points, there would have been no need to write an entire book. The first time I wrote about transgender athlete policy was in 2018. I thought it was going to be a one-off piece about a couple of high school athletes and the challenges they faced in those moments. I never imagined that it would develop into a professional specialty, or that it would dominate so much of the sports discussion in recent years.

While I was reporting for this book, sources regularly asked me what I believed in an effort to gauge how I might treat them. When I was covering Lia Thomas, I found that lots of people were assuming what I believed based on the fact that I'm non-binary. Candidly, I'm not a fan of people I don't know making assumptions about me, so I've decided to share my thoughts on the topics and issues we've explored in these pages, answering the questions I've often ducked.

I want to be clear: I am not advocating a position that I want you to believe. I hope that as you've read the first eleven chapters of this book you've been considering your own positions on these issues, your values, and what you believe to be true as it concerns gender and sports. If I'm asking you to do that, then I think it's only fair that you know unequivocally where I stand—though I do reserve the right to change my mind. As do you.

Because this question is so difficult to answer with a single

228 • FAIR PLAY

sentence describing policy, I've divided my thoughts across age groups, competition types, and relevant topics.

YOUTH SPORTS

My bright line concerns transgender youth. There is no scientific or empirical evidence to suggest that the categorical bans passing state Houses across the country are required to protect the integrity of women's sports. Many of the laws that have passed affect youth as young as elementary school. Frankly, there isn't even a need to sex-separate sports before puberty, let alone restrict access to those sports on the basis of what amounts to pure animus.

The American tradition of youth sports has tied those opportunities to education. I cannot accept a system that would allow for transgender youth to be affirmed in the classroom but be othered on a sports team. (Nor can I accept transgender youth being discriminated against in schools when it comes to being affirmed in the classroom and having access to bathroom and locker room spaces. That's a slightly different topic, but I want it on the record.) When it comes to high school, I understand that puberty is messy and there could be some concern about competitive advantage for transgender girls, but I also cannot accept a system that mandates hormone therapy or medical treatment to participate in school sports. Morally and philosophically, I simply cannot get there.

A big reason why I am not in favor of such measures is that I am not convinced that transgender youth participating in school sports is a problem. Yes, Andraya Yearwood and Terry Miller won a bunch of track championships in Connecticut.

That is an undisputed fact. Those are the only two athletes in the public consciousness who competed (and won) in a state without legal and/or medical requirements for transgender athletes to participate in accordance with their gender identities. If such policies created environments where transgender girls could dominate girls' sports, then it would stand to reason that there would be more examples in Connecticut and/or in other states that have similar policies. The truth is that there are not. Since Andraya Yearwood and Terry Miller graduated from high school in 2020, there has not been a single controversial case of a transgender athlete competing in school sports in the state of Connecticut. Even as legislation was passing from 2020 to 2022, lawmakers were citing *Connecticut* rather than cases in their own states . . . because there were no controversial cases in their states.

Furthermore, the laws that have passed have created a culture of fear and distrust among transgender youth. Many laws passed in late 2021 and 2022, such as the one in Texas, have gone back to using birth certificates as the point of delineation of sex for sports participation, only these laws specifically outline the "original" birth certificate, which they define as being "issued at or near birth." How birth certificates are amended vary from state to state, with some states outlawing the ability to amend the gender marker altogether. It is not always clear that a birth certificate has been amended, and therefore what is "original" cannot be easily deduced. So if a transgender young person socially transitioned at a young age, began a medical transition in adolescence, and changed their birth certificate, it should not be assumed that any of that information could be made public. Such a student, however, could feel an intense amount of pressure to keep their transgender identity a secret out of fear of retribution from the school and/or the state. Just writing this paragraph felt dystopian.

These laws prey on assumptions we, as a society, make about gender, as well as on the reality that many people are unfamiliar with transgender people. Going back to something Idaho Representative Barbara Ehardt said in chapter 9: "Our mind's eye will paint a picture when we're talking about something based on the descriptive words we use"; the use of "biological male" is meant to conjure an image of a cisgender boy masquerading as a woman for the express purpose of dominating girls' sports. That's not who transgender youth are at all. It's not who transgender adults are. The obsessive focus on biology in lower-stakes sports, particularly before high school, strips transgender young people of their humanity. They're kids who want to play sports with their friends. And we should let them.

Youth participation in sports is declining. If there's one thing that people on all sides of this issue agree on, it's that kids playing sports is a good thing. Creating more barriers for any group of young people to participate in sports is bad policy in my mind, especially if we are talking about elementary and middle school students. We should be encouraging all students in those age groups to play sports. The fact that legislation is creating an environment to push specific groups of young people out of sports in service of a particular political agenda is objectively terrible.

Transgender youth are offering us an opportunity to reconsider the entire business of how youth play sports and why. For decades, the stakes surrounding young people and their pastimes have continued to rise. Smarter people than me have

continued to highlight the ways in which the professionaliza-
tion of youth sports and activities have negative impacts on
kids and adults alike. Perhaps we should take this opportunity
to reevaluate.

COLLEGE SPORTS

When it comes to college athletics, what's appropriate depends on
the level of competition. Many of the recently passed laws affect
intramural sports at public universities. For all intents and purposes, intramural sports are recreational sports, and many intramural sports are co-ed. There is simply no reason for transgender
women to be banned from intramural volleyball or women's flag
football or softball or tennis. Even if there is a slight advantage in
terms of speed or size, it's intramural sports; there are no stakes.
By definition, it's for fun and to stay in shape.

For NCAA Division III athletics, there are no scholarships,
and there is no money to be made for the college or student-
athletes (unless a student-athlete is also an influencer on social
media). For that reason, there also is no need for restrictions
when it comes to the participation of transgender athletes, including those who are nonbinary and/or genderqueer. They
should be able to participate and compete wherever feels best
for them.

Sometimes there are concerns about more physical sports
like hockey and rugby. Frankly, that concern is overblown. Girls
and women have been playing competitive hockey in co-ed environments for decades; there's no reason to think that transgender women specifically pose any kind of safety threat that
would warrant a categorical ban at the Division III level. Hell,
a transgender woman played professional hockey in Canada

for years—and was a defensewoman, no less—and didn't send anyone to the hospital. Same goes for rugby, which has been inclusive of all genders in the United States, literally for decades, despite World Rugby passing a ban in 2020 on transgender women playing women's rugby at the international level.

There is the argument that while there may not be scholarships in Division III, athletics can be used for preferential treatment to gain admission to elite schools, but perhaps that issue should also be reexamined (by someone else, in another book). Regardless, that particularly thorny topic has nothing to do with transgender athletes.

For NCAA Division II and Division I athletics, I am not opposed to restrictions when they make sense and provide a pathway to participation for all transgender athletes, including transgender women, in a manner that is consistent with their gender identities. The recent policy shift toward embracing different rules for different sports makes sense to me, but it remains to be seen exactly what shape those policies will take (more on that in the next chapter). Even at the Division I and II levels, I think categorical bans are inappropriate, as are burdensome restrictions like a subjective medical panel operating with no publicly shared criteria.

PROFESSIONAL AND OLYMPIC-LEVEL SPORTS

My feelings on professional and Olympic-level sports mirror my views for the collegiate level. This is the highest level of competition that we have, and as such, restrictions are appropriate. There are already strict rules and regulations governing all athletes in elite sports as it pertains to doping and hormone levels, so it would make sense to me that a similar level of scrutiny be applied to questions of eligibility in gendered categories. I want to underscore, however, that a path to participation is my belief at all levels. The barrier to entry is already so high for elite sport that even getting into that level requires a tremendous amount of skill. There can be hoops, but those hoops should allow for an athlete to successfully jump through them to be able to compete. And that athlete may, in fact, win a race or an Olympic medal.

An emerging consideration is that of transgender men and nonbinary athletes who wish to take testosterone and remain eligible to compete in the women's category. This is a question mostly for those who did not medically transition prior to puberty and who are elite athletes not wanting to choose between their sport and who they are. I will be honest and say that I'm not sure where I net out on that question. In general, I feel comfortable saying that I have fewer hesitations when it comes to team sports. A single person taking testosterone for the purposes of transitioning on a hockey or soccer or basketball team doesn't feel like that much of an issue. Will that person gain some strength and speed? Absolutely. Is it enough to have an overwhelming impact on the performance of a team? That I don't know, but I'm inclined to say probably not.

Individual sports, however, are another issue altogether, especially those focused on strength and speed. Medically transitioning and continuing to compete in the women's category in sports like track or swimming doesn't feel appropriate to me. To be clear, this viewpoint is separate from questions about naturally occurring higher levels of testosterone in people assigned female at birth. They should absolutely be able to compete in the women's category. The difference is in how athletes in women's sports with naturally high levels of testosterone process and access that androgen. Those athletes, by definition, process androgen differently physiologically.

RECREATIONAL AND INTRAMURAL SPORTS

We seem to have forgotten that this is where the majority of us experience sports for most of our lives. Chances are that if you're reading this book, you didn't go to the Olympics (though if you did, congrats!). There is a very specific window of competitive high school sports where these questions become messiest. But other than that, unless we're looking at high-level elite sports, this just shouldn't be an issue. Let everyone play and let them participate in the ways that feel most comfortable for them. Does that mean if you're in a rec volleyball league, someone who is a transgender woman may wish to participate as well and she may be reasonably tall? I mean, sure. But she could not be that tall. And she could be bad!

There is this idea that somehow transgender people have sports superpowers. Just because a person is trans doesn't mean they will be good at sports. Some tall people are shitty basketball players. Some fast people are not great at soccer. Even if, in the abstract, you accept the premise that transgender women specifically might be a little "taller, faster, stronger" than cisgender women if they transitioned after puberty, it still takes skill to be good at sports. And being good at sports only matters if there are stakes. I don't think rec league trophies qualify. Or local 5K runs. Or your intramural basketball team. Or your kid's T-ball team.

FAIRNESS

What is fair? Whether sitting on a panel, chatting with friends, or fielding questions from my family at a holiday gathering, this question always comes up. And often it's asked out of a genuine desire to preserve the integrity of a sports competition. I define that integrity as being the public's belief that a competition result is just and the rewards were earned. For many, the participation of transgender girls and women in girls' and women's sports will *never* be fair, for all of the reasons we've explored in these pages. I reject that, for the simple reason that sports, by design, are not fair.

I want to be clear what I mean by that. I'm not suggesting that we shouldn't try to create a just system or that we should simply throw up our hands, or that fairness doesn't matter. But when we talk about fairness, there's this underlying belief that fairness means that there is an equal chance for everyone to win or be successful at sports. That is untrue regardless of how a person feels about transgender athletes.

For example, school districts with more resources have the ability to pay for better facilities, draw better enrollments, pay coaches more, etc. Is that fair? Some athletes who come from affluent families can hire specialized coaches to aid their development. Is that fair? Some athletes are taller in sports that preference height, and some are faster in those that preference speed. Is that fair?

The reality of sports is that we accept unfairness all the time. So what role does fairness play when it comes to transgender and gender-expansive athletes? One of the ideas Joanna Harper talks about is "meaningful competition." In this context, "meaningful competition" is acknowledging that, in some circumstances, transgender women in particular may retain some physiological advantages if they went through testosterone-driven puberty. Negating those advantages may not be entirely possible, but that doesn't mean the advantage is overwhelming or unfair. In other words, a transgender woman may win a race or be part of a winning team, but that doesn't mean the result was predetermined. Given the information available from a science perspective, it's hard for me to accept an argument that the mere *existence* of a possible physiological advantage amounts to an overwhelming performance advantage in all sports at all levels in all cases. There is not nearly enough evidence to make such a claim.

There has never been an example of a transgender woman competing in women's sports who is unbeatable, especially over time. Power lifter Laurel Hubbard had a very successful career and made it to the Olympics, where she finished last in her weight class, without completing a lift. All of the women who beat her were cisgender. Andraya Yearwood and Terry Miller won state championships, and they both lost races to their cisgender competitors. Juniper Eastwood won a conference championship in collegiate cross-country. She did not come close to the podium at nationals. CeCé Telfer won a Division II national championship in the 400m hurdles, but she placed fifth in that same meet in the 100m hurdles. And Lia Thomas, for all of the hullabaloo about how she was going to threaten Katie Ledecky's and Missy Franklin's records, won a national championship and placed fifth and eighth in her other races, and broke no national records. Everyone who beat her was cisgender, that we know of, with the exception of Henig. For every athlete who I just named, there are tens, if not hundreds, of transgender athletes whose names we don't know who have competed without incident because they never won or were never perceived as a threat. I struggle to find where the overwhelming unfairness is.

ATHLETES WITH DIFFERENCES OF SEX DEVELOPMENT

Caster Semenya and other athletes like her should be able to compete in the women's category. This is different for me than the question of transgender men competing in the women's category while medically transitioning, for a couple of reasons. The first is that to be 46 XY DSD and assigned female at birth, by definition there is a physiological anomaly that affects how the body processes androgens; otherwise, a person with 46 chromosomes who is XY would have been assigned male at birth. The second is that, at least in Caster Semenya's case, she clearly and explicitly has identified as a woman her entire life. Are athletes with intersex variations overrepresented in elite women's track and field? Maybe. But there has not been sufficient scientific evidence to remove them from the women's category.

WOMEN'S SPORTS

I wouldn't have a career without the existence of women's sports. I grew up playing girls' basketball. I coached girls' basketball. I cover women's sports at all levels. I can barely watch the NBA playoffs without succumbing to boredom, because I find it to be completely uninteresting compared to the WNBA. (If you love men's sports, I am not judging you. I watch football, soccer, and Formula 1. I'm just saying that I love women's sports more).

The natural conclusion of complicating the gender binary

is a movement to reorganize sports and do away with sex and gender categories altogether. However, I don't believe that is realistic. Selfishly, I enjoy women's sports, so I would like to keep them. Also, global sport is sex separated, and trying to undo that is a fool's errand. Another reason why I find that strategy to be unrealistic is that women's sports in the United States already do not receive the funding and resources that they are entitled to under the law. I have no confidence that without a protected category of women's sports anyone other than cisgender men would receive any funding and support at all, even if there were cisgender women who could successfully compete against and with boys and men. Just look at Esports, where there are few women competing professionally. There's no physiological differences between sexes that should push women out of competitive video games, and yet, sexism is one hell of a drug.

There is a fear that by allowing transgender women into women's sports, and thereby women's locker rooms, that those spaces cease to be safe for cisgender women. Often, these concerns are raised in service of needing privacy. I'm of the opinion that there should be more privacy in all locker rooms. Individual showers and bathroom stalls for all. But I also think it's important to acknowledge that the conversation about transgender girls and women participating in sports in accordance with their gender identity has opened the door to a vast amount of transphobia that extends far beyond a sincere question about the ways in which testosterone-driven puberty affects physiological and metabolic advantages in sports. I grew up playing sports, and the locker room was a bastion of team bonding. We had dance parties and cracked jokes. We did not sit around naked, staring at one another's bodies. Personally, I cannot think of a single instance when my bare behind was visible to my teammates. We were all pros at putting on underwear and shorts underneath our towels, strapping our bras on over the towels, and then pulling the towels off and doing our hair. Spending time with teammates in those casual environments is important for team chemistry. And, frankly, sharing space with a transgender woman is sharing space with another woman.

One of the most essential things we could do to heal our sports culture is to have more co-ed sporting experiences last longer in childhood. That Boys and Girls club basketball league I wrote about in chapter 5 was important for two reasons: one, it gave me confidence that I could compete with boys, and two, it showed boys that a bunch of "girls" could compete with and beat them. As a society, we constantly tell boys that they are better at sports because they are boys, and we tell the opposite to girls. Notice that we don't say that because of testosterone-driven puberty boys develop physiological traits that help them succeed in a sporting culture designed to exploit those traits. That would be too complicated to explain. A more gender-inclusive sporting culture at young ages is better for all kids of all genders. And I think it has the power to be transformative. Young girls would gain confidence, boys wouldn't be told that they're automatically better by birthright, and those with more fluid and gender-expansive identities wouldn't need to choose a category until physiologically necessary. And when that happened, the experience might be better!

13.

THE FUTURE OF POLICY

ON NOVEMBER 16, 2021, a group representing the International Olympic Committee announced sweeping changes to its policy governing participation for transgender and intersex athletes. I'd been hearing about possible changes and adjustments for years. First, I heard they would be announced before the Tokyo Games, and then after. And sure enough, barely three months removed from the conclusion of the Tokyo Games, an announcement was being made from Lausanne, Switzerland.

I, of course, was not in Lausanne, but instead was curled up on my IKEA chaise in my living room, attached to my computer, waiting to hear exactly what the IOC's update would be. In the years leading up to this moment, more transgender athletes had begun to emerge at various levels of competition, and there was ongoing debate around inclusion and eligibility for athletes with intersex variations. As discussed in these pages, laws in the United States had become more restrictive, and the World Athletics policy for track and field had also become increasingly restrictive. The IOC was undoubtedly under a lot of pressure and hearing from a lot of voices. What the organization would do was a question that had me on pins and needles.

What the IOC announced was not a policy. Instead, the IOC unveiled a framework of guiding principles to inform the international federations as they developed their own policies for each of their sports. Previously, the IOC's policy had been uniform and applied to all Olympic sports. Moving forward, that wouldn't be the case. The IOC's move also created a policy void that would have to be filled. Many international federations had previously deferred to the IOC's standards (with a couple of notable exceptions) to determine eligibility for transgender and intersex athletes. Without that guidance, more policies would have to be written and published in the coming years, upending the eligibility landscape for transgender and intersex athletes in women's sports.

Titled "IOC Framework on Fairness, Inclusion and Non-discrimination on the Basis of Gender Identity and Sex Variations," the document outlined ten principles. They were as follows: inclusion, prevention of harm, nondiscrimination, fairness, no presumption of advantage, evidence-based approach, primacy of health and bodily autonomy, stakeholder-centered approach, right to privacy, and periodic reviews.[1] I know, it reads kind of like word salad, but the message was straightforward enough. Basically, the IOC said that as federations developed their own policies, they shouldn't ban transgender and/or intersex people from women's sports based on the assumption that those athletes have advantages, and if the federations were going to impose restrictions, they should have "robust, peer-reviewed evidence."[2]

It seemed simple enough, but there was a bit of a catch. The IOC was only *recommending* the federations do this. There were no consequences unveiled should a federation enact a policy that grated against this framework. World Athletics already had a policy on the books that didn't comply with this new framework, but IOC representatives repeatedly declined to criticize World Athletics directly. Besides, what was the IOC going to do? Kick track and field out of the Olympics?

The IOC framework came with no teeth and no enforcement mechanism. The federations would likely do as they pleased, which, technically, they were entitled to do. Because again, it didn't seem like the IOC was willing to criticize, let alone punish, a federation for putting a policy in place that the IOC might find to be too restrictive. It didn't take long for the first domino to fall.

JUNE 2022 MARKED a new era for policy governing transgender athletes on the international level. Because of the announcements of the IOC and NCAA in late 2021 and early 2022, respectively, the policy landscape had been relatively open. Part of the reason there was such an intense focus and back-and-forth about Lia Thomas was due to these dynamics. When it came to regulating eligibility for the women's category, the direction of that policy had been unclear for half a year after having a shared framework for the previous decade.

The Union Cycliste Internationale (UCI), which is the international federation for cycling, governing the Tour de France, Olympic cycling, and other disciplines of international biking competition, was the first international organization to make a move in the new world order. The organization responded to transgender cyclist Emily Bridges' entering the British National

Omnium Championships in the women's category after twelve months of testosterone suppression by blocking her entry and announcing a new transgender athlete policy. That policy requires twenty-four months of suppression under a testosterone threshold of 2.5 nmol/L. On the international stage, it was the strictest policy to date, doubling the time of testosterone suppression and halving the previously used testosterone threshold of 5 nmol/L.

Bridges' mother, Sandy, wrote a statement on social media in response to UCI's policy update. "As you [can] imagine, this uncertainty and moving of goalposts has created a significant amount of distress and upset to Em, to us as a family, and the wider trans community," she wrote, in part.

At the 2022 FINA World Championships in Budapest, Hungary, representatives from the membership gathered for an "Extraordinary General Congress" to vote on a new policy for transgender athletes. Since World Aquatics is the international swimming federation, its policy will reorient the policies for each country's national governing body, including USA Swimming. The announced World Aquatics policy went a step further than UCI, defining eligibility for both the men's and women's categories as follows:

- Eligibility for the men's category will be open to anyone who wants to compete in that category regardless of legal sex and/or gender identity, including transgender men, transgender women, people who are gender expansive, and those with differences of sex development.
- Eligibility for the women's category will be restricted to cisgender women (and presumably transgender men who have

not started hormone therapy). Transgender women and athletes with differences of sex development will be eligible *only* if they can prove they never experienced testosterone-driven puberty.

That means that any transgender woman athlete who transitioned after the onset of puberty—the age World Aquatics' consulted medical expert used was twelve—will not be eligible to compete in the women's category at FINA-sanctioned contests, including world championships and the Olympics, under any circumstances. This is a marked departure from previous policies that provided a pathway to participation for athletes who transitioned in early or even late adulthood, after a time frame of testosterone suppression. Announced days after UCI's policy, World Aquatics' policy easily became the most restrictive one in the world. But, more important, World Aquatics' policy was the first indication of what could be the new direction of policy regulating transgender participation in elite sports.

"We are going in a much more restrictive direction in terms of policies," Chris Mosier said. "[Anti-transgender activists] are proactively reaching out to national governing bodies and international federations trying to get in front of them to create more restrictive policies or full-out bans."

"I think we are going to see a mix of incredibly restrictive policies with some more progressive policies," Anne Lieberman said. "I also think, though, that we are seeing a very clear intervention point by a number of different organizations working at the intersection of human rights and sport who are saying, 'No, you cannot support either scientifically or ethically outright bans on trans women and girls on women intersex variations, because the science simply does not support it.'"

Lia Thomas was in Greece when she got the news. Thomas was eating dinner with friends while on vacation. Her phone kept vibrating with text messages from loved ones checking in on her and asking if she'd seen the news. She didn't have the slightest idea what anyone was talking about. After some quick googling, Thomas realized what had just happened. She'd said previously that she wanted to swim at the Olympic Trials, like her brother had before her. She wanted to keep swimming, and keep competing. The World Aquatics decision took that off the table and effectively ended her career. She didn't say another word for the rest of dinner. "I was so shocked," she said to me. "I just retreated back into myself."

In its broadcast meeting announcing this policy, World Aquatics representatives took great care to say that all athletes are welcome to participate in aquatics and that this specific policy applies to World Aquatics events and World Aquatics events only. In service of that stated commitment to inclusion, World Aquatics announced the organization would explore what an open category of competition could look like. But the fact remains that for transgender girls, there will not be a spot in elite women's swimming competition unless they begin testosterone suppression by age twelve.

What does that mean in a country where transgender identity is rarely affirmed and access to care is scrutinized? In the United States, multiple states have considered and passed bills criminalizing access to the kind of gender-affirming health care that would allow for a transgender girl to transition in such a way that she could be eligible for World Aquatics events under the organization's new policy. Texas instructed its Department of Family and Protective Services to investigate parents of transgender youth receiving such care under suspicion of child abuse. Clinics such as GENECIS in Dallas, Texas, have been the site of protests by the far right. The existence of transgender young people, beyond their ability to play sports, has increasingly been politicized and scrutinized. World Aquatics, as an organization, wants to look at its policy in a vacuum, only weighing the science of testosterone, when in reality, these policies operate in conditions that are anything but a vacuum. *Everything* is politicized.

There's also the fact that even though World Aquatics explicitly stated that this policy was appropriate for only their elite competitions, there was no guarantee that national governing bodies wouldn't impose these types of restrictions on non-elite competition. There was also the reality that because World Aquatics took the first step to impose what was effectively a ban for most transgender women in women's sports, other organizations would likely follow. In the days and weeks following World Aquatics' announcement, that was exactly what happened.

The International Rugby League (IRL) banned transgender women from international competition "until further research is completed to enable the IRL to implement a formal transgender inclusion policy."[3] World Rugby, which sanctions union-style rugby, banned transgender women from women's competition in 2020.[4] Sebastian Coe of World Athletics weighed in, supporting World Aquatics. "We see an international federation asserting its primacy in setting rules, regulations, and policies that are in the best interest of its sport," Coe said to the BBC.[5] "This is as it should be. We have always believed that biology trumps gender and we will continue to review our regulations in line with this. We will follow the science."

In January 2023 World Athletics updated policy was publicly reported. The proposed policy would require transgender women and athletes with differences of sex development to suppress their testosterone level to 2.5 nmol/L for twenty-four months prior to being eligible for competition in women's events. When formally announced in March, however, the new regulations for transgender women mirrored World Aquatics' exactly, effectively banning them from competing in the women's category internationally. The DSD regulations were as previously reported.[6]

Previous policies have historically been seen as effective until a transgender athlete was successful. Inclusive high school policies became problems when two transgender girls found success in one state. The NCAA policy operated for a decade but suddenly became a problem after three transgender women were successful. The same can be said for the sports that were the first to announce updated policies at the elite level: cycling and swimming. Both sports responded to the prospect of transgender women competing in their ranks and those athletes being competitive and successful at the elite level. So what happens if a six-year-old transgender girl falls in love with swimming in Denver or Indianapolis or Seattle, never goes through testosterone-driven puberty, and makes the 2032 Olympic Trials? What if she wins?

What I keep coming back to is Lia Thomas in the pool, pulling her body through the water while staring down at the black line on the pool's tile bottom. She looked at that line for lap after lap after lap as she considered the fact that she knew she was transgender and she was swimming on the men's team, in the men's uniform, and she didn't know how she could possibly move forward. In the quiet of those moments, when the only thing she could hear was the swish of the water and her own thoughts, the thought she grappled with was whether she was willing to end her career to be who she was. Thomas learned in the subsequent months that she could still be a swimmer and there was a path forward for her. Had World Aquatics' policy been in effect, the outcome likely would have been different. And so the cumulative impact of this policy does, in fact, ensure that Lia Thomas will never be eligible to swim at the Olympics, but it also likely ensures that there will never be another Lia Thomas. Whether that is a measure of its effectiveness depends on the eye of the beholder.

But as some successfully advocated for more restrictive policies, others worked in the other direction, seeking to establish more open policies. Even in some professional leagues.

In October 2021, a month before the IOC handed down its new guidance, the Premier Hockey Federation (PHF), formerly the National Women's Hockey League (NWHL), announced a new policy for transgender athletes. Some of the first professional athletes to come out as transgender played professional women's hockey: Harrison Browne in the PHF/NWHL and Jessica Platt in the Canadian Women's Hockey League (CWHL). Both leagues put policies for transgender athletes into place as their respective players came out publicly. The CWHL, however, folded in 2019, leaving just the NWHL to carry the torch of professional women's hockey in North America. When the NWHL rebranded as PHF in September 2021, the league became the first professional women's league in North America without "women" in the title. It was an unconventional move, and so was the transgender athlete policy that followed. The policy was a strong departure from the status quo, designed to rethink the methods used to determine participation requirements for transgender athletes.

Typically in elite-level competition, whether collegiate, professional, or Olympic, the policies for transgender athletes hinge on hormone therapy and revolve around questions about when an athlete began hormone therapy, what kind, and what their hormone levels are. Even World Aquatics' new restrictive policy still hinges on testosterone and puberty. Those questions have very little to do with the person an athlete is and, for some advocates, continue the harmful pattern of dehumanizing transgender people by scrutinizing (and policing) their bodies. Of course, in elite athletics, body scrutiny and policing are not unique to transgender athletes, as we discussed in many of these pages. But a transgender policy that departed in a high-profile way from what has been the conventional scaffolding bracketing the rules and mores of transgender athletes hadn't been seen until PHF's policy.

The new policy adopted by PHF was different in a few key ways. For transgender women, there is no medical transition requirement. The policy is that transgender women must be "living in their identity for a minimum of two years."[7] Transgender men may participate in the PHF whether or not they have started hormone therapy. If taking testosterone for transition, transgender men can continue to play as long as they receive a therapeutic use exemption. There is no upper limit of testosterone given. All nonbinary athletes are also deemed eligible, regardless of sex assigned at birth. If an athlete was assigned female at birth, they are eligible without restrictions. For those assigned male at birth, they are eligible as long as they have been living in their identity for two years. No hormone suppression required.

PHF's policy made waves, both for the lack of hormone requirements for transgender women and for the longer wait time for transgender women to participate in the league. At the time, most policies used a twelve-month suppression requirement, so no suppression requirement but a two-year wait time had the unique distinction of being upsetting to pretty much everyone.

Personally, I think the policy raised good questions and ideas. Transgender inclusion policies (or exclusion policies) have been pretty much focused on hormones and the notion of competitive advantage for those who are assigned male at birth. The PHF benefitted from being a team sport. As I've said, I do think that team sports have the ability to be more flexible. One or two or a handful of athletes participating under this policy would not be likely to create a crisis. The policy also mentions an often-overlooked category of athletes in this conversation: those who don't fit the gender binary at all.

WHEN IT COMES to discussing transgender athletes in particular, the policy and public focus has been pretty fixed on binary transgender identities—transgender women and transgender men—and has been slow to begin a discussion that's more inclusive of athletes who don't identify in binary ways. There are a number of athletes who have competed at all levels of sports who identify as nonbinary or in other gender-expansive ways. Quinn, a professional Canadian soccer player, has publicly said they're nonbinary. G Ryan came out as genderqueer while swimming on the University of Michigan's women's swim team. Layshia Clarendon played in the WNBA for nearly a decade.

All of these athletes happen to spend their careers in women's sports, but there are gender-expansive athletes in men's sports as well. Griffin Brooks, the Princeton diver, is nonbinary. Jackson Harrison competes in men's club gymnastics at Arizona State University and is also nonbinary. Harrison started gymnastics at seven years old. They'd go to their older brother's football games but pay attention to the cheerleaders instead. When the game ended, Harrison trotted out to the grass and tried to copy everything the cheerleaders were doing. Eventually, their parents put them into gymnastics. They started competing soon after that.

Men's collegiate gymnastics, even at the club level, doesn't resemble cheerleading at all, however. "College teams are basically just frats with dedication," Harrison said. "I stand out more because I'm not a bro."

Harrison describes themselves as more feminine, which has given them a tense relationship with their sport at times. They came out as a freshman in high school, painting their nails and wearing makeup to school. While competing in gymnastics, Harrison battled an internal fear that they would be ostracized, "not because I was super tall or because I was good; it was because I was queer," they said. At six feet, Harrison was tall for a gymnast, even one competing in MAG.

Eventually Harrison started hiding themselves because of the pressure to conform in gymnastics. By the time they were a senior in high school, they stopped wearing makeup and painting their nails. They wore athletic clothes to school and didn't dress up. "I started to see myself as a gymnast," Harrison said. "I didn't see myself as a queer person. I was a gymnast first."

Gymnastics is an example, like softball and baseball, where the men's and women's equivalent of the sport are very different. For someone like Harrison, who competes in MAG, switching to WAG simply wouldn't be an option, nor would that quite fit with how Harrison sees themselves. As stated earlier, the only event that is technically the same in MAG and WAG is floor exercise, but Harrison can't do the kinds of skills on floor in MAG as they could if they competed in WAG. "It would be super dope if they put leaps and jumps and turns in the men's code because it's men's artistic gymnastics and those are artistic skills," Harrison said. "Those are skills that I like doing and they make me feel comfortable."

In such a gendered sport, creating something that's more gender-inclusive seems like an impossible task, but some are working toward that future. Morgan True started gymnastics because their sister did it first. They dutifully went to practice for a few years before taking a break due to a negative experience with a coach. They returned to the sport and started competing in sixth grade, which was late for gymnastics. Competing in college wasn't something that was going to be possible for True because they were only a level eight, which was below the level of a college competitor.

Instead, True continued in the sport by coaching. One of the things they did while coaching at a Bay Area gym was to establish a gender-inclusive gymnastics program for kids. Part of the desire to create such a program was philosophical, but some of it was also practical. It requires space and money to house all of the equipment necessary to run both boys' and girls' gymnastics programs. Most of the gymnasts who try the sport are children, many of them girls. But one of the best ways to efficiently use the space, in True's mind, was to just have everyone try everything. Of course, when not practicing sex separation in sports, there are inherent challenges, and the first one is usually about fairness followed by trophies. "I think our sport is so heavily, so deeply concerned with who's going to win and who could win and what fairness means," True said. "And the biggest damage of that is the lack of access. We can talk about how to lose gracefully and how to keep trying even though you're never going to be an Olympian."

Gymnastics isn't the only sport where these kinds of questions are being asked. Jake Fedorowski started running in college. They grew up in Minnesota and tried all kinds of sports: hockey, baseball, tennis, and soccer, just to name a few. But nothing really stuck until they started running. "I didn't know at the time, but like, I look back on it now, and I didn't feel welcome in those spaces," Fedorowski said. "I didn't see myself reflected."

Fedorowski participated in a lot of individual outdoor activities as a college student in Chicago. When they moved to Seattle, however, they found a community in the Seattle Frontrunners, a walking and running club for the LGBTQ+ community. "For the first time, this activity that I always kind of thought was an individual thing could actually be something you do with a team or with a group of people that celebrate you and accept you as who you are," Fedorowski said.

Fedorowski finished their first marathon in September 2021 in the middle of a downpour. They crossed the finish line into the arms of a bunch of Frontrunners who were also participating that day, all wearing their Frontrunners singlets. Fedorowski was able to register for the race as a nonbinary participant, but there wasn't a built-out division. As a nonbinary runner, Fedorowski started challenging the notion that they would have to run in either the men's or the women's category. For them, having a nonbinary category recognized their gender identity as they saw it: distinct. That meant being able to stand on a podium of nonbinary athletes and be awarded prize money in the nonbinary category—all of the things that would be available to runners in either the men's or the women's category. "I want my identity as a nonbinary person, someone outside of the men's and women's division, to be celebrated and to be affirmed," Fedorowski said.

Nonbinary runners are being included more in major road races, including the Philadelphia Distance Run, Chicago Marathon, and New York City Marathon, and the Boston and London marathons added the category in 2023. "To see a race of that size, with that large of a following step into this work is monumental," Fedorowski said of the Boston Marathon. "And it's, it's going to be very . . . I'm very excited to see how they, you know, kind of how they follow through with their commitment to creating space for nonbinary folks."

The changes being advocated for by nonbinary athletes are just the beginning of grappling with what nonbinary inclusion looks like. The participation of nonbinary athletes requires us to ask larger questions about how gender-expansive athletes can participate in a system that was explicitly not designed to accommodate them. The PHF policy was one of the first professional sports leagues to explicitly enumerate eligibility for nonbinary athletes. Another league also introduced nonbinary athletes in its policy.

Athletes Unlimited, a new women's professional sports league, adopted a policy in 2021 that included eligibility rules for nonbinary athletes. The policy requires nonbinary athletes who are assigned male at birth to suppress their testosterone. There are no hormone level or time requirements for the suppression, only that it's happening. It says nothing about athletes assigned female at birth who want to take testosterone for transition purposes, whether that athlete is nonbinary or a transgender man.

It is an important note that these are professional leagues. The thing about professional sports is that an athlete has to be *good enough* to gain entry into that league. That already creates a significant barrier. Whether it was a good policy decision could only be answered if, in fact, it was tested. The underlying truth of all of these policies governing elite sports is that most will remain untested for years, perhaps decades.

Not all nonbinary athletes, however, are elite-level competitors. True, Harrison, and Fedorowski all demonstrate that reality. But they've been involved in sports for much of their lives, which makes these questions pressing, and they shouldn't be left for down the road. Statistically speaking, few nonbinary athletes are elite, just as only the elite few of cisgender athletes make it to the professional ranks. To build the skill necessary for being a professional athlete, people start young. In women's swimming, for example, it's not uncommon to see teenagers compete at the World Championships or the Olympics. Of course, these are the best of the best, and very few people make it that far. Even so, the athletes that do make it that far almost always start as children. That's the important part of policy as it pertains to inclusion. If transgender and intersex athletes struggle to access sports from the beginning, it almost ensures that they will never have success at higher levels of sports. That shuts them out of scholarship opportunities, professional leagues, etc.

I'm not saying that the goal of policy should be to grow the numbers of transgender athletes playing elite sports, rather that the shutting of doors at the top has a trickle-down effect to youth and recreational sports. Many sports organizations take their policy cues from larger organizations like national governing bodies, international federations, the NCAA, and the IOC. A youth soccer league doesn't have the resources to commission studies and convene policy summits to consider what eligibility criteria should be for gender-expansive youth. But if professional leagues are considering these questions and enumerating nonbinary athletes in policy, that opens the door for more inclusive, participation-based policy in less competitive settings.

I'm not sure what that policy should look like, but there are options. True implemented an "everyone plays together" approach at their gymnastics gym, and I think that could make sense for a lot of team sports as well. A third nonbinary category for individual sports is interesting to me as well. I wonder how those ideas will develop in contrast to the "open" category that World Aquatics proposed, which would allow for transgender women who transitioned after the onset of puberty. Fedorowski's nonbinary category is a relatively closed category (albeit a more flexible one). The idea isn't an open category so much as it is a dedicated nonbinary category, similar to a men's or women's category. These ideas, while similar, are also in tension.

Policy simply reflects the values of its shapers. The idea that some scrub could simply walk off the street and dominate because there was no policy preventing someone assigned male at birth from joining a women's team ultimately devalues the skills of the women playing that sport. This assumption permeates the culture of sport and of gender. Perhaps it's time to explore policy solutions to weaken it.

"SPORT IS A binary, sex-segregated space and it's not built for the future of this conversation," said Athlete Ally executive director and founder Hudson Taylor. "We're just having a debate that is not really set up for success." I know that sounds like Taylor is about to advocate for the end of women's sports as we know it, but what if, instead, we looked at the issue as the end of sex-separated sports as we know it?

Perhaps that's a semantic without a difference for some people, but to me, it is a very key difference. So much of this debate, of this book up to this point, has been spent exploring questions of the perceived threats to the women's sports category, deconstructing them, decontextualizing them, and so on. All done in the service of *protecting* the integrity of the category. After all, that's what these policies and laws purport to do; it's stamped at the top of nearly all of the legislation. The means of that protection is to keep all those who are assigned male at birth out. When it comes to legislation in the United States, this is done in service of a greater gender policing (again, mostly a topic for a different book), but it's all propped up by the gendered norm that any athlete assigned male at birth is a better athlete than anyone assigned female at birth. A large part of why that assumption exists isn't because we sex-separate sports; it's because we sex-separate sports starting in kindergarten. "We sex-separate sport really early," Taylor said. "And that begins a socialization process for boys and girls, which is really damaging."

Though I had an amazing experience playing co-ed basketball during my childhood, when I started playing soccer at seven years old, we were already sex separated, which was different from my everyday experience at school. At recess, everyone played together. I regularly played football with the boys or against boys in basketball on the blacktop. So the boys I competed against during recess all played together, and I played with the girls. Don't get me wrong, I loved playing soccer and have tremendous memories from those experiences. I ended up playing travel soccer when I got older and eventually played a year of varsity in high school. But I also wonder what might have happened if all of us played organized sports together in elementary school? This kid Michael was known to be super fast, but in second grade, could Emily, our speedster, have outrun him? I think a lot about the possible lessons that could be learned by students of all genders if our sporting system wasn't so separated.

This isn't benign musing. So much of our discourse around these issues stems from the idea that the fundamental message underpinning sex separation at young ages is not that boys have a physiological advantage from testosterone that emerges at puberty (though, of course, some people dispute that claim, let's accept it here for the sake of the exercise), it's that boys are *better at sports* than girls. Otherwise, why bother having sex-separated teams for second grade soccer? And that message is one that shows up in our culture all the time. It's in the "kitchen" comments on Twitter underneath women's basketball highlights ("Why don't they just fix me a sandwich instead," etc., etc. . . .) and in the wild assertions that JV boys' basketball teams could beat the South Carolina women's basketball program in a game. Sure, teenage boys may be on average faster, stronger, taller, and can jump higher, and those traits may be beneficial in basketball players, but that does not make someone a good basketball player automatically.

Imagine a world where children of all genders play soccer and baseball together until middle school, where track meets are combined until age twelve, where play and movement are centered for all of our children until puberty. There is such a small sliver of the sporting experience where any of this angst dominating the news cycle matters. We've lost the plot. So let's write a new story. One that works better.

EPILOGUE

THE MARCH TOWARD RESTRICTION

A LOT HAS changed since I started writing about transgender athletes. When I pitched my first story on policy in the fall of 2016, I didn't expect to still be writing about the issue more than half a decade later. The story that came from that first pitch was published in May of 2018. The reporting had been long and arduous. I thought I was done after that. It became clear to me a year later while watching the Equality Act hearings that I wasn't done, and I might never be.

Writing this book in this particular moment was incredibly difficult. In the two years I spent drafting it, the issue of transgender people playing sports became unbearably heated. I initially wanted to write this book because I felt like most people in my life were talking past one another on this issue. I wanted the book to be the home for all of those ideas to be considered. In journalism, we focus a lot on objectivity, or the idea of being a neutral arbiter who is positionless. I don't think of my role that way. Instead, I think it's most important that my biases and positions are known, and that fairness and truth be my guide. None of us is neutral. On this topic, it became impossible to straddle a fence that increasingly seemed like a mirage.

It's become clear to me that we're at an inflection point. What began as a good-faith discussion about policy and physiological differences between sexes has given way to a level of intolerance and discrimination that is simply unconscionable. Health care is being attacked. Parents are being attacked. Children's right to *their* privacy is being attacked. Each time one of the bills restricting access to sports for transgender youth passes, states consider legislation that takes it a step further. And as long as there is no outcry, those steps become bolder.

Over the past few years, hundreds of bills were filed that targeted the LGBTQ+ community, particularly transgender youth in schools, though not exclusively. The bills restricting access to sports for transgender youth, however, were just the opening salvo for groups attacking LGBTQ+ rights. Advocates have called the bills that focused on sports a Trojan horse, and the 2022 legislative session may have proven them right. Health care, bathrooms, locker rooms, LGBTQ+ books, and even discussing LGBTQ+ people in schools all came up for debate in the 2022 session. Texas directed its Department of Family and Protective Services to investigate parents of transgender children under suspicion of child abuse. States have increasingly explored policy that would make it difficult for children to socially transition. It has become impossible to isolate the issue of transgender athlete participation from this broader legislative attack on LGBTQ+ people in the United States.

Separate from those legislative measures, however, is the movement in elite sports. After nearly a decade of moving toward inclusion, federations and national governing bodies have reversed course. Instead, each new regulation coming from top governing bodies is more restrictive than the last, with some inching close to outright bans for transgender women in women's competition specifically. If recent history is to be our judge, these policies will trickle down to affect youth.

I'm someone who owes my career to women's sports. I fell in love with sports through the 1999 World Cup team. I watched women's basketball with my dad all the time. My parents taped—literally recorded on a videotape—the 2003 Final Four game between UConn and Texas. I watched that game every morning for at least a year. I love sports, yes, but I love women's sports the most. So it comes as no surprise that both my fandom and my career have been anchored in covering women's sports. Many of the voices you've heard in this book have been from people who also love women's sports. Some of them disagreed, but I always felt like the question asked of me by that legislator was a good one. What will happen to women's sports? My answer to this question is that women's sports will continue growing. The USWNT vs. England soccer match sold out Wembley Stadium's 90,000 seats in twenty-four hours. More people are watching women's sports on television than ever before. The threat to that progress is not transgender girls; it's media who ignore women's sports, women receiving fewer opportunities to participate, and professional athletes still practicing in high school gyms or community centers. It's the stories of rampant abuse from coaches and doctors and administrators. I could almost write another book just listing the bullshit that undermines women's sports. Women's sports, however, will continue; I have no doubt about that.

Sports are important; all kids should be able to play them. That doesn't seem like it should be a controversial statement.

But today it can be. People like Lia Thomas are just the latest scapegoat. There will be another Lia Thomas, another Andraya Yearwood, another Mack Beggs, and so on. There are also many athletes whose names we don't know, and there are some whose names we've come to know only because they're suing for the right to play on their school sports team. Every restrictive policy, every law that enacts a prohibition on transgender youth participating in sports in accordance with their gender identity, pushes young people out of sports. What message does that send?

Many of the laws that are being passed have mechanisms that allow for parents, community members, school officials, and/or students to call out those whom they suspect are transgender to prove they belong in girls' and women's sports. I often think back to my own life as a kid with short hair who was often mistaken for being a boy. I was taunted on the basketball court all the time growing up, constantly being told that I was "a man" or something of the sort. Plenty of cisgender women have similar stories, some of which have been explored in these pages.

Ultimately, a more restrictive policy landscape means a more heavily policed gender landscape. From a sports perspective, we've already been here, stereotyping women as being lesser athletes, capable of smaller things. This is the opposite of where we should be, and that hurts all girls and women. After all, if policy hinges on defining womanhood, that requires placing limits on who does and does not count as a woman. It also creates a world where people who subvert gender norms experience heightened scrutiny, and that does not just apply to transgender youth. There are already examples of girls with short hair being singled out and having their gender questioned informally. Now, in many states, there are formal processes in place to challenge a student's gender. What counts as a reasonable question? Hair length? Height? Muscle size? We've already seen this happen in Utah, where parents of competitors who placed second and third in a state competition challenged the first-place finisher's gender with the high school association. The Utah High School Activities Association (UHSAA) investigated the complaint, asking the student's school to pull her records going back until kindergarten. There was no indication that this student was transgender. The UHSAA also said this wasn't the first complaint it had received. Most of the complaints, the organization said, are filed when a female student "doesn't look feminine enough."[1] That might be a perfectly fine space for some people. As I wrote earlier, I do think the conversation is a bit different at the elite level. We aren't just talking about elite athletes, however. The consequences of this more restrictive policy landscape remain to be fully seen. There is no doubt, though, that with intensely restrictive policy comes the policing of gender, a concept about which there is clearly little agreement. That is not a trade I am willing to make.

What about you?

ACKNOWLEDGMENTS

Every book is the culmination of work and belief by so many people. I'd like to thank my agent, Kiele Raymond, for being the first person other than myself to believe in this project and see me as an author. You gave me the strength to continue on a day when I felt that this book would never happen. I'd also like to thank Alice Pfeifer and Anna deVries for their notes, encouragement, and patience, along with the entire team at St. Martin's Press.

Thank you to everyone who spoke to me for this project and who has trusted me over the years, but especially to the transgender athletes: Mack, Andraya, River, Chris, Anne, Schuyler, Jackson, Aryana, Blake, Lia, Morgan, Jake, and Griffin.

A special thank-you to my ESPN family, past and present. To Alison Overholt, for hiring me and taking a chance on a kid writing snarky feminist columns on the internet. To all of those who have edited me through the years and turned me into the journalist, writer, and thinker I am today: Jena Janovy, Laura

Purtell, Elaine Teng, JB Morris, Jenn Holmes, Ross Marrinson, Ty Wenger, Ericka Goodman-Hughey, Scott Burton, and Becky Hudson. To Susie Arth, for whom I lack the words to describe the importance of our friendship and editing partnership. And to Lauren Reynolds: thank you for being you, and for your unwavering belief in what I can accomplish. I have been blessed to work at a company that supports the work that served as the foundation for this book. Thank you to Laura Gentile, Nate Ravitz, Norby Williamson, Rob King, and Tina Thornton, for valuing my voice and contributions. To Chris Buckle, for being a great boss. To Jimmy Pitaro, a special thank-you for never letting me question my place at the worldwide leader.

Community has been essential for me to get through the process of finishing this project. Thank you to all of my journalist colleagues and friends, who listened to me whine and cry over the years: Natalie Weiner, Aishwarya Kumar, Nicole Auerbach, Tyler Tynes, Seth Wickersham, Jessica Luther, and Lindsay Gibbs. To the Kids Table, for keeping me young and being some of my first friends in journalism. To Alexa Philippou, the best colleague and friend I could ever ask for. Thank you for your love and support and for helping me get over the finish line. To Jackie Powell and Tess Demeyer, for your encouragement and support. To Lyndsey D'Arcangelo, for helping me get started in the first place. It's not an exaggeration to say this book doesn't exist without you. To Kathleen Massara, for helping me find a place in this industry when I struggled to do so. To the queer and trans journalists covering our community: Kate Sosin, Jo Yurcaba, O'rion Rummler, Julie Kliegman, Lauren McGaughy, Nico Lang, and others, I see you and love you. This is so hard, but know that I'm in it with you.

To my mentors: Pablo Torre, Wade Davis, Kate Fagan, and

Taryn Callahan-Miller, thank you. You have all given me so much and helped me in ways that I could only hope to return someday. To Julie Foudy and David Epstein, for being early believers. To Heather Burns and Erin Spraw, for being exceptional colleagues and guiding lights. To my queer and trans elders, especially Mak Kneebone and Lynn Young. To Steph Laffin, for introducing me to Wade, and for being there from the beginning. To Jim Farrell, for teaching me how to think and make meaning in this world. Though you aren't here to read this, I have no doubt that you would be so proud of the dense-facting in this book. Thank you to literally all of my teachers, who stoked my passion for writing before I ever realized it was something I wanted to do and pushed me when I didn't want to be pushed: Leslie Shepard, Gayle Ploetz Beck, Marilyn Day, Ed Kelley, Jen Cerny, Richard Battersby, Catherine Battersby, Judy Kutulas, Anna Kuxhausen, Ben Percy, Peter Magolda, Marcia Baxter-Magolda, Elisa Abes, and Stephen Quaye. To my forever coach, Gary Christlieb, thank you for instilling my deep love of basketball that transcends anything I would ever accomplish on the court. I have a career because of all those scouting sessions.

Thank you to my family and friends, for your endless love and support. To my parents, Mitch and Cory, I'm so grateful for you. So many kids like me have negative experiences with parents who refuse to see them for who they are. Your love for and belief in me has never wavered, and, in so many ways, you saw my authentic self before I ever did. Thank you to my Grandy, who has been such a cheerleader for this book. To my Grandpa, for instilling my love of learning. And to my Nana, who isn't here to read this book herself, but who I know is proud of me. To Hayes, thank you for always showing up. To Marin, thank you for always being in my corner. To Willie and James, you both love to challenge me in different ways, and I am always grateful for our chats, whether they are about football or politics. To Sarah, thank you for giving me another sister and for putting up with my antics all these years, especially when it comes to playing cards. To Ann Marie, for welcoming me into your family with open arms. To Doug and Clara, thank you for your support from afar. To Grace, thank you for your inquisitive phone calls and the laughs. To Kendal, thank you for being there for me and Elizabeth, and for always keeping me in line. To Groupy Group, thank you for your love and patience as I disappear for long stretches and then pop back up. Thank you to Zoe, for being my first writing buddy and, perhaps, the only person in the world to truly understand why I stopped watching *Grey's Anatomy*. To Mollie and Christian, thank you for always seeing all of me, including the person who loves reality competition shows. To Joshua, my oldest friend, you are my brother, and fourteen-year-old me is stunned we're still friends.

And to my wife, Elizabeth, this book is as much yours as it is mine. Thank you for being patient with me as I promise you the world and then take longer than expected to deliver. I've been grumpy for years and thrown more fits than I should have. I would not have gotten through this without you and, man, am I grateful you gave me another chance and went on a second date with me. I love you so much and I love our little life.

NOTES

CHAPTER 1. THE TWO GENDERS

The information in this chapter comes from interviews with Michelle Warnky-Buurma, Jessie Graff, Meagan Martin, and Allyssa Beird, first-hand observations and analysis, other firsthand sources, and multiple seasons of *American Ninja Warrior*. Also:

1. Kathrine Switzer, "The Girl Who Started It All," excerpted from *Marathon Woman*, https://kathrineswitzer.com/1967-boston-marathon -the-real-story/. All quotes from Switzer are from this excerpt unless otherwise noted.
2. Boston Athletic Association, "History of the Boston Marathon," www.baa.org/races/boston-marathon/history.
3. Roberta "Bobbi" Gibb, "A Run of One's Own," http://runningpast .com/gibb_story.htm. All quotes from Gibb are excerpted from this writing unless otherwise noted.
4. International Olympic Committee, "Who Was Pierre de Coubertin?," https://olympics.com/ioc/faq/history-and-origin-of-the-games/who -was-pierre-de-coubertin.
5. Ellyn Kestnbaum, *Culture on Ice: Figure Skating & Cultural Meaning* (Middletown, CT: Wesleyan University Press, 2003).

CHAPTER 2. THIRTY-SEVEN WORDS

The information in this chapter comes from interviews with Erin Buzuvis and Libby Sharrow, firsthand observations and analysis, and other firsthand sources. Also:

1. National Federation of State High School Associations, "Sports Participation Survey," www.nfhs.org/media/1020206/hs_participation_survey_history_1969–2009.pdf.
2. National Federation of State High School Associations, "Sports Participation Survey."
3. NFL Communications, "2021 NFL Regular Season Averaged 17.1 Million Viewers," https://nflcommunications.com/Pages/2021-NFL-Regular-Season-Averaged-17.1-Million-Viewers.aspx.
4. Jon Lewis aka Paulsen, "Ratings: Stanley Cup, MLB, Softball, Lacrosse," *Sports Media Watch,* June 2021, www.sportsmediawatch.com/2021/06/stanley-cup-playoff-ratings-first-round-mlb-fox-ncaa-softball-lacrosse-espn/.
5. Jon Lewis aka Paulsen, "NBA Season Is Most-Watched in Three Years," *Sports Media Watch,* April 2022, www.sportsmediawatch.com/2022/04/nba-ratings-most-watched-regular-season-three-years/.
6. Katie Barnes, "Jonquel Jones and the Untold Story of the WNBA's Reigning MVP," ESPN, June 22, 2022, www.espn.com/wnba/story/_/id/34109460/jonquel-jones-untold-story-wnba-reigning-mvp.
7. Elizabeth Sharrow, "'Female Athlete' Politic: Title IX and the Naturalization of Sex Difference in Public Policy," *Politics, Groups, and Identities* 5, no. 1 (2017): 46–66.
8. Glynn A. Hill, "NCAA Responds after Coaches Criticize Conditions at Women's Volleyball Tournament," *The Washington Post,* April 9, 2021, www.washingtonpost.com/sports/2021/04/09/ncaa-womens-volleyball-tournament-conditions/.
9. Nancy Hicks, "Title IX Exemptions Unlikely for 'Revenue-Producing' Sports," *The New York Times,* October 2, 1975, www.nytimes.com/1975/10/02/archives/title-ix-exemptions-unlikely-for-revenueproducing-sports.html.
10. Dale E. Plyley, "The AIAW vs. the NCAA: A Struggle for Power to Govern Women's Athletics in American Institutions of Higher Ed-

ucation 1972-1982," National Library of Canada, September 1997, www.collectionscanada.gc.ca/obj/s4/f2/dsk2/ftp03/MQ28637.pdf.

11. Ibid.

12. Ibid.

13. Kristi Dosh, "NCAA Bullish On Change For Women's Basketball Tournament Revenue and Distribution," *Forbes,* March 31, 2022, www .forbes.com/sites/kristidosh/2022/03/31/ncaa-bullish-on-change -for-womens-basketball-tournament-revenue-and-distribution/?sh =cd973362303b.

14. U.S. Department of Education, "Dear Colleague Letter," April 4, 2011, www2.ed.gov/about/offices/list/ocr/letters/colleague-201104 _pg3.html.

CHAPTER 3. NO BOW LESBO

The information in this chapter comes from interviews with Ben Smith, Cathy Renna, Miranda Elish, Kayla Lombardo, Blake Bonkowski, and Ella Douglas, firsthand observations and analysis, and other firsthand sources. Also:

1. Ben Smith, "Kagan's Friends: She's Not Gay," Politico, May 11, 2010, www .politico.com/story/2010/05/kagans-friends-shes-not-gay-1529809.

2. Ed Pilkington, "Photo of US Court Hopeful Elena Kagan Sparks Debate over Sexuality," *The Guardian,* May 14, 2010, www.theguardian .com/world/2010/may/14/elena-kagan-baseball-photograph.

3. Jennifer Fermino, "Does a Picture of Elena Kagan Playing Softball Suggest She's a Lesbian?" *New York Post,* May 13, 2010, https: //nypost.com/2010/05/13/does-a-picture-of-elena-kagan-playing -softball-suggest-shes-a-lesbian/.

4. Rebecca Dana, "Elena Kagan Lesbian Controversy and Softball," *Daily Beast,* May 19, 2010, www.thedailybeast.com/elena-kagan -lesbian-controversy-and-softball.

5. Howard Kurtz, "A Question of Boundaries," *The Washington Post,* May 13, 2010, www.washingtonpost.com/wp-dyn/content/linkset /2005/04/11/LI2005041100587.html.

6. Graham Hays, "Stereotypes Haunt Softball," ESPN, October 10, 2010, www.espn.com/college-sports/columns/story?columnist=hays _graham&id=5671978.

7. Cyd Zeigler, "Out LGBTQ Women Outnumber Out Men at the To-kyo Olympics by about 9-to-1. Why?" *Outsports,* August 3, 2021, www.outsports.com/olympics/2021/7/21/22583016/olympics-lgbtq -athlete-women-men-gay-tokyo-why.

8. Elizabeth King, "A Short History of the Tomboy," *The Atlantic,* January 5, 2017, www.theatlantic.com/health/archive/2017/01/tomboy /512258/.

9. Jan Felshin, "The Triple Option . . . for Women in Sport," *Quest* 21, no. 1 (1974): 36–40.

10. Laurel R. Davis-Delano et al., "Apologetic Behavior Among Female Athletes," *International Review for the Sociology of Sport* 44, no. 2 (2009): 131–150.

11. Laurel R. Davis-Delano et al., "Apologetic Behavior Among Female Athletes."

CHAPTER 4. THE RUNNER IN SOUTH AFRICA

The information in this chapter comes from an interview with Anne Lie-berman, firsthand observation and analysis, and other firsthand sources. Also:

1. Christopher Clarey, "Gender Test After a Gold-Medal Finish," *The New York Times,* August 19, 2009, www.nytimes.com/2009/08/20 /sports/20runner.html.

2. Christopher Clarey, "Gender Test After a Gold-Medal Finish."

3. Ruth Padawer, "The Humiliating Practice of Sex-Testing Female Ath-letes," *The New York Times Magazine,* June 28, 2016, www.nytimes .com/2016/07/03/magazine/the-humiliating-practice-of-sex-testing -female-athletes.html.

4. Ibid.

5. "Dutee Chand vs. Athletics Federation of India (AFI) & The Interna-tional Association of Athletics Federations (IAAF)," www.doping.nl /media/kb/3317/CAS%202014_A_3759%20Dutee%20Chand%20 vs.%20AFI%20%26%20IAAF%20%28S%29.pdf

6. "IAAF Introduces New Eligibility Regulations for Female Classifica-tion," April 26, 2018, https://worldathletics.org/news/press-release /eligibility-regulations-for-female-classifica.

7. "Mokgadi Caster Semenya vs. International Association of Athletics Federations," www.tas-cas.org/fileadmin/user_upload/CAS_Award_ -_redacted_-_Semenya_ASA_IAAF.pdf.

8. Stephane Bermon and Pierre-Yves Garnier, "Serum androgen levels and their relation to performance in track and field: mass spectrometry results from 2127 observations in male and female elite athletes," *British Journal of Sports Medicine* 51, (2017), 1309–1314

9. Ibid.

CHAPTER 5. IT'S BIOLOGY, AND WE CAN'T CHANGE THAT

The information in this chapter comes from interviews with Myron Genel, Katrina Karkazis, Joanna Harper, Hayes Barnes, Cory Barnes, and Mitch Barnes, firsthand analysis and observations, other firsthand sources, and the pilot episode of *Pitch*. Also:

1. Chris Chavez, "Sha'Carri Richardson Cruises to Tokyo Winning Women's 100m Olympic Trials Title," *Sports Illustrated,* June 20, 2021, www.si.com/olympics/2021/06/20/sha-carri-richardson-punches -ticket-tokyo-olympics-trials-track.

2. Connecticut Interscholastic Athletic Conference, "2021 CIAC Spring Championships: Open Outdoor Track," https://content.ciacsports .com/ot21o.shtml.

3. Katie Barnes, "How Two Transgender Athletes Are Fighting to Compete in the Sports They Love," *ESPN,* May 29, 2018, www.espn.com /espn/story/_/id/33460938/how-two-transgender-athletes-fighting -compete-sports-love.

4. M. L. Healy et al., "Endocrine Profiles in 693 Elite Athletes in the Postcompetition Setting," *Clinical Endocrinology* 81, no. 2 (2014): 294–305.

5. Marley Dickinson, "Journal Publishes Correction to World Athletics Testosterone Study," *Canadian Running Magazine,* August 18, 2021, https://runningmagazine.ca/the-scene/journal-publishes-correction -to-world-athletics-testosterone-study/.

6. Joanna Harper, "Race Times for Transgender Athletes," *Journal of Sporting Cultures and Identities* 6, no. 1 (2015): 1–9.

7. Timothy Roberts et al., "Effect of Gender Affirming Hormones on Athletic Performance in Transwoman and Transmen: Implications

for Sporting Organisations and Legislators," *British Journal of Sports Medicine* 55, no. 11 (2021): 577–583.

8. Anna Wiik et al., "Muscle Strength, Size, and Composition Following 12 Months of Gender-affirming Treatment in Transgender Individuals," *The Journal of Clinical Endocrinology & Metabolism* 105, no. 3 (2020): e805–e813, https://doi.org/10.1210/clinem/dgz247.

9. Leonardo Azevedo Mobilia Alvares et al., "Cardiopulmonary Capacity and Muscle Strength in Transgender Women on Long-term Gender-affirming Hormone Therapy: A Cross-sectional Study," *British Journal of Sports Medicine* 56, no. 22 (2022): 1292–1298.

10. Simon Burton, "Childhood Move to Barcelona Was Medicine for Lionel Messi," *The Guardian*, April 20, 2010, www.theguardian.com/football/2010/apr/20/childhood-barcelona-medicine-lionel-messi.

11. E-Alliance, "Transgender Women Athletes and Elite Sport: A Scientific Review," Canadian Centre for Ethics in Sport, November 3, 2022, www.cces.ca/sites/default/files/content/docs/pdf/transgenderwomenathletesandelitesport-ascientificreview-e-final.pdf.

12. D. W. Lawrence, "Sociodemographic Profile of an Olympic Team," *Public Health* 148 (2017): 149–158.

13. Pooja S. Tandon et al., "Socioeconomic Inequities in Youth Participation in Physical Activity and Sports," *International Journal of Environmental Research and Public Health* 18, no. 13 (2021): 6946.

14. Roman Stubbs, "The Next Youth Sports Arms Race," *The Washington Post*, July 29, 2022, www.washingtonpost.com/sports/2022/07/29/youth-sports-business-facilities/.

CHAPTER 6. THE WRESTLER

The information in this chapter comes from interviews with Mack Beggs and Nancy Beggs, firsthand observations and analysis, other firsthand sources, the ESPN 30 for 30 Short "Mack Wrestles," and archived video coverage of debate and testimony in the Texas Senate. Also:

1. Bradford Richardson, "Mack Beggs, Transgender Wrestler, Prompts Questions about Steroids, Fairness," *The Washington Times*, February 28, 2018, www.washingtontimes.com/news/2018/feb/28/mack-beggs-transgender-wrestler-prompts-questions-/.

2. U.S. Department of Education Office for Civil Rights, "Questions and Answers on Title IX and Sexual Violence," April 29, 2014, www2 .ed.gov/about/offices/list/ocr/docs/qa-201404-title-ix.pdf.
3. U.S. Department of Justice and U.S. Department of Education, "Dear Colleague Letter on Transgender Students," May 13, 2016, www2.ed.gov/about/offices/list/ocr/letters/colleague-201605-title -ix-transgender.pdf.
4. Patrick Svitek, "Patrick Wants Fort Worth Superintendent to Resign," *The Texas Tribune,* May 9, 2016, www.texastribune.org/2016/05/09 /patrick-wants-fort-worth-superintendent-resign/.
5. Morgan Smith, "Texas AG Shopped Transgender Policy to Second School District," *The Texas Tribune,* May 26, 2016, www.texastribune .org/2016/05/26/paxton-shopped-transgender-policy-second -school/.
6. *State of Texas et al v. United States of America,* https://clearinghouse .net/doc/75263/.
7. Alexa Ura and Ryan Murphy, "Here's What the Texas Bathroom Bill Means in Plain English," *The Texas Tribune,* June 9, 2017, https://apps .texastribune.org/texas-bathroom-bill-annotated/.

CHAPTER 7. THE RUNNERS IN CONNECTICUT

The information in this chapter comes from interviews with Andraya Yearwood, Ngozi Nnaji, Rahsaan Yearwood, Aryana Brown, and Karissa Niehoff, firsthand observations and analysis, and other firsthand sources. Also:

1. Matthew Conyers, "At Cromwell High, Transgender Athlete Competes with Girls for First Time," *Hartford Courant,* April 7, 2017, www.courant.com/sports/high-schools/hc-hs-cromwell-track -andraya-yearwood-0407–20170406-story.html.
2. "Student Who Lost Track Championship to Transgender Athletes Speaks Out," *The Ingraham Angle,* February 26, 2019, https://video .foxnews.com/v/6007625250001#sp=show-clips.
3. Tina Detelj, "Petitions Circulate after Transgender Athletes Take Top Spots in State Competition," WWLP22 News, June 13, 2018, www .wwlp.com/news/connecticut/petitions-circulate-after-transgender -athletes-take-top-spots-in-state-competition/1237640247/.

4. *Selina Soule et al. v. Connecticut Association of Schools,* https://adflegal
   .org/sites/default/files/2020–04/Soule%20v.%20Connecticut%20As-
   sociation%20of%20Schools%20-%20Complaint.pdf.
5. *Selina Soule et al. v. Connecticut Association of Schools.*
6. Katie Barnes, "The Battle over Title IX and Who Gets to Be a Woman
   in Sports: Inside the Raging National Debate," *ESPN,* June 23, 2020,
   www.espn.com/espnw/story/_/id/29347507/the-battle-title-ix-gets
   -woman-sports-raging-national-debate.

CHAPTER 8. THE BREAKUP IN WOMEN'S SPORTS

The information in this chapter comes from interviews with Pat Griffin, Donna Lopiano, Nancy Hogshead-Makar, Anne Lieberman, Felice Duffy, Doriane Coleman, and Neena Chaudhry, firsthand observations and analysis, and other firsthand sources. Also:

1. Doriane Lambelet Coleman, "Sex in Sport," *Law and Contemporary Problems* 80, no. 4 (2017): 63–106, https://scholarship.law.duke.edu
   /cgi/viewcontent.cgi?article=4849&context=lcp.
2. Erin Buzuvis and Nancy Hogshead-Makar, "Participation of Intersex Athletes in Women's Sports," Women's Sports Foundation, www.womenssportsfoundation.org/wp-content/uploads/2016/08
   /participation-of-intersex-athletes-in-womens-sports.pdf.
3. Doriane Coleman et al., "Pass the Equality Act, but Don't Abandon Title IX," *The Washington Post,* April 29, 2019, www.washingtonpost
   .com/opinions/pass-the-equality-act-but-dont-abandon-title-ix
   /2019/04/29/2dae7e58–65ed-11e9-a1b6-b29b90efa879_story.html.

CHAPTER 9. THE QUEST TO SAVE WOMEN'S SPORTS

The information in this chapter comes from interviews with Chris Mosier, Anne Lieberman, Barbara Ehardt, and Eliza Byard, firsthand observations and analysis, and other firsthand sources. Also:

1. South Dakota High School Activities Association, "SDHSAA Transgender Procedure."

2. "'Visual Inspection' Could Be Part of State Law to Determine Gender Identity," *Rapid City Journal,* August 23, 2015, https://rapidcity journal.com/news/local/visual-inspection-could-be-part-of-state-law -to-determine/article_18b24dba-550f-5de9-b805-37409c4a7f5c.html.

3. Bryan Toporek, "Idaho Strengthens Youth-Concussion Law by Passing Revision," *Education Week,* April 6, 2012, www.edweek.org /leadership/idaho-strengthens-youth-concussion-law-by-passing -revision/2012/04.

4. Alabama House Bill 20 (2020), www.bamapolitics.com/alabama/bills /2020-alabama-legislative-regular-session/2020-alabama-house -bills/hb-20/.

5. Iowa House File 2202 (2020), www.legis.iowa.gov/legislation/BillBook ?ga=88&ba=HF2202.

6. Kentucky Senate Bill 114 (2020), https://apps.legislature.ky.gov/record /20rs/sb114.html.

7. Kevin Richert, "Transgender Athletics Bill Clears Its First Legislative Hurdle," *Idaho Education News,* February 12, 2020, www .idahoednews.org/news/transgender-athletics-bill-clears-its-first -legislative-hurdle/.

8. Kevin Richert, "Idaho Press: Little Says Signing House Bill 500 Was the 'Right Thing' to Do," *Idaho Education News,* April 8, 2020, www .idahoednews.org/kevins-blog/idaho-press-little-says-signing -house-bill-500-was-the-right-thing-to-do/.

9. *Lindsay Hecox et al. v. Bradley Little et al.,* www.aclu.org/sites/default /files/field_document/hecox_v_little_-_order_granding_preliminary _injunction.pdf.

10. James Madara, "AMA Letter to National Governors Association," April 26, 2021, https://searchlf.ama-assn.org/letter/documentDownload ?uri=%2Funstructured%2Fbinary%2Fletter%2FLETTERS%2F2021 -4-26-Bill-McBride-opposing-anti-trans-bills-Final.pdf.

11. Vanessa Romo, "Arkansas Gov. Asa Hutchinson on Transgender Health Care Bill: 'Step Way Too Far,'" NPR, April 6, 2021, www .npr.org/2021/04/06/984884294/arkansas-gov-asa-hutchinson-on -transgender-health-care-bill-step-way-too-far.

12. Department of Justice Statement of Interest in *Selina Soule et al. v. Connecticut Association of Schools et al.,* www.aclu.org/sites/default

/files/field_document/soule_et_al_v._ct_association_of_schools_et _al_-_trump_admin_statement_of_interest.pdf.

13. United States Department of Education, "Letter of Impending Enforcement Action," https://adfmedialegalfiles.blob.core.windows.net /files/SouleDOEImpendingEnforcementLetter.pdf.

14. Luke Broadwater and Erica L. Green, "DeVos Vows to Withhold Desegregation Aid to Schools over Transgender Athletes," *The New York Times,* September 18, 2020, www.nytimes.com/2020/09/18/us /transgender-students-betsy-devos.html.

15. Emily Hays, "Breakthrough Reached on Trans Athletes," *New Haven Independent,* September 23, 2020, www.newhavenindependent.org /index.php/archives/entry/trans_athletes_showdown_resolved/.

16. Shawne K. Wickham, "NH College Rescinds Transgender Sports Policy after Federal Case," *New Hampshire Union Leader,* October 18, 2020, www.unionleader.com/news/social_issues/nh-college-rescinds -transgender-sports-policy-after-federal-case/article_687943f7-66c8 -5682-a0cd-a30f74d7ced8.html.

17. United States Department of Education, "Letter to Kim Mooney," October 16, 2020, www2.ed.gov/about/offices/list/ocr/docs/investiga tions/more/01202023-a.pdf.

18. Shawne K. Wickham, "NH College Rescinds Transgender Sports Policy."

19. Chris Johnson, "10 Years Later, Firestorm over Gay-only ENDA Vote Still Informs Movement," *Washington Blade,* November 6, 2017, www .washingtonblade.com/2017/11/06/10-years-later-firestorm-over-gay -only-enda-vote-still-remembered/.

20. Dwight Adams, "RFRA: Why the 'Religious Freedom Law' Signed by Mike Pence Was So Controversial," *The Indianapolis Star,* April 25, 2018, www.indystar.com/story/news/2018/04/25/rfra-indiana-why -law-signed-mike-pence-so-controversial/546411002/.

CHAPTER 10. THE CASE OF LIA THOMAS

The information in this chapter comes from interviews with Lia Thomas, Bob Thomas, Carrie Thomas, Riley Gaines, Nancy Hogshead-Makar, Schuyler Bailar, and Griffin Maxwell Brooks, firsthand observations and analysis, and other firsthand sources. Also:

1. Valerie Richardson, "Transgender Swimmer Lia Thomas Smashes Women's Records, Stokes Outrage," *The Washington Times,* December 5, 2021, www.washingtontimes.com/news/2021/dec/5/transgender-swimmer-lia-thomas-smashes-womens-reco/.

2. Adriana Diaz, "EXCLUSIVE: 'It's Impossible to Beat Her': Despondent Female Rival Says Swimming against Trans Lia Thomas Is 'Intimidating' and 'Discouraging' after Teammates Spoke Out and Said 'Everyone Knows It's Wrong," *Daily Mail,* December 15, 2021, www.dailymail.co.uk/news/article-10310305/Female-competitor-speaks-saying-IMPOSSIBLE-beat-UPenn-transgender-swimmer-Lia-Thomas.html.

3. Yaron Steinbuch, "Transgender Swimmer Lia Thomas' Teammates Considered Boycotting Final Meet in Protest," *New York Post,* December 29, 2021, https://nypost.com/2021/12/29/transgender-swimmer-lia-thomas-upenn-teammates-considered-boycotting-final-meet/.

4. Katie Barnes, "Ivy League Executive Director Robin Harris: NCAA 'Missed Opportunity' with New Transgender Athlete Policy," *ESPN,* January 25, 2022, www.espn.com/college-sports/story/_/id/33145647/ncaa-missed-opportunity-new-transgender-athlete-policy.

5. Anne Lepesant, "Stanford's Brooke Forde Says She's Okay with Racing Lia Thomas at NCAAs," *SwimSwam,* January 25, 2022, https://swimswam.com/stanfords-brooke-forde-says-shes-okay-with-racing-lia-thomas-at-ncaas/.

6. "An Act Relating to Athletics," https://apps.legislature.ky.gov/record documents/bill/22RS/sb83/bill.pdf.

7. E. Coleman et al., "Standards of Care for the Health of Transgender and Gender Diverse People, Version 8," *International Journal of Transgender Health,* September 15, 2022, www.tandfonline.com/doi/pdf/10.1080/26895269.2022.2100644?cookieSet=1.

8. Jake Zuckerman, "She's Ohio's Only Trans Female Playing Varsity Sports; Lawmakers Want Her Out," *Ohio Capital Journal,* June 13, 2022, https://ohiocapitaljournal.com/2022/06/13/shes-ohios-only-trans-female-playing-varsity-sports-lawmakers-want-her-out/.

CHAPTER 11. WHY AREN'T WE TALKING ABOUT TRANSGENDER MEN?

The information in this chapter comes from interviews with Chris Mosier, River Coates, and Schuyler Bailar, firsthand observations and analysis, and other firsthand sources. Also:

1. International Olympic Committee, "IOC Approves Consensus with Regard to Athletes Who Have Changed Sex," May 17, 2004, https://olympics.com/ioc/news/ioc-approves-consensus-with-regard-to-athletes-who-have-changed-sex.
2. International Olympic Committee, "IOC Consensus Meeting on Sex Reassignment and Hyperandrogenism," November 2015, https://stillmed.olympic.org/Documents/Commissions_PDFfiles/Medical_commission/2015–11_ioc_consensus_meeting_on_sex_reassignment_and_hyperandrogenism-en.pdf.
3. Stephanie Yang, "NWSL's Transgender Player Policy Needs Work," Allforxi.com, April 3, 2021, www.allforxi.com/2021/4/3/22360802/nwsl-transgender-player-policy-needs-work.
4. Paul Krotz, "PHF Updates Transgender and Nonbinary Inclusion Policy," Premier Hockey Federation, October 15, 2021, www.premierhockeyfederation.com/news/phf-updates-transgender-and-nonbinary-inclusion#:~:text=Transgender percent20Athletes&text=Transgender percent20men percent20are percent20eligible percent20to,physicians percent20and percent20applicable percent20medical percent20experts.
5. Tennessee House Bill 0003 (2021), https://wapp.capitol.tn.gov/apps/BillInfo/default.aspx?BillNumber=HB0003&ga=112.

CHAPTER 13. THE FUTURE OF POLICY

The information in this chapter comes from interviews with Chris Mosier, Anne Lieberman, Lia Thomas, Morgan True, Jackson Harrison, and Jake Fedorowski, firsthand observations and analysis, and other firsthand sources. Also:

1. International Olympic Committee, "IOC Framework on Fairness, Inclusion and Non-discrimination on the Basis of Gender Identity and Sex Variations," https://stillmed.olympics.com/media/Documents/News

/2021/11/IOC-Framework-Fairness-Inclusion-Non-discrimination -2021.pdf?_ga=2.5799347.1681228443.1655989099–665612058 .1655989099.

2. International Olympic Committee, "IOC Framework on Fairness, Inclusion, and Non-discrimination."

3. Ian Ransom and Jill Gralow, "Rugby League Joins Clampdown on Transgender Athletes in Women's Sport," Reuters, June 21, 2022, www.reuters.com/lifestyle/sports/international-rugby-league-bans -transgender-players-womens-competition-2022–06–21/.

4. World Rugby, "Transgender Guidelines," www.world.rugby/the- game/player-welfare/guidelines/transgender.

5. Simon Evans, "FIFA, World Athletics Review Transgender Rules Af- ter Swimming's Change," Reuters, June 20, 2022, www.reuters.com /lifestyle/sports/fifa-world-athletics-review-transgender-rules-after -swimmings-change-2022–06–20/.

6. World Athletics Council press release, March 23, 2023. https:// worldathletics.org/news/press-releases/council-meeting-march -2023-russia-belarus-female-eligibility.

7. Premier Hockey Federation, "PHF Transgender and Nonbinary Player Inclusion Policy," www.premierhockeyfederation.com/phf-transgender -and-nonbinary-policy.

EPILOGUE

1. Courtney Tanner, "Utah Parents Complained a High School Athlete Might Be Transgender After She Beat Their Daughters," *The Salt Lake Tribune,* August 18, 2022, www.sltrib.com/news/education/2022/08 /18/utah-parents-complained-high.

INDEX